The Causes of Demographic Change

Social Demography

Series Editors
Doris P. Slesinger
James A. Sweet
Karl E. Taeuber
Center for Demography and Ecology
University of Wisconsin–Madison

The Causes of Demographic Change

Experimental Research in South India

John C. Caldwell
P. H. Reddy
Pat Caldwell

The University of Wisconsin Press

The University of Wisconsin Press
114 North Murray Street
Madison, Wisconsin 53715

The University of Wisconsin Press, Ltd.
1 Gower Street
London WC1E 6HA, England

Library of Congress Cataloging-in-Publication Data
Caldwell, John Charles.
    The causes of demographic change.
    (Social demography)
    Include bibliographical references and index.
    1. Demographic transition—India, South.
2. Fertility, Human—India, South. 3. India, South—
Population. I. Reddy, Palli Hanumantha, 1938–
II. Caldwell, Pat. III. Title. IV. Series.
HB3640.S6C35 1988   304.6'0954'8   88–40189
ISBN 0–299–11610–7
ISBN 0–299–11614–X (pbk.)

Contents

Tables and Maps

Tables

Maps

Preface

The major social change of the last hundred years has been the shift in much of the world from large families, eroded by many deaths, to controlled fertility with lower mortality rates. This has resulted from socioeconomic change and has given rise in turn to vastly more change. It has been described and inadequately explained by a body of literature known as *demographic transition theory*.

Working in tropical Africa during the 1960s and 1970s, Pat and Jack Caldwell became convinced that the most hopeful research direction for explaining why these revolutionary changes had taken place lay in a combination of anthropological and demographic field methods—what has become known as the *micro approach* to population research. They progressively reshaped their field methods. However, it was only when they joined P. H. Reddy in India that the three of them mounted a full-scale program devoted solely to developing this research approach and to applying it to a range of basic problems in transition theory.

India was a good place, and the time was right, for such research. Most mortality decline had occurred during the lifetime of older people, while the steepest fertility decline had occurred during the previous few years. The research program raised as many new questions as the ones it helped to solve. Fertility change clearly could not be explained by confining oneself to the study of fertility, or by restricting the research to a survey approach.

The chapters that follow come out of that program. They represent a frustratingly small part of what we learned.

Some of them clearly pursue certain theoretical problems raised in a previous publication (John C. Caldwell, *Theory of Fertility Decline*, Population and Social Structure: Advances in Historical Demography Series [New York: Academic Press, 1982]).

Acknowledgments

The research described in this book is the product of the collaboration of individuals and their institutions. The individuals are the authors of the book. The institutions are the Population Centre, Bangalore, and the Department of Demography, Australian National University, Canberra. Field work was made possible by the provision of staff from the Population Centre. Additional funding came from both the Australian National University's Department of Demography and from its parent body, the Research School of Social Sciences. Subsequent analysis benefited very greatly (and, indeed, made possible the appearance of the book at this stage) from the receipt of a Population Council International Fertility Research Award. The Ford Foundation also provided support. In Karnataka, the project benefited at every stage from the support of the Ministry of Health, with original encouragement from its Additional Secretary, Dr. Saksena, and from its program (supported by the Indian government and the World Bank), the Indian Population Project.

Some of the individuals who played major roles in the research work should be named even at the expense of leaving others out. Parallel rural studies were carried out during residence in other villages for an entire year by Sumitra K. Potnis and P. N. Sushama, while work was undertaken in Bangalore by Sheila Chandra Mauli and Shashikala Kempawadkar, all members of the Population Centre staff. We have also benefited from other related studies by Ph.D. candidates of the ANU Department of Demography (all former staff members of the Population Centre): A. Shariff in Karnataka, M. Guruswamy in Tamil Nadu, K. Raju in Andhra Pradesh, and P. N. Sushama in Kerala. Many others played important roles in Canberra or in Karnataka: Wendy Cosford, who has been very actively involved with the project since the beginning, Jennie Widdowson, Pat Quiggin, S. Begum, Revathi N., Kusum Kumari, and P. Ananda Shetty. In addition, Bruce Caldwell has made a major input into the anthropological side of the work, but has reported his own research elsewhere (*Stability and Challenge: Caste Responses to Changes in Occupation and Education in an Indian Village* [Delhi: Hindustani Press, 1988]).

We acknowledge, with gratitude, permission to republish the following papers: "The Determinants of Fertility Decline in Rural South India," in *India's Demography: Essays on the Contemporary Population*, ed. Tim Dyson and Nigel Crook (New Delhi: South Asian Publishers, 1984), 187–207; "The Family Planning Programme at the Local Level," in *The Demographic Transition in Asia*, ed. Gavin W. Jones (Singapore: Maruzen Asia, 1984), 111–24; "The Causes of Marriage Change in South India," *Population Studies* 37, No. 3 (1983): 343–61; "The Determinants of Family Structure in Rural South India," *Journal of Marriage and the Family* 46, No.1 (1984): 215–29; "The Social Component of Mortality Decline: An Investigation in South India Employing Alternative Methodologies," *Population Studies* 37, No. 2 (1983): 185–205; "Educational Transition in Rural South India," *Population and Development Review* 11, No. 1 (1985); 29–51; "Periodic High Risk as a Cause of Fertility Decline in a Changing Rural Environment: Survival Strategies in the 1980–83 South Indian Drought," *Economic Development and Cultural Change* 34, No. 4 (1986): 677–701; "The Causes of Demographic Change in Rural South India," *Population and Development Review* 8, No. 4 (1982): 689–727.

In addition, the chapter, "The Support of the Aged in Rural Karnataka," was first presented to a conference on aging, organized by T. Nair and held at the University of Kerala in January 1985.

Two other particular notes of gratitude should be expressed. The first is to the people of the nine villages, and particularly to those of the "large village" where we were welcomed so warmly every time we stayed there. The second is to the Karnataka government and its Ministry of Health who were the hosts to a conference held in April 1983 in the magnificent location of Karnataka's Legislative Assembly building in Bangalore, where many of the core findings of this book were first publicly discussed with a wide range of persons from Karnataka, India, and beyond. At that conference, "The Micro Approach in Demographic Investigation: Toward a Methodology" was also first presented; it was later read at a meeting in Mexico arranged by the Social Science Research Council.

The Caldwells are extremely appreciative of the warm home that the Population Centre, Bangalore, provided for their work, and the Reddys have similar feelings with regard to the Australian National University.

The Causes of Demographic Change

Chapter One

Focus and Approach

A major challenge to social scientists is that of explaining world demographic transition. The decline of both mortality and fertility levels has been one of the most fundamental processes in recent history, and its occurrence underlies much of subsequent social change. Mortality had been falling slowly for centuries in some parts of Western Europe, but, even there, expectations of life at birth at the beginning of the present century were still under 50 years, and those in much of Asia and Africa were below 30 years. Now, most of the world has attained at least 50 years, with industrialized countries exhibiting levels usually over 70 years. Before 1870, marital fertility was falling nowhere but in France. Subsequently, levels began to decline in Western Europe and in English-speaking countries of overseas European settlement. This gave rise to demographic transition theory,[1] but, in contrast to what might have been anticipated from the classical version of that theory, fertility has declined significantly during the last 20 years in such poor

---

1. See, especially, F. W. Notestein, "Population—The Long View," in *Food for the World*, ed. T. W. Schultz (Chicago: University of Chicago Press, 1945), 36–57, and F. W. Notestein, "Economic Problems of Population Change," in *Eighth International Conference of Agricultural Economists, 1952* (London: Oxford University Press, 1953), 13–31. For a discussion and criticism of this theory, see J. C. Caldwell, "Toward a Restatement of Demographic Transition Theory," *Population and Development Review* 2, nos. 3–4 (1976): 321–66. For threshold theory, see United Nations, Department of Economic and Social Affairs, *Population Bulletin of the United Nations, no. 7—1963, with Special Reference to Conditions and Trends of Fertility in the World* (New York: United Nations, 1965).

agrarian countries as India, Indonesia, and China, where most development indices are well below those which obtained at the onset of fertility decline in the countries experiencing the earlier fertility transition.

Much theory has been rendered obsolete by the fact that mortality and fertility apparently have no common socioeconomic threshold throughout the world that determines the onset of their declines. This has also weakened confidence in the most widely employed research approach for identifying the conditions of decline, namely, the use of large data sets of populations for the correlation of various social and economic characteristics with mortality and fertility levels. Specialized demographic surveys focusing on mortality and fertility have illuminated some of the intermediate mechanisms involved in demographic change, but have been rather less than successful in showing why these mechanisms begin to change and why they do so in certain conditions but not in others. Difficulties lie both in the approach and in the defective research instruments employed (see Appendix).

This book presents the findings of a rather different method for investigating the nature of demographic change, particularly the onset of fertility and mortality decline. We were determined to work and live in an area where the beginning of major change—at least with regard to fertility—had occurred recently, and to draw not only on the methodology developed by demographers but also on that employed by anthropologists. Our aim was not solely to attempt the development of a new methodology but also to explore ways of strengthening existing methodologies.

We were, for instance, convinced that most fertility surveys had major structural weaknesses that could at least be partly overcome. One was a concentration on married women of reproductive age as if the rest of the household and community either played no role in reproductive decisions or these could be adequately reported by these women. Another was a totally inadequate methodology for deciding what mechanisms should be probed in order to explain demographic change in any particular society. Most questions in the surveys were derived from older surveys, often carried out in quite different societies, or by the apparently logical decision that certain additional information would provide a sufficient picture—a decision made by researchers often of a different culture and far removed from the specific demographic arena. Thus, our work was based on two premises. The first was that existing research approaches and instruments could be improved, provided that they were made more culturally specific and provided that methods were developed for feeding them with information on the appropriate questions to be asked and on what was minimally sufficient for an adequate investigation. The second was the belief that many aspects of human change could be explained—in contrast to being measured—only if demographers and other social scientists were to develop and retain a methodological approach which rested on an intimate knowledge of particular societies. This book is the record of an attempt to experiment with such an approach.

The analysis of census figures and other large statistical aggregates has provided a kind of map of demographic change over time, and statistically significant correlations in these data have indicated areas for further study. That study, especially if it aims at explaining the nature of demographic change, is likely to have to employ other methods, both historical and anthropological. The work described in this book is posited on the assumption that the actors in the great demographic dramas of our times were not mere automatons, but had, in many cases, some idea of why they acted as they did. They may even have had an inkling as to why their behavior differed from that of others. This anthropological or (in current demographic parlance) micro approach does not rest on their ability to fully appreciate or explain these differences. The investigator can do that, given the different personal testimonies to individual behavior. Nor is there a necessity for these explanations to be correct in the sense of being complete and being aware of all the forces impinging on the individual—the investigator can supply supplementary evidence, often using macro data. The essential point is that the individual can provide enough information on motivation to allow hypotheses to be developed. In the study of society, these can rarely be rejected with absolute certainty (in the statistical study of society, null hypotheses can be rejected, but only by the use of selective measures, which are neither comprehensive nor an accurate representation of underlying reality). Rather, information can be accumulated which weakens or strengthens the hypotheses. That evidence may come from continued anthropological work, or it may be documentary and archival, dating from an earlier time when some change was just beginning. Our choice of India was wise in the sense that most of our adult respondents had lived through a period of great changes in demographic behavior. We placed much emphasis on probing the memories of those who had experienced the greatest change, and most old people became very accustomed to our continuing questions. Often, with practice, their ability to analyze changes in behavior improved markedly with the months and years.

The Identification of a Research Site

The project, which began in 1979, involved collaboration between the Population Centre, Bangalore, India, and the Department of Demography, Australian National University. The planned investigation was within the area of Karnataka which had been allocated to the south Indian section of the Indian Population Project, a program of the governments of India and Karnataka funded by the World Bank. An early decision was that the exact site chosen, although in the large project area which covered half the state, should be in a locality where there had not yet been any health or family planning activities beyond the normal government program.

In many ways, this was an ideal location. In India as a whole the expectation of life at birth was almost certainly lower than 25 years at the beginning of the century and little over 30 years in 1941. Between then and the late 1970s the expectation of life at birth had risen by 20 years, so that persons still under 40 years of age had been subject to a risk of infant mortality of a type which prevailed in Europe centuries ago and has now almost completely disappeared from the world. The level of infant mortality had fallen in a quarter of a century from around 180 per thousand births to perhaps 130.[2] In Karnataka, all measures of mortality were better still, so that the unadjusted infant mortality rate from the Sample Registration Scheme (SRS) was, for 1976 (the latest data available during the field work), 129 for the whole country, compared with 89 in Karnataka and only 99 even in its rural areas.[3] Indeed, the only parts of India where levels were certainly lower were Kerala, Goa, and Maharashtra.

The chosen research area was probably more happily chosen still with regard to fertility decline. A recent estimate of the decline in India's crude birthrate is that between the 1960s and 1970s it fell from 41 births per thousand population to 35, with Karnataka being two points lower in each period.[4] Only Kerala, Maharashtra, Punjab, and Tamil Nadu exhibited lower levels. Indeed, the unadjusted SRS figures showed Karnataka as 28.9, with only Kerala below it. Much of the

2. Samuel Preston and P. N. Mari Bhat, "New Evidence on Fertility and Mortality Trends in India," *Population and Development Review* 10, no. 3 (1984): 500; Anrudh K. Jain and Arjun L. Adlaka, "Preliminary Estimates of Fertility Decline in India During the 1970s," *Population and Development Review* 8, no. 3 (1982): 600–603.
3. Family Welfare Programme in India, *Year Book: 1980–81* (New Delhi: Government of India, 1982), 1, 31.
4. Preston and Bhat, "Fertility and Mortality Trends."

fertility fall had occurred during the Emergency, only three years before field work began.[5] A recent survey in three different areas of Karnataka concluded that, in the years between 1960–69 and 1975–79, the total fertility rate fell by 40 percent from 6.8 to 4.1, one-third of this decline being explained by later marriage and two-thirds by a decline in fertility within marriage (almost entirely attributable to sterilization).[6]

A series of criteria were compiled so that the chosen locality would contain a representation of the major population groups in south India and would be typical of those rural populations which had been little affected by proximity to large urban areas or to modern irrigation schemes. Ultimately, a village was chosen about 75 miles west of Bangalore and at a slightly greater distance from Mysore. This is in the southern part of Karnataka and was part of the princely state of Mysore prior to Independence. It is on the *maidan*, or plains, though in fact the country is gently undulating. This is the high country of the southern Deccan, around 2,500 feet above sea-level. Its most spectacular feature is the great granitic hills, huge piles of rock, the highest of which rise an additional 1,500 feet. The area is dry, and often dusty, being in the rain shadow cast by the Western Ghats. The annual rainfall is little over 25 inches, which, at 13 degrees from the equator, is barely sufficient for agriculture even at this altitude. The area is almost always dry, and is subject to dangerous droughts when the monsoon falters, as it does quite frequently.

The major crop is *ragi* (Indian finger millet), which is usually grown without irrigation and is eaten as a kind of plastic ball to be quickly swallowed or as a kind of tough chapati. It grows on dry land and is the major crop precisely because there is little irrigated land. The subsidiary dry-land crop is *jowar* (sorghum). In southern Mysore, red *jowar* predominates. It is used as cattle food or is eaten as a supplement or in a crisis by the very poor. Further north, white *jowar*

---

5. The Emergency is the name given to the period between June 1975 and January 1977 when Prime Minister Indira Gandhi suspended India's constitution and ruled by decree. From early 1976 a much more vigorous family planning program, with elements of compulsion, was pursued with most emphasis on sterilization. This program was undoubtedly an important factor in explaining the defeat of Mrs. Gandhi and the Congress Party at the election in March 1977.

6. N. Baskara Rao, P. M. Kulkarni, and P. Hanumantha Rayappa, *Determinants of Fertility Decline in Rural Karnataka: A Survey of Selected Villages in Dakshina Kannada, Dharwad and Mandya*, Population Research Centre, Institute for Social and Economic Change in collaboration with the World Bank and UNFPA (Washington: The World Bank, 1983), (xvi).

is a staple. On the edges of the fields, horsegram and other pulses are grown. Where there is irrigation, usually below old tanks, rice is cultivated (the tanks can usually supply water for only a single crop each year) for local consumption by the rich or for sale to the city. There are also areas with higher water tables where coconut plantations can be raised or those where tube-well irrigation can support fields of sugarcane. Wealth depends on owning land suited to growing rice, sugar, or coconuts. Cattle are grazed by small boys (and occasionally by girls), and are tethered near the house at night where they are given additional food (including cows' milk). A major capital item is a pair of working bullocks for plowing, and another is a bullock cart for transport. No tractor nor mechanized rotary hoe was found in the study area during the period of research.

This is a general area well known to social science. Mysore society was extensively and sensitively reported on by the Abbé Dubois, Francis Buchanan and Mark Wilks in the late eighteenth and early nineteenth centuries,[7] all reporting to the East India Company on the new areas that had been opened up by the defeat of the Mysore Sultanate. In the last third of a century, a significant number of anthropological studies have been carried out in the region. Alan Beals, Scarlett Epstein, and Sarah Hobson have all worked within fifty miles of our research site, and M. N. Srinivas worked around one hundred miles away.[8] The same is true with regard to demographic studies.

7. J. A. Dubois, *Hindu Manners, Customs and Ceremonies*, trans. H. K. Beaumont (Oxford: Clarendon Press, 3d ed., 1906); Francis Hamilton Buchanan, *A Journey from Madras through the Countries of Mysore, Canara and Malabar Performed under the Orders of the Most Noble the Marquis Wellesley Governor General of India for the Express Purpose of Investigating the State of Agriculture, Arts and Commerce, Religion, Manners and Customs; the History Natural and Civil and Antiquities in the Dominions of the Rajah of Mysore and the Countries Acquired by the Honorable East India Company* (London: T. Cadell and W. Davies, 1807); Mark Wilds, *Historical Sketches of the South of India, in an Attempt to Trace the History of Mysoor; from the Origin of the Hindoo Government of the State, to the Extinction of the Mohammedan Dynasty in 1799. Founded Chiefly on Indian Authorities Collected by the Author while Officiating for Several Years as Political Resident at the Court of Mysoor* (London: Longman, Hurst, Rees & Orme, 1810).

8. Alan R. Beals, "Interplay Among Factors of Change in a Mysore Village," in *Village India: Studies in the Little Community*, ed. McKim Marriott (Chicago: University of Chicago Press, 1955), 78–101; T. Scarlett Epstein, *Economic Development and Social Change in South India* (Manchester: Manchester University Press, 1962); idem, *South India: Yesterday, Today and Tomorrow—Mysore Villages Revisited* (London: Macmillan, 1973); Sarah Hobson, *Family Web: A Story of India* (London: John Murray, 1978); M. N. Srinivas, *Religion and Society Among the Coorgs of South India* (Oxford: Clarendon Press, 1952); idem, "The Social System of

C. Chandrasekaran sampled the area in the early 1950s while carrying out the Mysore Population Study, and he was followed a quarter of a century later by K. Srinivasan and colleagues at the Bangalore Population Centre with the Bangalore Population Study.[9] They all left one problem untouched, that of the reasons for changing demographic behavior, although data from the two demographic studies have recently been employed to construct a theory of demographic change for Karnataka.[10]

Research Methodology

The methodology was progressively developed in the course of the work. We were determined to draw on the research approaches both of demographers engaged in social surveys and of anthropologists working on village studies. The unalterable decision was that there would be a substantial and continuing contact with a relatively small population so that the principal investigators knew a large number of people personally and understood the history of individuals as they sought marriage and faced parenthood, illness, and death.

Initially, the usual pattern of rural research in India was followed. A village was chosen with approximately 2,500 inhabitants. This was on the larger side of the distribution of villages chosen by anthropologists, but was consistent with most previous work in that it was multicaste in structure, the site of a weekly market, on a road, and something of a local service center.[11] In spite of all this, it was remote (30 miles from where the nearest gasoline could be purchased), and, at first sight, tiny. When driving, one could easily pass through it in one minute, wondering all the time whether there were enough people there to disclose a range of demographic truths.

a Mysore Village," in Marriott, *Village India*, 1–35; idem, "The Dominant Caste in Rampura," *American Anthropologist* 61 (1959): 1–16.

9. United Nations, Department of Social and Economic Affairs, *The Mysore Population Study*, Population Studies, no. 34 (New York: United Nations, 1961); K. Srinivasan, P. H. Reddy, and K. N. M. Raju, "From One Generation to the Next; Changes in Fertility, Family Size Preferences, and Family Planning in an Indian State Between 1951 and 1975," *Studies in Family Planning* 9, nos. 10–11 (1978): 258–71.

10. K. Srinivasan, Shireen J. Jejeebhoy, Richard A. Easterlin, and Eileen M. Crimmins, "Factors Affecting Fertility Control in India: A Cross-Sectional Study," *Population and Development Review* 10, no. 2 (1984): 273–96.

11. Asok Mitra, *India's Population: Aspects of Quality and Control* (New Delhi: Abhinav Publications for the Family Planning Foundation, 1978), 404; Census of India 1981, *Series–1, India (Part 2, Special: Report and Tables Based on 5 Per Cent Sample Data* (New Delhi: P. Padmanabha, Controller of Publications, 1984), 78.

However, this was not the central problem posed by size. In fact, as we attempted to get to know family after family, the total number of families even in a village of this size became daunting. In our spare time, we set out to learn more about the surrounding hamlets and found them to be usually dominated by a single caste and sometimes to contain but one caste. They had none of the relative self-sufficiency of the larger village, and economically and in many other ways survived only as part of a network of villages. More important, their demographic behavior so contrasted with the larger village that in many ways, such as the age of the women at marriage or the duration of breast-feeding, the larger village stood intermediate between the hamlets and the city of Bangalore. Noting that at the 1971 census around one-sixth of the rural population of both India and Karnataka lived in centers with fewer than 500 inhabitants and two-thirds in centers with less than 2,000, we moved to double the population being investigated by including eight additional hamlets with populations ranging from 62 to 543. The final area of investigation was an elliptical area with a longer axis of about seven miles and a total population in late 1979 of 4,773. It should be noted that the concept of a local population is far from simple and that the total number of persons residing at one time or another in the course of the next four years in these villages was almost 350, or 7 percent, higher than the number recorded by our 1979 census. At any one time, the total figure was very similar to the census figure, but large numbers of persons with various kinds of rights to accommodation come and go: wives returning after having given birth in their parental villages, daughters coming back temporarily to their parents' homes to give birth, migrant sons and their families visiting from Bangalore, laborers spending a few weeks or months repairing a road or finding seasonal agricultural employment, toddy tappers coming and going and building makeshift houses during their biennial tapping visit, and many others.

The village work was not to be statistically isolated. In keeping with most micro-approach research in demography, we had studied all available large-scale data sets relevant to the area before we started. We knew the district, state, and national levels and trends with regard to a range of demographic behavior. We knew the important questions to be answered before we entered the field. We carried out our own measures of local demographic levels and trends, and would have been disconcerted if these had not approximated the broader trends. In the work described in this book there was a close approximation, so at no time did we doubt that we were answering the questions for a larger population. If this similarity in demographic measures had not been found, we would have persisted with the research in order to establish either why this was an unusual population or why large-scale methods of data collection tended to err with regard to some kinds of information.

We were in agreement that we would not dispense with any part of the survey-taker's research armory which was useful for our purposes. In practice we carried out much more detailed mapping than is common in surveys, showing every house. These maps were used for sampling, but their greatest value lay in marking the households by a range of family and individual characteristics so that many aspects of the social and demographic ecology became clear. Even many of the local people expressed surprise when they saw testimony on the maps as to how impermeable were caste residential borders. Similarly, there can be no proper understanding of the mechanisms for assisting the aged without a realization of just how tightly everyone (including the old) grouped together not only with their fellow caste members but also with their relatives.[12]

Soon after the mapping came the initial census. This was intended to provide not only a sampling frame but also a baseline from which demographic and other change could be measured. Even the first census was more a census-survey in that a considerable range of information was gathered without restriction to that which was completely straightforward and quantitative. Nevertheless, we were worried on several counts. Would this prove sufficiently satisfactory to dispose us toward doing much of the subsequent work by successive surveys? Would the impact on households be sufficiently great that they would thereafter feel that they had told us everything that we should know and would be reluctant for us to probe deeper? Would they become convinced of the truth and exactness of everything that they had told us to the point where this information would be repeated again, no matter to what extent it misrepresented the whole truth?

None of these fears were borne out. Successive surveys provided valuable distributional patterns. But they hardly ever produced new ideas or the basis for a new range of questions previously not thought valuable. The new ideas emerged solely from the more anthropological type of work. Furthermore, because our presence was continuous, friendly later visits were never regarded as intrusive in the sense that subsequent survey rounds may be. A more interesting occurrence was that most families seemed to have little idea of the information previ-

---

12. This aspect of Indian society has been explored further by K. N. M. Raju in Andhra Pradesh.

ously given and certainly did not feel constrained by it. In fact, so valuable was the baseline information that we later regretted almost all of the restrictions that we had placed on it, and enlarged the initial census-survey when it was carried out in the smaller villages some months afterwards.

The initial census-survey also served as a register, to which changes could be made as a result of later work both of a formal and a more informal type. The changes included births and deaths revealed when collecting vital statistics. Most of these changes were real, but some involved correcting erroneous information in earlier censuses. The major source of error arose from marked differences in how the researchers and the respondents defined *residence*. In spite of very great emphasis on our definition, many families at first refused to admit that children and grandchildren living in Bangalore or elsewhere for the great majority of the year were not resident members of the local family. M. N. Srinivas found this in his own ancestral village, where he first enumerated double the population who genuinely resided there according to his definition, admittedly in this case not only because of genuine disagreement of the kind explained above, but also because of deliberate deception arising from apprehension about the implications of recent land-reform legislation.[13] The latter problem was on a much reduced scale at the time of our work. What did surprise us was that the tendency to provide incorrect information was no lower among the more educated, who often had a stronger concept of the real and continuing home of the family, no matter how dispersed it was in fact. This was partly related to the possession of more fixed property, especially larger houses and more land.

Originally, we had intended that nearly all subsequent work should be participant observation and relatively unstructured interviewing. In fact, whenever we explored new areas of behavior and developed new hypotheses, we felt that a useful, indeed indispensable, addition would be a highly focused survey-round establishing distributional patterns for a large population (either the total population or perhaps every second household) and allowing the establishment of some statistical correlations. However, even these surveys allowed for a great deal of flexible probing and the reporting of new and related information with exploratory open-ended questions. Such surveys investigated aspects of off-farm employment, land tenure, child labor inputs, defenses against drought, use of health facilities, family structure, education, and aspects of marriage.

13. M. N. Srinivas, personal communication.

Related work of a more formalized type was also conducted employing a case-study approach. This was particularly important when collecting life histories showing successive attempts to arrange marriages or the history of individuals' experiences with education, training, and employment.

Nevertheless, the heart of the work lay in local residence and in a participant-observation approach. The local residence occurred for a sustained period each year between 1979 and 1983. Because the Australian participants were usually constrained to the November-March period, the experience did not include the full annual cycle of agriculture, but always covered the period through the *ragi* harvest to the next plantings. This clearly had certain disadvantages, but it also provided the opportunity to compare measurements at annual intervals. On two occasions there were also visits at other times of the year. The Indian researchers, however, visited more frequently. In addition, members of the research team, either in their capacity as staff members of the Bangalore Population Centre or as graduate students of the Australian National University, spent full years in six other villages, three in adjacent areas of Karnataka and three in neighboring states of south India. This additional experience, reported elsewhere,[14] provided an invaluable opportunity for comparison and a means for assessing whether we were measuring uniquely local phenomena or demographic behavior that was the more general experience. The latter was by far the most common.

Because time was short and there was much to be studied, and doubtless also as a result of social science experience of a nonanthropological type, the principal investigators worked with a team of collaborators. Many of the latter were staff members of the Population Centre with many years of rural research in demographic surveys. Others were chosen because of their social science background and rural origins. There were initial difficulties in recruiting sufficient female research worker who could live in villages and we failed at the time to attain our 50 percent target. In addition to the village research

14. A. Shariff, "The Beginning of Fertility Decline in South India: A Microstudy of a Cluster of Four Villages" (Ph.D. thesis, Australian National University, Canberra, 1984); M. Guruswamy, "The Measurement of Labour Inputs in Family Work and Activities, and Their Relation to the Economic Value of Children and the Control of Fertility" (Ph.D. thesis, Department of Demography, Australian National University, Canberra, 1986); K. N. M. Raju, "Family Functions: Dynamics of Households in a Village of Coastal Andhra Pradesh," (Ph.D. thesis, Australian National University, Canberra, 1988); P. N. Sushama, "The Causes of Fertility Decline in Kerala" (Ph.D. thesis, Australian National University, Canberra, 1988).

team, two other women, staff members of the Population Centre, carried out similar and parallel work in Bangalore, one in a slum and one in a middle-class area.[15] This was later supplemented by further city work undertaken by two returning investigators from the rural area.[16] In the large village, the principal investigators lived in a room which alternated as a store for the assistant engineer's cement, whereas the male collaborators stayed with village households—usually of the same caste—and female collaborators were either similarly housed or stayed with the female health workers. The latter arrangement provided valuable insights into the working of the health and family planning programs. The villagers were well disposed toward the researchers and unflagging in their attempts to throw light on the matters being researched.

There were no problems with regard to participant observation. We participated around the clock and were invited to ceremonies and happenings of every kind. We were endlessly welcomed to the houses and institutions (such as schools, health centers, temples, and mosques). The heterogeneity of the group led to a surprising range of contacts with different sections of the community. The number in the team varied, with research collaborators totaling at various times between eight and twelve. There was a selective process involved according to the liking and aptitude for the particular type of work. The best work was probably done with the smaller number, which allowed tighter contact to be maintained.

Participant observation provides a background context which permits a general interpretation of one's findings and experience. However, it would probably need a lifetime for one to be provided randomly with sufficient information on specific matters of interest. Thus, we needed to have discussions which had a substantial element of direction, and we required some plan to decide which families were to be investigated. Possibly because of prior experience with surveys, we were suspicious of purely random contacts, which we believed could be highly selective. At least in the first investigation, we could not attempt to get to know all households in depth, because they totaled 786. Our first study was focused on the decision whether to restrict family size or not. We decided to begin only with the larger village and then to confine our attention to the situation where there was a high

15. Sumitra K. Potnis worked in a remote, backward village; P. N. Sushama worked in a relatively economically advanced village; Sheila Chandra Mauli studied a middle-class area and Shashikala Kempawadkar a slum in Bangalore. The Population Centre will report on these studies.

16. Revathi N. and Kusum Kumari.

likelihood that decisions one way or the other had been made. We did this by identifying those households with one or more couples, with spouses living together, where there were three or more living children, and where the wife was 30–39 years of age. This sounds highly restrictive, yet in the larger village, 194 households, or 47 percent of the total, were of this type. We found that we could cope with this number and we later used the same method of selection for the smaller villages. Even so, we became increasingly unhappy at not having comparable data for younger couples or smaller families. Thereafter, for the other investigations, we reverted to systematic sampling, usually of every second household. By the time the research was complete, we had some knowledge of all families and a considerable amount of both anthropological and demographic data on each.

A major emphasis in the investigation was that the focus of interest was the entire household. Even if we were discussing female sterilization, we were equally interested in the roles played by both husband and wife, and indeed in finding out where the parents of each spouse fitted into the whole picture. The family economy and the education of young children were clearly central matters for probing. All members of the household were repeatedly brought into discussions, sometimes along the lines indicated by probing lists and sometimes quite informally.

There were two types of interviews, one done by the collaborating researchers and the other by the principal investigators. The former type tended to be guided more by probing lists than the latter and were documented by notes from which reports could be made, rather than being taken into anthropological notebooks. Most of the comparable data came from the former. Most of the new leads and material for fresh hypotheses came from the latter, doubtless because of a greater feeling of individual freedom to take the investigation anywhere, coupled with a conviction that there must be important areas, yet undetected, which must somehow be discovered and be brought into the whole picture. Only the principal investigators can feel this overall research responsibility, and this is one reason why they must continually participate. At first, great care was taken to speak to individuals on their own. Later, we discovered that some of our most valuable findings surfaced in group interviews, through interactions and even arguments among village participants. This was particularly true when we were discussing social change over time and when we were asking about the reasons for alteration in behavior. We rarely attempted to structure or balance groups but let them form naturally. Over several houses, the composition of groups changed as people disappeared to undertake tasks or reappeared from the fields. Often, when new topics had been broached, word appeared to have been sent to relatives or neighbors who had some specialized or relevant experience, for suddenly a person with specialized knowledge, previously unnoticed, would speak up. Another reason for the key role played by the principal investigators in their interviews was their greater knowledge of other research and of the theoretical literature on the subject.

We were initially concerned about the problem of provoking discussion or of convincing villagers that there was something to be discussed at all. Our first plan, when investigating fertility control behavior, was to ask people why they differed in this respect from other specified persons of similar background and characteristics. Soon, we realized that this meant revealing confidential information. We substituted an approach whereby we first asked about the birth control practices of siblings or friends and then sought explanations of similarities and differences. On the whole, these triggers were not needed, but we gained interesting insights into how little may be known about siblings' behavior and grounds for decisions when the siblings do not live close by. We trained our investigators not to resolve all conflicts in testimony, but rather to report the conflicting evidence after exploring it further, so that we could eventually decide where truth probably lay, or, more important, gain insights into conflict situations where interacting persons interpreted the position and the actions of their relatives in quite different ways. This was particularly the case with the complex interactions that lead to the adoption of fertility control—an area which is usually quite unsuited for examination by survey methods.

Our first intention was to define for our collaborators the problem to be investigated and then to let them get to know each household well while compiling notes on all relevant matters. The degree of independence was too great. There was some fascinating material, but there were also great gaps and much that was not comparable. Reluctantly, we began to construct probing lists, but these always remained subtopics and never jelled into questions. They could be explored in any order, and, if seemingly irrelevant, did not need to be asked at all. There was always an encouragement to follow new leads, and to report these in full. The important point was that the probing lists were not only flexible but were living instruments. They changed from day to day as new items were added and some were dropped. Individual interviewers could add items of their own.

The heart of the research, that which held it together providing form, and from which new probing items were constructed, was the daily meeting. Here, everyone discussed and argued, and proudly presented new findings and new ideas based on these findings. In this type of research, much of the motivation to do innovational interviewing and to discover new but important facets of the problem comes from knowing that within hours these discoveries can be presented to the whole group. This is the fundamental mechanism for developing the spirit of research and the feeling of being on the frontier of knowledge.[17]

The basis of this kind of work is the construction and testing of hypotheses at all kinds of levels. In the older research areas of anthropology, many of the hypotheses can be derived from other research, from books, and from theoretical formulations. The conditions of change in demographic behavior are not yet such an area. Most of the hypotheses have to be generated and strengthened or discarded during the research project. The ideas pursued by the principal investigators during their long and very flexible interviews and the ideas put forward in the daily discussion groups were emerging hypotheses, often only partly formed, which were the new probes added to the lists for the next day's work. Much of the discussion took the form of strengthening or weakening hypotheses. We progressively developed what we called the "playback method," where we put our hypotheses and related intellectual problems to the respondents themselves, often in group situations. Whatever this did to lead their ideas was of small importance compared with the invaluable dissection of the hypotheses. Villagers often added further valuable evidence once the situation received a theoretical structuring of this kind; sometimes they were able to destroy what had seemed to be a valuable idea before we wasted too much effort on it.

Two very important problems confronted us: how to record the information, and how to analyze it.

During discussions, interviewers took notes, some more comprehensively than others. Soon afterwards they discussed the whole interview with one of the principal investigators in a kind of debriefing session. This had three purposes. The first was to search for incomplete investigations, so as to direct the researcher back to the household. The second was to allow the research worker to put the whole position into perspective before writing a report and also to think over the total picture to see if more information or more consideration was needed.

17. This aspect of the research had been developed in Africa. See J. C. Caldwell, *The Study of Fertility and Fertility Change in Tropical Africa*, no. 7 in *Occasional Papers* (Voorburg: International Statistical Institute/WFS, 1974).

The third was to help the principal investigator to build a growing mental picture of the whole matter. These discussions, because they allowed readier rejoinders, and, indeed, cross-examination, played a distinctly different role from reading the reports. Subsequently, possibly after one or more revisits, the research worker wrote a report. Each family had a separate file to which the reports could be added. Subsequent knowledge of the family, from other villagers, could lead either to the depositing in the file of supplementary reports or to the amendment of reports already there.

The major research decision was how to use this material. There was a temptation, which we resisted, to code it. Our decision not to do this was determined partly by the nature of the material, where each report did not cover all the points raised by other reports, but might instead contain quite elaborate descriptions of matters dealt with passingly or not at all by other research workers. We believed that as soon as we made any decision to code, this would affect the way both we and our collaborators regarded the household visits. There would be more emphasis on covering every point and less on following to their limits those discoveries which appeared to be important. Thus, we made a clear distinction between these semistructured interviews and the highly focused specific surveys which often concluded each topic that we investigated.

These reports were quite distinct from the additional conclusions drawn by the principal investigators and included in their notebooks. These notebooks were also used to record information offered by villagers or actions observed or experienced when living in the village. We did not employ paid informants because of a belief that there was often a strong element of self-selectivity, which might mean a determination to offer a certain type of interpretation together with supporting evidence. We did, however, talk to villagers continuously, often directing our conversations to specific matters, and much of this material we recorded.

The main use of the files was for reading and rereading from the very beginning of the work until after all fieldwork had been completed. The purpose of this was to seek ideas and to generate hypotheses. These readings during the fieldwork interacted with interviewing, daily discussions, and the debriefing of interviewers. As the work proceeded, the reports were increasingly used to sustain or reject hypotheses, and this became their major function at the end of the work.

Perhaps the most important single element in this research approach is that the same persons participate fully in every aspect of the research. Those who designed the work, participated fully in the field research, and generated the hypotheses are also those who ultimately draw conclusions and write papers. There is no problem of gaps or misunderstandings which can lead analysts to conclusions which would differ from the experience or interpretations of field-workers. Social science creates gaps between data collection and analysis only at its peril, but it is common in survey research for such role differentiation to exist.

When we began the village work, we thought of it as being largely a means for generating plausible hypotheses, which would later be confirmed by correlation analysis from large-scale data sets. We subsequently modified this attitude for a number of reasons. First, many of our hypotheses concerned social and economic change from the preexisting conditions, so that confirmatory or supporting evidence was to be found in archives, libraries, reports, or books. Other hypotheses were best supported by local records on land holdings or production. Second, the research clearly came ever closer to validating itself for the area being studied. Ever more strongly supported hypotheses tended to become explanations. That these explanations had wider currency could be deduced partly by their own internal logic within the broader area of cultural near-homogeneity and partly from the fact that the demographic behavioral patterns that resulted could be shown by census or other large-scale data to exist over a broader area and to be changing in much the same way and at a similar pace as those found in the research area. Third, although we believed that correlation findings could add strength to the hypotheses, we continued to feel that the data from such large-scale work were often so defective that surveys alone could not with complete certainty disprove a hypothesis, but that the best approach would remain a combination of micro and macro work. Fourth, small-scale surveys for the five thousand inhabitants of the area often provided quite satisfactory numbers for correlation analysis. The case for large-sample surveys was mainly for showing that similar patterns persisted over larger populations.

There is, then, a case for a micro-macro mix. This does not mean that every demographic village researcher should feel that work cannot begin unless plans and funding have been completed for a final large survey. It does mean that when large surveys are undertaken, they will benefit from designing questions based on hypotheses arising from village surveys in the area or other similar-culture areas. Larger projects can help to set up the village studies, preferably beginning some time before the surveys.

When we began the work one of our aims was to formulate better survey questions over a more complete range and to test survey data to see where it was least reliable. It became clear that the survey household was probably largely an artifact of the survey interviewer or supervisor (because of problems of applying definitions or obtaining agreement from respondents to use that definition), and that, consequently, out-migration was understated, infant mortality was probably usually understated (especially of the newly born), and traditional fertility control was probably always underestimated. Complex matters, such as the suggestions and pressures leading to the control of fertility, are often unsuited to study by surveys (which all too frequently record merely the final concession or surrender that leads a woman, for instance, to consent to sterilization). However, the most interesting finding was that the range of responses provided with precoded questions may often be a product of the survey procedure itself. To many questions there was often broad agreement in the village, as could be ascertained by lengthy household discussions. This frequently is not equally clear in surveys—even in our own—because respondents give responses with slightly different emphases, or, more commonly, begin a complex answer explaining each aspect or component in a different order from that adopted by other respondents. The precodes tend to select the first aspect mentioned, and so produce a broad distribution of responses even when near-consensus exists in the community (usually not as to a single point but regarding several points, all of which are relevant).

Originally, we intended to give invented names to all nine settlements, in order to identify them to readers while protecting our respondents. In fact, the smaller villages were, in terms of demographic behavior, rather similar, and are usually grouped here during analysis. We started to report that analysis as a contrast between *the large village* and *the smaller villages* and we will continue this rather prosaic usage.

The Chosen Area

The villages were situated only near small streams. Although dry, the area had once been covered by sclerophyllic forest and scrub, inhabited by tribal hunters and gatherers. From the beginning of the present millennium, the area was first on the outskirts of the Chola Empire based on the Tamil-speaking area of India's east-southeast, and then on that of the Hoysala Kingdom with its capital 50 miles to the west of the study site. Both assigned settlement rights to groups of Hindu farming families to move toward the frontiers, to clear forests and establish settled communities. These often took the form of *brama-deyas*, or Brahmin settlements with associated Harijan laborers and peasant farmers. The large village appears to have been established in this way, as a settlement of Vaishnavite Brahmins (followers of Vishnu, also known as Iyengars) who moved out from the predominantly Shaivite (followers of Siva) Tamil Nadu coastal areas.[18] This is believed to be one of 25 settlements made in the eleventh century. Some of these families are still found there, speaking medieval Tamil. Thus, the large village still is the home of all the Brahmins and most of the Harijans (untouchables) who were their laborers. The smaller villages are predominantly the preserve of the peasant castes and some backward castes who were originally occupied in such work as sheepherding.

In the eighteenth century the area became part of the Sultanate of Mysore, and was then ruled by the Maharajah of Mysore after the defeat of Tippu Sultan's armies by the East India Company. The larger village was situated on one of the radial roads built from the city of Mysore. So important was this road in the nineteenth century that the Maharajah's government built a series of travelers' bungalows along it for journeying officials. In 1880, an earthen wall, half a mile long, was thrown across the largest stream of the area (probably on the site of an earlier smaller dam) to form a tank of considerable size near the larger village, so ensuring its predominance in the area. This led to the two most decisive events in the village's history. The first was the breaching of the earthen dam wall and the consequent inundation of the village during the unusually heavy rains of the 1898 monsoon, and the second was the decision the following year by a high official of the Maharajah's court that the village was to be moved to confiscated land, provided free to the householders, beyond flood level about half a mile to the south. In 1901 the transfer began and street alignments were set out, so that the residents have ever since boasted of their planned town. Temples were moved only slowly. It was often more practicable to move the gods to a new building, and the process has only recently been completed.

During this century the history of the larger village, unmarked by communal violence or other dramatic events, has mostly been one of acquiring institutions. In 1911 the Agricultural Cooperative Society of the DCC Bank began to give credit, and in 1971 the Mysore State Bank opened a full branch—one of the area's larger buildings. In 1910–13 a

18. *Mysore State Gazetteer: Tumkur District* (Bangalore: Government Press, 1969), 591.

mosque was constructed by the Muslim population, and in the decade from 1924 to 1934 three government schools were built. In 1929 the Mysore Government established a health center, and in 1947–48 the area suffered for the last time from a plague epidemic. After Independence came the Rural Veterinary Dispensary in 1949, the first rice mill in 1955, and electricity in 1957, making possible the first electrically driven rice mill and the first radios in the same year. In 1951 elections were held for the new *panchayat* council, and the appointed, and largely hereditary, headman or *patel* went into retirement and increasing obscurity. Shortly after, a sugar mill was established. Buses were nationalized in 1960, and the bus stand, still the most crowded single place in the district, was built. In 1964–64 a sub–post office was established and in 1964 the government sank a bore well. In 1965 a villager bought the first privately owned truck (and by 1980 four entrepreneurial families owned trucks).

The 1970s began with the establishment of a police outpost in 1970, the tarring of the main road in 1970–71, and the appointment of an assistant agricultural officer in charge of soil conservation at the same time. The construction of a rural water supply system began in 1975 and a large new post and telegraph office was built, with the first telephones being connected the following year. The Karnataka State Government began to enforce new land reforms in 1975–76. In 1978 the first private doctor, a member of a prominent Brahmin family, opened a clinic, although his clientele are not nearly as numerous as are those of the Government Health Sub-Centre. In the same year a modern water tank with piped water was constructed. In 1980 the first local farmer bought a tractor, the government established a small enterprise, a branch of the National Textile Corporation, and a small private commercial institute was established for typing.

We have concentrated on the large village in the system, and have shown the changes to have been enormous—something not always clear when first looking at villages remote from the cities. The communications revolution has been extraordinary. Until 1940, no one could be sure of arranging any transport beyond the village except at walking pace by bullock cart; now buses endanger the lives of people every half-hour by roaring into the village. Until 1957 no instantaneous message had even been received in the area; then electricity allowed powered radios to be used and within three years the new transistor radios were being listened to in all villages. It is only in the last 25 years that the large rice and sugar mills have appeared, and only in the last 15 years that powered grain mills in the smaller villages have begun to appear.

The educational revolution has been even more extraordinary, but that will be dealt with separately.

An important element in the society was the cinema. When our study began, the nearest cinema was six or seven miles away; during the research, a temporary or "tent" cinema (built of bamboo and palm thatch) was given a license outside the large village; by the end of our work a small permanent cinema was being constructed. Even in 1980 almost half the population had been to the pictures, one-third of these within the previous week. Most young men went quite regularly, and their elders gave this as the reason for social and demographic change more often than any other factor.

Clearly, social and economic relations must be changing. We were working in the field on the day when *jajmani* debts were traditionally settled by a disbursement of grain, but saw no sign of such transactions. However, we were told of one large village not very far away where such postharvest grain payments are still the common pattern.

The District and Its Occupations

As can be seen from map 1.1 and table 1.1, the survey population consists of two parts, a large village and eight smaller villages, approximately equal in total to the population of the large village. Each of the smaller villages except one ((1) in the table) is essentially within the larger village's commercial catchment area in that the larger village provides the weekly market and small shops which they mostly patronize. Even the exceptional village, which is situated furthest from the larger village and which has a small weekly market of its own, still provides a substantial number of customers for the larger village. The

Table 1.1. Populations of Survey Villages, January 1980

Village	Males	Females	Persons	Households
Large village	1,342	1,215	2,557	413
Smaller villages:				
(1)	272	271	543	100
(2)	219	189	408	63
(3)	163	185	348	51
(4)	147	146	293	48
(5)	132	143	275	48
(6)	95	101	196	31
(7)	44	47	91	19
(8)	33	29	62	13
Total	2,447	2,326	4,773	786

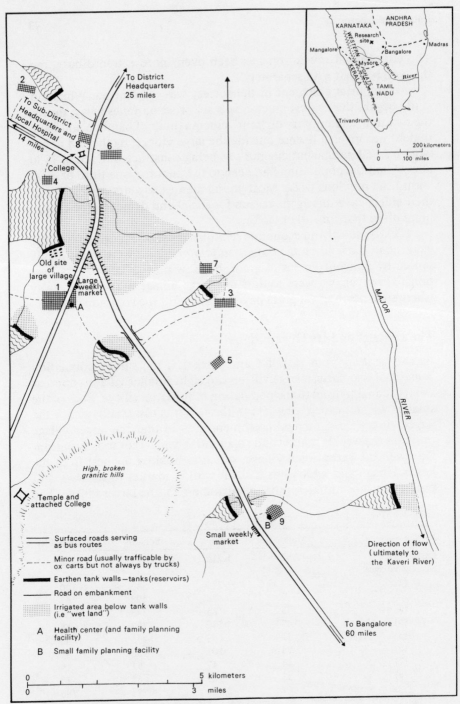

Map 1.1. The Study Area

catchment area also includes some villages to the south and southeast which were not studied.

This contrast between the large village and the smaller villages is not merely one of size. It is largely a distinction in function, which has as yet been inadequately handled by social scientists in India. The large village, unlike the smaller villages, has had a weekly market, the *sandy* or *shandy* (the latter the Tamil version), since at least far back into the last century. Every Wednesday, on both sides of the road on the northern outskirts of the village, people from the district and beyond gather from early morning to midafternoon, in temporary stalls or on the ground, to sell merchandise: foodstuffs, areca nuts, areca nuts wrapped in betel leaves with lime (*paan*), tobacco, cigarettes, matches, nails, soap, and hundreds of other items. There are some specialized areas selling only cow shoes or pots (some villages elsewhere specialize in making earthenware pots), jaggery (blocks of unrefined local sugar), *beedies* (local cigarettes), coconuts, or bananas. No one sells religious posters as is common in markets in northern India. The large village also has over twenty permanent shops: cloth merchants, bicycle repairers, coffee grinders, hotels (for selling tea, coffee, and food), a toddy bar, a barber, several small grocers' shops, and so on. By contrast, the smaller villages rarely have more than one or two tiny shops. The total contents of one we listed were a few of each of the following: *beedies*, matches, candles, razor blades, lollies, onions, tea bags, jaggery, incense sticks, split peas, rubber bands, washing blue, local and commercial soap, coconut and groundnut oil, kerosene, thread, needles, aspirin, and salt. These items took the form of a few scattered piles across dusty wooden shelves, and apparently were as numerous as this because it was in the one small village with a considerable Muslim population which is therefore more given to trading. It is no accident that the large village is on a main road, near to where four roads meet, whereas every other village is away from the main roads, down earth tracks, which, although mostly usable by trucks in the dry season, are normally traversed only by bullock carts and pedestrians. The total number of business outlets in the area doubled over four years—one index of commercialization and a measure of the speed with which the economy is being monetized.

In addition, over the last 50 years, accelerating in the last 20, the large village has become a center for governmental services connected with education, roads, health, veterinary activities, agriculture, agricultural credit, engineering and water services, and the police. The result is that the merchant class has been supplemented by a considerable bureaucracy.

The effect of this is surprising. Even though the large village seems a typical agricultural village to the outsider, a majority of its workforce (excluding housewives and students)—admittedly a bare majority, 52 percent—are engaged in nonagricultural occupations. The figure for the smaller villages is 10 percent. But, in the large village, 29 percent of the work force are merchants or their assistants, 15 percent are the bureaucracy and other government employees, and 8 percent are other nonagricultural workers, such as the day laborers employed to maintain the road.

Nevertheless, in the district as a whole the chief activity is farming. Of the total agricultural population, one-fifth own no land at all, in spite of persistent attempts in Karnataka to provide the landless with some land. They are agricultural laborers or *coolies*. Nearly four-fifths own some land which they work with their own hands, with or without assistance. The actual position is not as simple as this description might imply, because the full-time *coolies* are not the only source of agricultural labor. Many members of families that do possess land, especially those with smaller holdings, also earn money by hiring themselves out as laborers, particularly at times of peak demand. Those with land either own it or are tenants. Here again, the position is far from simple. Many tenants have rights that are more or less hereditary, while many landowners have been tenants of this kind but have gained title to their land under land reform legislation. Many farmers are both landowners and tenants; indeed, a considerable number are landowners, tenants, and agricultural laborers. There is no simple class stratification in rural areas, although the area of land farmed is an important source of prestige and power.

There is an important distinction between the large village and the others in terms of the type and scale of agriculture. The large village is not only a center for bureaucrats and traders, but also for landlords. The six large landowning families in the district who only oversee physical work (half are Brahmins, the rest Jains) live there. So do a disproportionate number of the other large families, especially those with irrigated land. The result is that although the large village is the home of just over one-fifth of all landowners, almost three-fifths of landless laborers live there. Thus, it has a radically different farming structure. The major reason for this contrast is the existence of the large tank and hence of the majority of irrigated or wet land there. With land reform, large landowners have had to surrender much of their dry land to tenants, but little land to *coolies*, and they have been especially successful in retaining the wet land for rice cultivation with *coolie* labor.

Religion and Caste

Unlike much of south India, the survey district contained no Christians; nor were there any Parsees or Buddhists. Of the total population, 22 percent were Muslims, 6 percent Lingayats, 3 percent Jains, and the remaining 69 percent more orthodox Hindus. The larger village again showed itself to be more heterogeneous, with 32 percent Muslims, 4 percent Lingayats, 6 percent Jains, and 58 percent Hindus. The Lingayats are a thousand-year-old sect of followers of Siva who originally disdained caste. They are found mostly in Karnataka, but their main concentration is much further north than the survey district.

The description above—a fairly standard one in terms of social science—is, nevertheless, far from complete. It is very much a description employing the outlook of the *great tradition* (favored by the Learned), whereas the truth is that the *little tradition* (found among simple villagers) is also very much alive in the villages (see chap. 6). Much respect is paid to the ancient female gods who ward off disease and other disasters. They can be specific to a single village, as is the goddess Marayama to the large village, or known more widely, as is the goddess Miriama who wards off smallpox and also infertility. Cults of these goddesses have taken over the old temple buildings at the previous site of the large village, and in every village there are frequent sacrifices of goats and sheep to deities of this type. In the smaller villages, even Muslims absorb Hindu practices from both traditions into their religious practices.

Outside the large village, Muslims were found in only one other village (they had probably been Harijans before the establishment of the Muslim Sultanate in the eighteenth century), where they formed half the population; Lingayats were in only one other village, where they made up two-thirds of the population, and Jains nowhere else. Six of the villages were homogeneously orthodox Hindu.

There are interesting parallels in terms of caste distribution. M. N. Srinivas, studying another large village of southern Karnataka, believed his village to be unusually complex in that it contained 16 castes (counting Muslims and Lingayats as castes and condensing his three Brahmin castes to a single one).[19] This may, in fact, be the nature of larger villages which act as service centers, for our large village, with two-thirds as much population again as Srinivas's Rampura, contained 24 castes (counting Muslims, Lingayats, and Jains). The largest four castes in Rampura constituted five-sixths of the whole popula-

19. Srinivas, "The Social System of a Mysore village," in Marriott, *Village India*, 1–35.

tion, but the four largest in our large village contributed only three-fifths of the total, and it needed the 10 largest castes to make up five-sixths.

In the whole district there were 26 castes (two of them unrepresented in the large village but numbering no more than 0.4 percent of the district population) and at least 69 endogamous subcastes (the note of caution is sounded here because the true endogamous group amongst people like the Vokkaligas is usually the sub-subcaste, which members sometimes had difficulty in identifying by name).

Apart from the large village, every village was characterized by one caste being in an absolute majority of the population. Indeed, one village was made up entirely of one caste, and four others had populations of which over 80 percent were from a single caste. The numerically dominant caste in four of the eight smaller villages was the Vokkaliga, the main peasant caste of southern Karnataka, but in the other four it was Muslim, Lingayat, Tigalaru (a poor peasant caste, once hunters) and Ganigaru (a service caste, once oil crushers). Smaller villages are often, then, havens for a single caste, where members of that caste may be rich landowners or poor landless laborers. Small villages may be characterized by dominant subcastes, three of the eight studied consisting of over 80 percent of one or other of the Vokkaliga subcastes.

It is something of a misnomer to label Vokkaligas as a caste. The term means *peasant-farmer* and in the 1881 census was employed as an occupational category for over 60 similar peasant castes, often distinguished more by place of residence that by hierarchical distinctions. In the next four censuses they were formed first into a caste-occupation group, and then into a caste.[20] This situation has now been accepted by the statewide caste association, but not by the village marriage market.

The classical picture of each village containing a significant proportion of Harijans to serve as landless laborers and scavengers, say at least 10 percent of the population, was the case only in the large village, and, in a less definite form, in one other. The same was true of the service castes, especially of those working in their traditional occupations. Only the large village could provide a range of services, a situation that has perhaps always been true only of the larger villages which act as service centers, visited by those in need of services on the

20. Cf. the discussion in James Manor, *Political Change in an Indian State: Mysore, 1917–1955*, Australian National University Monographs on South Asia, no. 2 (New Delhi: Manohar, 1977), 34–36.

shandy day or at any time for urgent needs, and sometimes sending out itinerant craftsmen to visit the smaller centers.

The castes of the district can be condensed by adding together those of similar level in the caste hierarchy (see table 1.2).

Clearly, this distribution, as in most of south India, is not the classical Indian split among the twice-born (Brahmins or priests, Kshatryas or warriors, and Vaisyas or merchants), the Shudras or peasant castes, and the Harijans or untouchables. Strictly speaking, one-third of the population, Muslims, Jains, and Lingayats, lies outside this classification. The upper castes are represented only by Brahmins, who make up no more than 5 percent of the population. The Harijans form only 8 percent of the total, little more than half the

Table 1.2. Distribution of Population by Caste Group

Caste group	Constituent castes	Persons No.	%	Households No.	%
Brahmin	Brahmin	239	5	41	5
Jain	Jain	166	3	25	3
Lingayat	Lingayat	296	6	55	6
Muslim	Muslim	1,132	22	170	20
Vokkaliga	Vokkaliga	1,627	32	274	32
Service Castes	Kumbar	19	(0.4)	3	(0.3)
	Achar	34	1	9	1
	Ajamaru	41	1	8	1
	Madivala	95	2	18	2
	Kshatriya	6	(0.1)	1	(0.1)
	Shetty	25	(0.5)	5	(0.6)
	Banajiga	9	(0.2)	2	(0.3)
Poor Peasants	Edigaru	42	1	8	1
and	Tigalaru	292	6	53	6
pastoralists	Kuruba	13	(0.3)	3	(0.3)
	Nayakaru	156	3	24	3
	Ganga Matha (or Bestharu)	149	3	24	3
	Uppernaru	35	1	7	1
	Ganigaru	111	2	16	2
	Bovi	9	(0.2)	3	(0.3)
Harijan	Adikarnataka	180	4	28	3
	Adidravida	211	4	34	4
Others		56	1	10	1
Not Stated		174	2	45	5
Total		5,117	100	866	100

Note: The numbers in this table are of all persons resident in the villages at any time during the survey period. It exceeds the January census by 344 persons and 80 households.

national average. In between lies a vast middle group, which is typical of the caste structure of south India, and goes far toward explaining the emerging social flexibility of the region. This group forms a majority of the population. Any of them might own land, and, if they do, will work it with their own hands. The real peasant caste of southern Karnataka is the Vokkaliga, many of whom take this identity so much for granted that they assert that their real caste name is *gowda* or farmer.

Caste is still of absolute importance with regard to marriage, as was demonstrated by the occurrence of only one cross-caste marriage —an elopement—during the years of the study. Although people of different castes mingle together and even eat together more easily than in the past, notions of hierarchy, especially in terms of purity, and the concept of pollution are very much alive. In one of the smaller villages pure water is available from the tube well installed by the government near the Harijan quarter, but only the Harijans enjoy this, for the other castes insist on drawing their water from a distant well which has been shown to be unsafe.

The continuing significance of caste is well demonstrated by the settlement pattern (see map 1.2). The core institutional area of the large village is occupied almost exclusively by the three elite groups, Brahmins, Jains, and Lingayats, each having specific areas of concentration. One corner of the village is, with the exception of a single household, exclusively Muslim, whereas in the opposite corner are found the Harijan settlements. The latter are separated by some distance into the settlements of the Adikarnataka, who were once called Madigas and traditionally were scavengers and leather workers, and the Adidravida, once called Holyas and who were agricultural laborers and watchmen. The middle castes exhibit greater overlap, but there are nuclei of settlement for each caste. There are only two exceptions. The first is the residence area for officials where the government allocates housing, and the second is the new *janata* (people's) housing area where the government provides loans for the backward castes. In spite of statements by *panchayat* (council) leaders and others that this project provides a melting pot for castes, there are no Brahmin, Jain, or Lingayat families there, and only one Harijan family, where the head is a teacher. It is in fact a melting pot of Muslims with Hindu middle castes, and already exhibits some nucleation of caste. The pattern in the smaller villages is similar but simpler. That these are not primarily socioeconomic patterns is shown by the much more confused picture presented by the mapping of households by their heads' occupations.

There is, of course, a relation between caste and occupation, as shown in table 1.3 where caste has been condensed further.

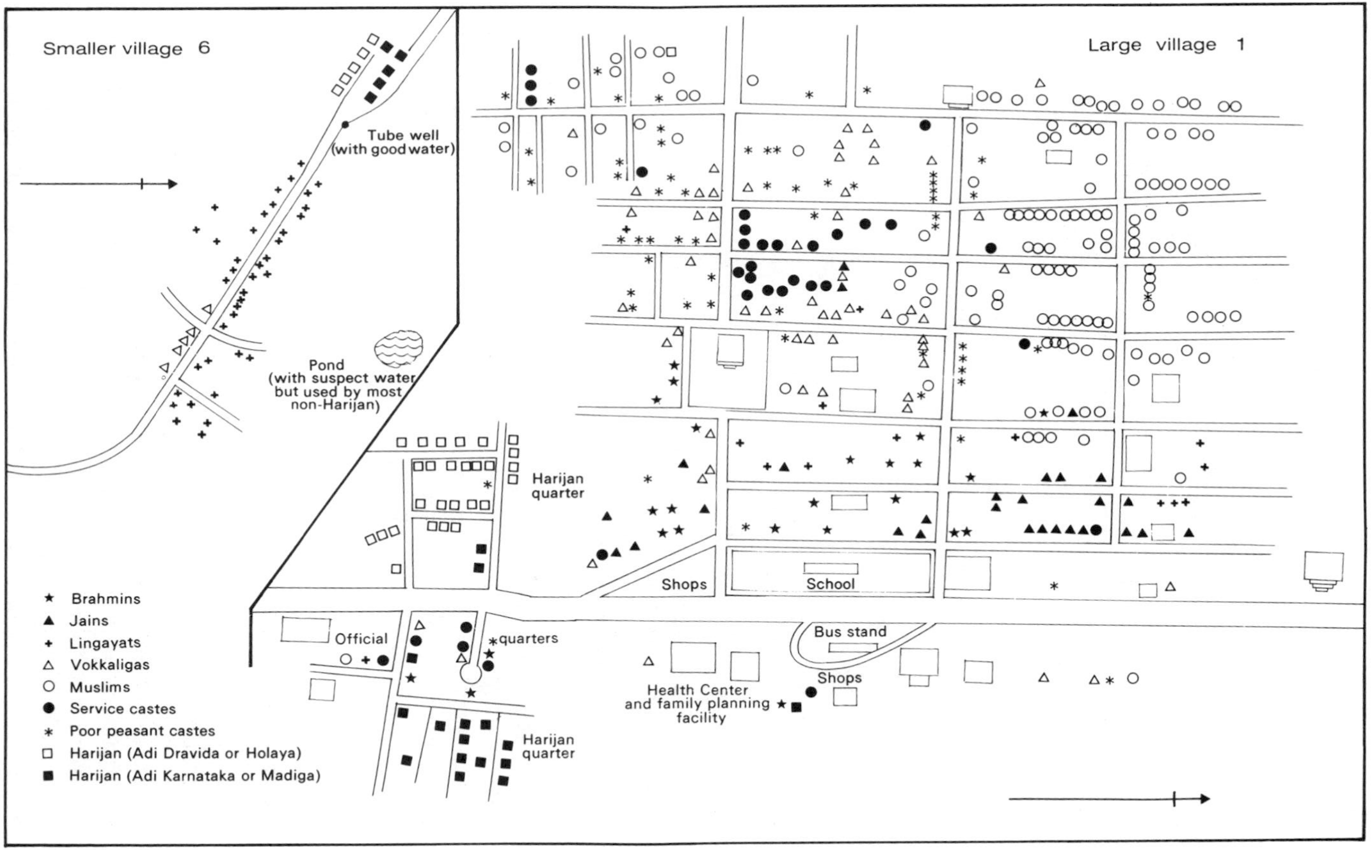

Map 1.2. Residential Location by Caste Group

Large village 1

Smaller village 6

Tube well
(with good water)

Pond
(with suspect water
but used by most
non-Harijan)

School

Bus stand

Shops

Health Center
and family planning
facility

Shops

Harijan
quarter

*quarters

Harijan
quarter

Harijan
quarter

Official

★ Brahmins
▲ Jains
+ Lingayats
△ Vokkaligas
○ Muslims
● Service castes
✱ Poor peasant castes
□ Harijan (Adi Dravida or Holaya)
■ Harijan (Adi Karnataka or Madiga)

31

Table 1.3. Caste Group by Occupation of Household Head

Percentage of caste group in each occupation

Caste group	White collar	Landlord	Farmer	Laborer[a]	Other non-agricultural occupation	Home duties[b]	%	N
Elite[c]	30	4	40	0	11	15	100	301
Merchant/Service[d]	12	1	28	9	39	11	100	1,048
Peasant/Middle[e]	7	0	70	5	7	11	100	1,597
Harijan/Scheduled[f]	8	0	42	22	10	18	100	999

Percentage of occupation contributed by each caste group

Elite	22	65	6	0	5	9
Merchant/Service	30	35	15	25	64	22
Peasant/Middle	27	0	58	22	16	34
Harijan/Scheduled	21	0	21	53	15	35
%	100	100	100	100	100	100
N	401	20	1,962	405	641	516

Notes: Letters denote castes as in table 1.2.
[a] Laborers with no land.
[b] Almost entirely widows.
[c] Brahmin, Lingayat, Jain.
[d] Muslim, Service Castes.
[e] Vokkaliga and Poor Peasants and Pastoralists.
[f] Harijan.

Muslims and the service castes make up little more than one-quarter of the population, but contribute two-thirds of urban work outside the professions, mostly as merchants and artisans. The lower castes make up another quarter of the population and provide the majority of *coolie* labor. The elite (Brahmins, Jains, and Lingayats) have three times the representation in the bureaucracy and professions that their numbers alone might have indicated, whereas the under-represented group is not the scheduled castes, for whom there are educational and occupational reserved places, but the peasant castes.

Education

Table 1.4 presents the educational pattern for the district and the significant difference between the large village and the smaller villages.

Some of the contrast can be explained by the earlier establishment of schools in the large village. This is not the whole explanation, however; differentials persist among the young at a time when most villages have primary schools and all have reasonably easy access to them (table 1.5).

Table 1.4. Population Distributed by Educational Level (Percentage distribution)

Educational level	Large village		Smaller villages		All villages	
Persons under 5 years of age						
Not at pre-school or school	11.3		12.2		11.7	
At pre-school or school	2.3		0.4		1.4	
Persons 5+ years of age	% of 5+		% of 5+		% of 5+	
No schooling	22.8		54.9		37.7	
Schooling:						
less than 7th standard	31.6		15.9		24.6	
7th standard	7.6		5.1		6.4	
some secondary	15.4		7.6		11.7	
some university	3.3	70%	0.5	34%	2.0	53.5%
tertiary (not necessarily requiring completed secondary)	2.9		0.7		1.8	
Not stated	2.8		2.7		2.7	

Table 1.5. Proportion Educated by Age, Sex, and Residence
(Percentages of each residence-age-sex-division)

Age	Education[a]	Large Village		Other villages		Total population	
		Males	Females	Males	Females	Males	Females
5–19	NS	21	29	32	63	27	46
	PS	62	57	54	31	57	44
	SS+	17	14	14	6	16	10
20–34	NS	18	38	52	84	33	60
	PS	35	32	22	12	29	23
	SS+	47	30	26	4	38	17
35–39	NS	33	59	66	93	48	74
	PS	33	37	27	6	30	23
	SS+	34	4	7	1	22	3
50+	NS	34	75	68	97	51	85
	PS	48	22	24	3	36	13

[a]NS = schooling; PS = primary schooling (up to grade 7); SS+ = secondary or higher schooling.

If the criterion of education is the proportion with any schooling, the large village had reached the position thirty years ago that the other villages have now attained. If the measure is secondary education, the large village led the smaller villages by almost the same period in the case of females and by over half a century for males.

The Two Societies

We are concerned, then, with two societies which might be expected to behave demographically in somewhat different ways. The large village, although officially a village, is really a service center, occupationally a small town. The complexity of its caste composition allows a full range of caste distinctions to be drawn, but also means that caste must to some extent be ignored in the many confrontations of everyday life. The stereotype of the illiterate Indian village is not wholly wrong for the smaller villages. There, among the population over five years of age, three-quarters of the females and almost half the males have never been to school. But in the large village, half of the females and three-quarters of the males have at least some schooling, and, amongst those under 20 years of age, 71 percent even of girls now go to school.

These contrasts are based on fundamental economic differences. The small villages are nucleated settlements of persons with access to land, mostly either owning or renting some land. The lives of these agricultural people, and their decisions about their children's education and future, revolve around land. In the large village, probably a considerable majority of all families believe that the future of at least some of their children will not lie in agriculture and might well be outside the district. Such contrasts may well have implications for the value of high fertility, and this dichotomy of the population was kept in mind throughout the study.

Trends in Vital Rates

The initial census-survey provided both short- and long-term retrospective measures of fertility and mortality. These were the levels and trends that demonstrated that the demographic situation of the locality was not essentially different from that of the whole state. The births and deaths recorded during the period of fieldwork, although limited and subject to capricious variability in a population of 5,000 compared with longer retrospective series, essentially supported the indirect estimates.

The simplest measure is the crude birthrate (births per thousand population over the previous year). This measure, derived from the direct question to each household about the number of babies born in the previous twelve months, yielded a crude birthrate of 25 for the whole area, 27 for the large village, and 23 for the smaller villages.

There was, clearly, some understatement. For instance, in the large village the addition of disclosed deaths over the preceding twelve months to the number of living children under one year of age yielded a number of births which converted into a crude birthrate of 29 per thousand. The understatement was probably even greater in the small villages because of lower levels of education amongst those reporting these events. This suspicion was supported by the lack of significant difference between the proportions of the total population in each of the childhood age groups between the large village and other villages.

On the other hand, there was probably not gross understatement. The use of stable population analysis[21] suggested crude birthrates for the whole area of 27.5, 32, and 39 when employing the proportion of the total population under 5, 10, and 15 years of age respectively. Age statement was almost certainly not bad enough to imply that such results had been obtained from a genuinely stable population with constant fertility. There had certainly been a considerable decline in fertility, which, strictly speaking, limits the value of stable fertility analysis (and of the Brass methods discussed below). Nevertheless, it is pertinent to note that although the proportion of the population under 5 years of age implied a recent crude birth rate of 27.5 per thousand, the proportions for ages 5–9 and 10–14 implied birthrates in the early 1970s and late 1960s of 43 and 50 per thousand.

The trend just suggested may be exaggerated by distortions in the age data. Nevertheless, it is difficult to avoid the conclusion that the birthrate at the end of the 1970s was in the vicinity of 30 per thousand, had been near 40 per thousand in the first years of the decade, and had been higher still in the 1960s.

This was, then, precisely the kind of population we wished to study. Birthrates were already moderate and had recently declined steeply. The onset of pronounced fertility decline may not have been more than a dozen years before the census-survey, and the steepest fertility decline had almost certainly occurred in the preceding half-dozen years. Participants in that decline should have been able to explain what had happened.

Table 1.6 shows the distribution of women by age and by their number of live births. Distributions are restricted to age-education groups containing more than 35 women, and hence among older women there are no distributions for those with schooling.

21. Cf. W. Brass and A. J. Coale, "Methods of Analysis and Estimation," in *The Demography of Tropical Africa*, ed. W. Brass, A. J. Coale, P. Demeny, D. H. Heisel, F. Lorimer, A. Romaniuk, and E. van de Walle (Princeton: Princeton University Press, 1968), 88–139; and A. J. Coale and P. Demeny, *Methods of Estimating Basic Demographic Measures from Incomplete Data*, Manuals on Methods of Estimating Population, no. 4 (New York: United Nations, 1967).

Table 1.6. Number of Live Births per Woman, by Age and Education
(Percentage distribution)

Education	Age	Number of live births							Total	
		0	1	2	3	4	5	6+	%	N
No	15–19	82	12	4	2				100	133
schooling	20–24	35	20	22	23				100	113
	25–29	24	8	15	36	5	12		100	114
	30–34	13	7	6	25	16	24	9	100	105
	35–39	15	6	3	16	22	16	22	100	102
	40–44	13	5	5	21	29	18	9	100	62
Primary	15–19	83	12	3	2				100	66
schooling	20–24	44	18	18	18	2			100	51
only	25–29	20	3	15	56	2	2	2	100	41
	30–34	3	3	5	40	23	17	8	100	35
Secondary	15–19	95	5						100	63
schooling or	20–24	84	8	8					100	39
more	25–29	37	18	16	0	5			100	38

Note: Distributions are only for age-education groups with 35 or more women.

The full distribution available for women with no schooling suggests that sterility levels—at least among this group—may be as high as 13 percent. This distribution shows that for women over 30 years of age the typical pattern has been 3–5 live births, with larger families something of an exception.

There is little in the table that cannot be explained by later age at marriage with increasing education. Indeed, once age at marriage and education are controlled, other socioeconomic characteristics of the population seem to play a minor role in determining fertility. Nor is the type of family in which a woman lives a determining factor.

Higher Muslim than Hindu fertility has been reported for India as a whole and for Karnataka often around 10 percent.[22] In the area we studied there were no significant differentials for women under 30 years of age. Above that age Muslims were pronouncedly more likely to have five or more children, the phenomenon being sufficiently common to yield a completed family size around 10 percent greater than among the rest of the population. This dividing point at about 30 years of age seems to be largely the result of the type of fertility control favored by the family planning program (sterilization) and by differ-

22. Cf. K. Balasubramaniam, "Differential Fertility in India: Evidence From a Survey in Karnataka State" (Ph.D. thesis, Australian National University, 1981); also J. C. Caldwell, "In Search of a Theory of Fertility Decline for India and Sri Lanka," in *Dynamics of Population and Family Welfare 1983*, ed. K. Srinivasan and S. Mukerji (Bombay: Himalaya Publishing House, 1983), 103–37.

ential acceptance (or resistance) by the religious communities. These are important points to remember when analyzing the fertility decline and are examined in a later chapter.

The use of Brass methods to estimate mortality levels from the proportions of children[23] who have died suggests an expectation of life at birth of about 52 years for the whole district, or of about 54 years for the large village and 50 years for the smaller villages. Probably the true levels are somewhat lower, there being an overstatement because of greater underreporting of children who were born and died soon thereafter. Perhaps an overall expectation of life at birth of 50 years, or of 52 in the large village and 48 in the other villages, would be closer to reality. The latter figure implies an infant mortality rate around 130 per thousand,[24] which is in accord with the number of recorded births reported in the previous twelve months as having been followed within the year by a death (see table 1.7).

The difference between the mortality levels of the large village and the smaller villages is to be expected. The large village has a government health subcenter, together with a small hospital. It has both a government and a private doctor. However, the latter has as yet been able to attract only a small clientele, mostly from the better-off groups. Only one of the smaller villages has any health facility at all. It is manned by an auxiliary nurse midwife, although the government doctor in the large village, who once visited it weekly, has discontinued doing so. The contrast is not so extreme as this might imply. Most of the residents of the smaller villages do use the health center, especially on the weekly market day when long queues of people are found outside the hospital, but clearly they cannot use it so easily, and help in an emergency cannot always be obtained quickly. Often they postpone treatment for up to a week, until market day.

The contrast between child survival in the two types of villages explains two of the otherwise anomalous features of table 1.7. The first is the slightly better survival rates among Harijan children than among peasant caste children, and the second is the considerably better figures for Muslims than for Hindus. Three-quarters of all Harijans live in the large village, compared with less than a quarter of the families of the peasant castes; 80 percent of Muslims are found in the large village, in contrast to only 45 percent of Hindus. The division in

23. Cf. Brass and Coale, "Methods of Analysis"; and *Indirect Techniques for Demographic Estimation*, Manuals on Methods of Estimating Population, no. 10 (New York: United Nations, 1983).

24. Employing "West" model tables in A. J. Coale and P. Demeny, *Regional Model Life Tables and Stable Populations* (Princeton: Princeton University Press, 1966).

Table 1.7. Differential Mortality Levels, Derived from Child Survival Data by Brass Methods and Converted to Expectation of Life at Birth

Characteristic	Sub-group	Expectation of life at birth derived from data (in years)	Suggested corrected expectation of life at birth (in years)
(1) Total population	—	52.3	50
(2) Location	Large village	54.4	52
	Smaller villages	50.3	48
(3) Caste groups	Elite	—[a]	—[a]
	Merchant	56.8	54
	Peasant	51.2	49
	Harijan	52.2	50
(4) Mother's education	No schooling	50.0	48
	Primary school only	58.5	56
	Secondary school or more	60.5	58
(5) Occupation of head of household	Elite	—[a]	—[a]
	Merchant	61.4	59
	Agricultural	49.1	47
	Home duties	43.6	41
(6) Religion	Muslim	57.5	55
	Hindu	51.0	49

[a] Numbers too small to yield consistent estimates.

health services between the large village and the smaller villages explains some, but not all, of the difference in mortality between the merchant castes and the remainder and by education of mother. The contrast in mortality rates between households headed by merchants and those headed by agriculturalists is due to a blend of greater urbanization, better economic position, and higher levels of education among the children's mothers. Household heads whose occupation is shown as home duties are either widows or separated or divorced women. Such households are often destitute and child mortality levels are high.

In spite of these contrasts, the most striking feature of the area is the limited mortality range—much more restricted in terms of the characteristics listed above than is the case in rural Africa.[25] Child survival appears to depend largely on the income of the household, the access to health services, and, above all, the education of the mother. With regard to the latter, the most important step is having any schooling at all.

25. J. C. Caldwell, "Education as a Factor in Mortality Decline: An Examination of Nigerian Data," *Population Studies* 33, no. 3 (1979): 395–413.

The mortality level in the district is no higher than it was in Western Europe when fertility began to fall steeply in the late nineteenth century. The situation in India is by no means analogous to Europe of that time. Hindu widows have a lesser chance of remarriage than did widows in Europe, and widows in rural India depend for their well-being on having a son to a relatively greater extent than did European widows of a century ago. It is, therefore, pertinent to inquire about the survival chances of sons in the various sections of the society, as is done in table 1.8 (assuming the same understatement in the reporting of mortality as was done in the discussion above).

The table is based on the survival of the sons to 35 years, when, on average, their mothers are 60 years of age, the average age for entering widowhood. The table is not multiplicative, although mother's education and father's occupation have a distinctly separate effect. Nevertheless, most women with secondary education are married to either bureaucrats or merchants, and the survival chances of sons of mothers with secondary education married to bureaucrats is above 85 percent, although not by a large margin.

The data show clearly that families with only one son, unless they belong to the elite, do subject the mothers to a considerable risk of entering widowhood without sons. This is an important point because once couples have two children they are the object of considerable pressure by the family planning program to have one or other of the parents sterilized. Admittedly, table 1.8 lists survival chances from birth, but, in fact, there is considerable encouragement to undergo such operations shortly after a birth.

This was, then, the kind of society which might well reveal the secrets of early fertility transition. Fertility undoubtedly declined steeply during the 1970s. It did this in circumstances where mortality

Table 1.8. The Probability of One Son Surviving until the Parents' Old Age

Section of Society			Family with one son (%)	Family with two sons (%)
(1)		Whole district	70	91
(2)	(a)	Large village	72	92
	(b)	Smaller villages	67	89
(3)	(a)	Mother with no schooling	67	89
	(b)	Mother with primary schooling only	77	95
	(c)	Mother with at least some secondary schooling	80	96
(4)	(a)	Father in bureaucracy[a]	85	98
	(b)	Father a merchant	81	96
	(c)	Father an agriculturalist	66	88

[a] Approximate estimate from a small sample.

had been slowly declining and where the risk of death was no greater
than it was in the early years of the European fertility transition, but,
nevertheless, in circumstances where child survival was by no means
guaranteed. The family system appeared to have experienced no radical transformation in structure. Nevertheless, something significant
was clearly happening to the family and its internal relations, as indicated by a marked increase in the age of female marriage. It is probable, moreover, that couples who marry later have much more exclu-
sive say over their own fertility than couples who marry at an age when
the parents and parents-in-law must still regard them as children to be
advised and directed.

Change over Four Decades

Much of our search for reasons for change in the areas of demographic
behavior, and in attitudes and circumstances which are influential,
delved into socioeconomic transition. Repeatedly, we sought the
advice of the old. Fortunately, for the large village there is a source for
comparison of a perhaps more trustworthy sort. The large village was
included in the Economic Survey of Mysore carried out as part of the
1941 census program by the government of Mysore.[26]

The information for 1941 appears to be for the large village with
boundaries as defined in our study, and hence the comparison in table
1.9 is warranted.

The population of the large village increased by 87 percent
between 1940 and 1981. Some of this growth can be explained by the
effect of declining mortality in swelling the number of survivors in
each family; indeed, the number of households increased by only 65
percent as average household size climbed from 5.4 to 6.2. In passing,
one might note that these statistics provide little support for any claim
that significant nuclearization of family residential patterns occurred
during this period.

Longer-term population trends are more difficult to quantify
because individual settlements cannot be identified in the earlier censuses. The settlements were grouped, but it does appear that the
population of the group of study villages multiplied by about two-and-
a-half between 1901 and 1980. Thus, the area of land per capita was by
the latter date only 40 percent of what it was at the beginning of the
century. This is a measure of land pressure, but not of pressure on all

26. Mysore Government, *Economic Survey [volume of the 1941 Census]* (Bangalore: Government Press, 1941), 11–13, 117–19.

Table 1.9. Large Village: Comparable Statistics, 1941 and 1980

Characteristic	1941	1980
Population:		
Persons	1,367	2,557
Males	711	1,341
Females	656	1,216
Sex ratio (males per 100 females)	108	110
Households	251	413
Average household size	5.4	6.2
Age structure (years):		
Under 5	15%	12%
5–14	28%	28%
15–49	45%	48%
Over 50	12%	12%
Caste/religion structure:		
Muslim	28%	35%
Jain	6%	6%
Brahmin	16%	5%
Vokkaliga	14%	14%
Harijan	10%	11%[a]
Other	26%	29%
Education/literacy:		
Proportion literate	28%	61%
Proportion of 5–14 age group in school: Boys	55%	62%
Girls	31%	57%
Land:		
Proportion of families with some land	60%	78%
Of families with land, proportion with over 7.5 acres	15%	12%
Family income source:		
Only agriculture	14%	18%
Agriculture and nonagriculture	59%	51%
Nonagriculture	27%	31%

Source: Government of Mysore, *Economic Survey*, 1941 Census of Mysore (Bangalore, 1948): 11–13.

[a] In 1941, listed only as Adikarnataka, but it appears probable that Adidravida were also included.

resources because potential nonagricultural employment both in the district and further afield during the period has increased enormously. The magnitude of this change does not appear in the figures in the table comparing family income source between 1941 and 1980. The problem is probably that the measure employed for 1941 was that of any income, whereas in 1980 it was of the employment of individuals. Retrospective data in 1980 showed that the off-farm employment of individuals had increased very substantially and persistently. The table shows an actual increase in the proportion of families owning land. This is a tribute to the success of land reform, and nearly all agricultural families now have at least a little land. However, that owned by the Harijans is usually very small, whereas the large land-owners have been remarkably successful in retaining the wet land below the tank while dispensing with dry land, particularly that suited only for grazing. Even so, there has been a marked drop in the number of holdings of more than 7.5 acres.

If the large village grew at the same rate as all the villages during the first four decades of the century, then its annual rate of growth was, between 1901 and 1941, around 0.7 percent per annum. Between the 1941 and 1961 censuses this increased to 1.9 percent as mortality declined. Between 1961 and 1980 the rate slowed again to 1.4 percent, the major explanation being rising levels of out-migration to Bangalore, other towns, and areas such as that around Mandya on the Cauvery River, where extended irrigation and new crop varieties were producing a "green revolution." Indeed, between 1979 and 1983, during the years of research, the rate of population growth was zero, as net emigration equalled natural increase. This may have been a short-term phenomenon, encouraged by a drought period, but it may well be the emerging pattern for dry-land villages without modern irrigation systems in regions like southern Karnataka, where employment in urban areas (especially in Bangalore) and in some rural areas (especially the irrigation areas along the Cauvery) has been available. At the time of the census-survey, before the drought intensified, 8 percent of household members were living and working outside the village.

The change in age structure shown in table 1.9 indicates a marked decline in fertility in the years immediately preceding 1980, in that it had affected the group aged 0–4 but not that aged 5–14. This conforms with other evidence that the major impact of the government's family planning program up to 1980 had been during the years of the Emergency, especially 1976 and 1977. The slight deterioration in the sex ratio over four decades, opposite in direction to the general experience of south India, is probably just incidental and can hardly be taken to indicate a worsening in the position of women.

The caste structure of the village has remained remarkably stable, with two exceptions. The first is the reduction in the proportion of Brahmins by over two-thirds, clear evidence for Srinivas's argument that the urbanization of India's Brahmins is one of the major social trends.[27] One of the reasons for urbanization in the research area has

27. M. N. Srinivas, *The Remembered Village* (New Delhi: Oxford University Press, 1976), 5.

been land reform, and, more importantly, fear of land reform. But the major mechanism is the extended education of children, who are thus fitted for city jobs; each generation is more urbanized, and, although the old usually do not follow their children, they are not replaced in the village when they die. The relative increase in the Muslim population owes something to the in-migration of traders, but is mostly the result of higher birthrates and resulting higher rates of natural increase.

Table 1.9 shows that in 1941, 55 percent of males and 31 percent of females 5–14 years of age were in school (they were aged 44–63 years in 1980). This can be compared with the figures in Table 1.5 which show that 66 percent of males and 25 percent of females over 50 years of age had ever been to school. The figures are compatible, and discrepancies with regard to females are explained by the fact that the large village had a better educational record than most villages and, on average, a higher proportion of the girls sent out as wives to other villages had been to school than was the case among the girls imported as wives. What the table does not show is the much greater improvement in education over those four decades in school attendance in the smaller villages. Indeed, in the large village the educational revolution had occurred in the years immediately before 1941, as is evidenced by the contrast between the proportions of children in school at that date and the low level of literacy in the whole population.

The Studies

The research team initially set out to study fertility decline and fertility control. As time passed, those studies led directly to related interests and then to more distant ones. All, nevertheless, were aspects of the area's demographic transition: marriage, family structure, health care and mortality, survival strategies during famine, educational change, and the support of the aged. All reports refer to the research period 1979–83. Reports on those studies follow. Finally, an appendix records our initial unhappiness with existing research on demographic transition which led us to begin this work.

Chapter Two

The Determinants of Fertility Decline

Perhaps the most important question in population studies is concerned with the circumstances leading to the onset of sustained fertility decline. It is a matter which has proved particularly unamenable to examination by large cross-sectional surveys, partly because such projects can hardly ever be planned before decisive decline has occurred. Yet, the fundamental concern must be the nature of society immediately before fertility falls, at a time when crucial changes ultimately determining the beginning of fertility transition are already under way. It would be pointless to survey large numbers of pretransitional societies with near stability in their levels of fertility in the hope that some would be subsequently shown to be nearing the time of decline, partly because of the waste of effort and money involved, but mostly because there would be insufficient clarity about the questions that should be asked, in that the nature of the questions is largely determined by the nature of the decline.

The Evidence for Fertility Decline

Analyses of Indian census data suggest that crude birthrates were around 40 per thousand in the 1940s, a moderate pretransitional level, perhaps 2–3 points higher in the 1950s, and probably close to 40 again in the 1960s.[1] The national Sample Registration System indicates decisive subsequent change with, by the late 1970s, a birthrate of 33 in the whole country and 28 in Karnataka, implying falls of around 17.5 percent and 30 percent respectively in perhaps fifteen years.[2] Although no research denies that sustained fertility decline has occurred, there is considerable debate about its magnitude. Two 1977 projects of the Bangalore Population Centre have contributed to the available information for Karnataka. The first, resurveying a quarter of a century later the same sample areas as the 1951–52 Mysore Population Study, claimed a fertility decline of only 10 percent.[3] The second, a dual record system, calculated a 1977 crude birth rate of 34, although produced from considerably lower survey and registration levels.[4] Controversy arising from the preliminary results of the 1981 census has produced arguments tending to support a birthrate of this level, although it remains possible that both immigration from other states and mortality decline have been underestimated. Similarly, the statistics of the government family planning program cast doubts on whether particularly low birthrates should be anticipated in Karnataka.[5]

Nevertheless, the focus of microresearch must be more specifically on the area of investigation, and here there is definitely something to explain. The two calendar years 1980 and 1981, a period of intensive fieldwork when persons and demographic events could not easily be overlooked, yield, with a small correction for undisclosed births followed almost immediately by deaths, a birthrate of 25 per thousand. Twelve-month retrospective statements for 1979 yield an uncorrected rate of 25 and a corrected rate of 28. The use of stable population analysis, in an area with apparently moderately good age statement as judged by single-year age statement, indicated, at the beginning of 1980, crude birthrates of 27, 32, and 39 from the proportions of the

1. R. H. Cassen, *India: Population, Economy, Society* (London: Macmillan, 1978).

2. Registrar General, *Sample Registration Bulletin* (New Delhi: Registrar General, various dates).

3. K. Srinivasan, P. H. Reddy, and K. N. M. Raju, "From One Generation to the Next: Changes in Fertility, Family Size Preferences, and Family Planning in an Indian State Between 1951 and 1975," *Studies in Family Planning* 9, nos. 10–11 (1978):258–71.

4. P. H. Reddy, A. Shariff, M. Guruswamy, and A. V. Diwakar, *Dual Record System* (Bangalore: Population Centre, 1980).

5. Ministry of Health and Family Welfare, *Family Welfare Programme in India: Year Book, 1979–80* (New Delhi: Ministry of Health and Family Welfare, 1981).

population under 5, 10, and 15 years of age respectively. The population is, of course, not stable if there have recently been steep fertility falls. Nevertheless, an analysis of fertility by age of woman at each birth produces much the same picture: a birthrate of no more than 30 in the early 1980s, close to 40 in the early 1970s, and possible as high as 45 in the early 1960s. If such declines are largely the result of sterilization or contraception, then the retrospective data closely support this picture: the first sterilization in 1962, with the tempo accelerating from 1970 and doing so dramatically from 1975. By 1980, among married couples where the wife was of reproductive age, 31 percent were practicing birth control (above average for Karnataka), five-sixths of them through sterilization. Furthermore, the sterilization of one or the other of the couple, the wife in 81 percent of cases, increased steeply with parity, covering two-fifths of couples after the third birth, and close to half after the fourth.

The Microdemographic Research Approach

The methodology and its evolution have been described in detail elsewhere (see Appendix), but some points must be emphasized. The minimum condition agreed upon at the outset was living in the villages and participating in everyday life. We found early on that there was no advantage in dispensing entirely with the apparatus developed by demographers, and we carried out detailed mapping, annual censuses, and vital registration surveys, as well as a series of small, highly focused surveys usually arising from the findings of in-depth interviewing.

We had assumed from the anthropological literature that the essence of successful anthropological investigation was participant investigation. Observation, even when structured, is highly appropriate and even essential for certain types of work; for instance, the relative access to food of different family members. We participated continually, but we now doubt whether this is the prime anthropological tool, at least in the study of change, where there has to be a historic perspective, and where causes and reasons (at least as believed or stated) have to be probed all the time. The fundamental instrument is the long probing discussion, often taking hours and usually taken up again after breaks, having an agenda but flexibly following chance leads (which often increase the general agenda). Such discussions are usually with more than one interviewee, and often involve a floating population, dictated both by work needs and by the self selection of persons with specialized knowledge or experience. It is necessary to work with persons of every age and often to contrast deliberately the experience and attitudes of different generations. A sample of families treated this way is safer and better than relying too greatly on self-selected informants. A hundred family interviews of this type over months will inevitably provide any reasonably sensitive investigator with a depth of knowledge about demographic behavior and change that no administration of a large-scale survey can ever do. Participant observation is a valuable supplementary device in that it may yield testimony which tends to confirm, deny, or modify the information provided in such areas as intergenerational relations.

This chapter examines the testimony and tests it both with our own survey data and with other data available for the region. All statements and hypotheses are backed by interview reports. If they occasionally give the impression of being unsubstantiated assertions, it is because we have deliberately forsworn the approach of estimating that X percent of the files indicate this, whereas Y percent indicate that. In fact we are near consensus in much that is reported, and increasingly suspect that the distributions achieved by surveys in all but simple quantifiable evidence are artifacts of questions not properly understood and of responses necessarily sufficiently complex in reality to yield an almost random distribution when they have to be assigned to one box or another.

The Conditions of Stable High Fertility

Only thirty years ago, there appears to have been little control of marital fertility with any intention of limiting the ultimate number of children. The birthrate may have been as high as 45, in spite of considerable youthful widowhood and little remarriage. There is some point in first examining the demographic situation, even though the impact of the intermediate variables and their rates of change are not the ultimate conditions of high fertility but only evidence of the underlying determinants. Subsequent change involved complex interrelations of movements in marital fertility, family structure, marriage, and mortality (see chapters 4, 5, and 6).

The picture of pretransitional fertility was obtained both from in-depth studies and from a survey of adults in the area. Copious testimony from older people enabled us to put together a reasonably clear account of the situation from the 1940s onward. However, the old were much less sure of their parents' behavior, and there appear to be limits to any attempt to re-create accurately the situation earlier in this century.

It is clear that attempts in the 1940s—and this is largely true for the 1950s, too—to restrict fertility in order to limit ultimate family size were virtually unknown. In terms of marital fertility, this was definitely a pretransitional period. In rural Karnataka there were a few women and some men (perhaps no more than one in half-a-dozen villages) who could prepare herbal concoctions which could be taken orally to provoke abortion. But these abortions were carried out not to limit family size but to hide the evidence of conceptions which should never had taken place, especially during times when sex should not have occurred: the first months of marriage, even for a postpuberty marriage; in auspicious months such as those during the harvest; after having become a grandmother; and before marriage. Later, conceptions resulting from extramarital relations, detectable because of low levels of coitus within the marriage, were to increase in number; these were also grounds for abortion. Contraception appears to have been practically unknown—even withdrawal, which was little practiced then or now. Even some of the traditional abortionists are described as employing "English medicines," which tends to undermine one's belief in the continuity of even this tradition.

However, it is improbable that marital fertility was constant during the first half of the century. There were forces upon it which were subject to change: coital frequency and the duration of postnatal sexual abstinence and breast-feeding.

It is claimed that until at least the 1940s, few Brahmins in south India, and fewer still in rural areas, would have had sexual relations except on the 15 or 16 auspicious days of the year. Even some of the otherwise auspicious days would have been avoided because of the wife's menses. For the rest of the population, total lifetime coitus was kept low, partly because of little female premarital sexual activity (not very important because of almost universal prepubescent or pubescent marriage) and fear of conceiving during inauspicious periods. There were probably two more important mechanisms. The first was a low level of sexual activity in marriage, especially in joint families where couples usually did not sleep together on most nights, and where mothers-in-law were deeply suspicious of sexuality on the part of daughters-in-law and would not make it easy for the couple to find privacy except prior to the birth of the first son.[6] The second was a belief that by the time a husband was in his forties—and his wife typically in her thirties—sexual relations should be reduced to a minimum, or abandoned, so as to allow the man to retain what strength and

6. S. Hobson, *Family Web: A Story of India* (London: John Murray, 1978).

health he still had. (Even our contemporary interviews are full of references to the detrimental effect of sexual relations on men over 35, and to good health being explained by continence.) There was, and still is, considerable aversion to grandmothers conceiving, although, at least during the last 40 years, it does not seem to have been as strongly prohibitive as the taboo found in other parts of the world.[7]

In rural southern Karnataka, postnatal sexual abstinence, of sufficient duration to affect fertility, has been practiced extensively and is believed to have been a universal Indian cultural phenomenon. Further, it has been practiced for the same reasons as it was in other parts of the world:[8] to achieve a spacing that would maximize the chance of the child's survival, to allow the mother to regain her health, and to not endanger the quality of the milk (reported to be a greater danger in the early period of breast-feeding than subsequently). The primacy of the first reason is shown by a considerable proportion of women who abstain for longer after a male than a female birth. The period of postnatal abstinence has been shortening for so long that there are no longer even folk memories of what the ideal period once was, but it was certainly at least two years. Among women who married during the 1940s, 15 percent of those living in the small villages, but only 5 percent of those in the large village, abstained for that period or longer, and a substantial majority did so for more than a year. Among women who have married since 1960, abstention for longer than 18 months has almost disappeared in the large village and is around 20 percent in the smaller villages. Even in middle-class Bangalore, it has not fallen substantially below six months.

Breast-feeding was of even longer duration and was controlled not by the concept of a proper duration but of a proper time for cessation, namely, when the woman had reached a certain stage of the next pregnancy (three months was most commonly quoted). Thus, in the 1940s, the great majority of women breast-fed for over two years, and many for three to five. Those doing so for less than 24 months were usually the victims of sickness, problems with their supply of milk, or the death of the infant. The majority of women in the smaller villages

7. J. C. Caldwell and P. Caldwell, "The Role of Marital Sexual Abstinence in Determining Fertility: A Study of the Yoruba in Nigeria," *Population Studies* 31, no. 2 (1977):193–217.

8. P. Caldwell and J. C. Caldwell, "The Function of Child-Spacing in Traditional Societies and the Direction of Change," in *Child-Spacing in Tropical Africa: Traditions and Change*, ed. Hilary J. Page and Ron Lesthaeghe (London: Academic Press, 1981), 73–92.

still wean later than 24 months, but in the large village (as in the poorer areas of Bangalore) the period now averages around 18 months.

For the theses that follow in this chapter, two very important matters arise from this examination of intermediate variables: the timing of change and the decision-making variables involved. With regard to timing, the position concerning breast-feeding is clearest. In the large village, the period began to shorten in the 1950s as an increasing number of women began to break the connection between weaning and the next pregnancy. In the smaller villages this change was delayed until the 1960s. With regard to abstinence, there has probably been some increase in the proportion of women not waiting for the full two years for decades before the 1940s, but there appears to have been an acceleration of these changes from the 1950s, with no marked difference by village size in the onset of the acceleration.

An important mechanism of these movements appears to have been a change in the intergenerational balance of decision-making. The older women claim that until the 1940s, decisions on both postnatal abstinence and breast-feeding were mostly controlled by the older generation: the mother-in-law, with whom they usually lived, with the backing of her husband; and, to a lesser extent, their own parents. The role of the latter was enhanced because most women returned to their own parents' house in the third, fifth, or seventh months of their pregnancy and stayed there until seven, nine, or even thirteen months after the birth (often not in the case of the third birth, and less often, or for shorter periods, in the case of later births). Taking all births together, a majority of new mothers stayed for at least six months after the birth in the 1940s, whereas this has now fallen to around one-quarter. The older generation were the major authorities on the traditional morality, having the primary right to advise and direct their sons, and having a direct and major interest in the health and survival of their grandchildren.

The evidence seems to be that this decision-making situation was first eroded in the case of postnatal abstinence, thus creating important precedents for the later changes in the areas of weaning and birth control. Furthermore, the action was taken not by the younger couple in concert, but by the younger husband exerting pressure on his wife and parents because of an increasing feeling that he could no longer be denied access to sexual relations. It is now commonly reported that after 6–12 months of abstinence men begin to nag their wives, "What did I marry you for?" Their mothers are shocked, and they and the wives are acutely apprehensive about the child's health. Significantly, the husbands' fathers attempt to stay out of the conflict, apparently an acknowledgement that they feel, to some degree at least, the validity of the protest. A related point is also important. Changes between the generations in the periods of postnatal sexual abstinence and in duration of breast-feeding appear to occur early in the marriage, at the time of the first, or, less often, the second birth. Then an intergenerational agreement is reached, and also an interpersonal one, and the pattern set remains surprisingly constant for the rest of married life.

This ceding of decision-making powers over demographic behavior is of central importance and is not a facet of a more general seizing of economic and other powers from the older married generation by the younger generation. The major reason for the cession has been a transfer of these areas of behavior from religious moral concern to the secular domain. The gods are no longer particularly worried by these matters. The nature of the change is agreed upon by most families, but few can suggest reasons. Certainly it has something to do with an external world—an urban and more educated one—which has increasingly invaded the study area over the last decades. Neither the Hindu great tradition nor the forces of "Westernization" have the same concern with postnatal behavior as the village goddesses of south India whose approval has until the last few decades dominated local morality. As these matters have become secularized, there has no longer been a strong moral imperative on the parents or on society to monitor behavior. Nevertheless, the failure to interfere with the younger couple as much as in the past is based not only on the growth of a belief that these are perhaps intimate matters of individual rather than family concern, but also on an increasing doubt on the part of the old as to what is appropriate and right with regard to these matters. Confusion is as important an element as the democratization of family decision-making.

One other demographic change has been occurring. Over the last 40 years infant and child mortality rates have fallen, the decline in southern Karnataka's infant mortality rates being from perhaps 230 to 100 per thousand, thus increasing the chance that each child will grow to adulthood from around half to four-fifths.[9] This change, too, is far from simple (see Appendix). Governmental intervention in times of famine has helped, but so has family change which allows a greater share of food to the weak at times of crisis. There have been no major

9. The use of Brass mortality methods on the child survival data from the 1941 census (for Mysore), the 1951–52 Mysore study, and the 1975 Resurvey by the Bangalore Population Centre yields infant mortality rates of around 230, 180, and 105.

epidemics in the area for a third of a century, and during this time the penetration of modern medicine has increased. The large village now has a health center with two doctors, in addition to two private doctors and a pharmacy. Nevertheless, the increase in the use of medical facilities, which has been moving consistently but slowly upward for four decades, has depended more on consumer demand than on government inputs. Most diseases have had divine explanations, and, accordingly, appropriate treatments. This has been—and is still—particularly the case with the very young and the very old, who are close to other worlds. Infant malnutrition, the common childhood cirrhosis,[10] and dehydration from infantile diarrhea are still described by nearly everyone in the study area as *balagraha* (Kannada for divine visitation to a child), and the preferred treatment by most of the population is the chanting of *mantras* and the wearing of *yantras* (charms). Similarly, fears of arousing jealousy and attracting the evil eye still lead to the appearance and reality of casualness with regard to behavior before and after childbirth. However, concepts of disease and its treatment are also passing into the secular domain, a process in which schooling has played a significant role. In the case of severe childhood illness, around half of the cases are now brought at a reasonably early stage to the health center (although, in a society with a pronouncedly plural attitude toward much of life, other treatments are usually carried out at the same time), and decision-making about treatment is being transferred from the grandparental to the parental generation, accompanied by an increasing right of the mother to draw attention to the child's condition and advocate treatment. Admittedly, twice as many boys as girls are brought for treatment (although adult women outnumber men, because of the high incidence of anemia).

It might be noted that this assessment of infant mortality, together with the level of widowhood prior to the last half-century, renders estimates of Indian birth rates prior to 1921 as around 49 per thousand,[11] doubtful unless they were products of very considerably higher infant mortality rates and the effect of these on disrupting periods of postnatal abstinence. Indeed, it would seem more plausible to suggest birthrates in the 40–45 range, perhaps reaching 45 only just before marital birthrates began to fall in the 1960s. It is, however, entirely consistent with a minor rise in the birthrate in the 1950s.[12]

10. A. Singh, S. S. Jolly, and L. Kumar, "Indian Childhood Cirrhosis," *Lancet* 1 (1961):587–91.

11. K. Davis, *The Population of India and Pakistan* (Princeton: Princeton University Press, 1951).

12. Cassen, *India: Population, Economy, Society.*

Fundamental Change in Society

When the research was first planned we doubted if large numbers of children imposed any real burden on rural families. Incomes were so low that it seemed unlikely that major social changes had occurred in rural areas, particularly with regard to relationships within the family. Children clearly worked obediently, especially among the farming families, who formed the substantial majority. If fertility was falling, the explanation probably lay in the pressure exerted by the family planning program.

Every one of these points still has considerable validity, and this is the reason that fertility has not fallen more rapidly. Yet, we increasingly gathered evidence that there is now a considerable demand for family limitation and that a major component of this demand is the economic burden of the large family. Clearly, the crux of the research was whether this had always been the case. If not, how had it arisen: because change in the intermediate variables threatened higher fertility than in the past; because the society had changed in such a way that children, beyond a certain number, were a burden; or because the family planning program had made families aware of difficulties, and of options, in areas which they had previously not regarded as subject to analysis or change?

These are matters which we have now probed for three years, with due regard to the experience of older people. Rarely does the social scientist find near-consensus, but on this matter not only is there a surprising amount of agreement, but some of the earlier apparent conflicts in testimony turn out to be more matters of perspective and morality than disagreement about facts. The whole exercise has raised the doubt as to whether the spread of responses in many survey questions is not more a matter of random reaction to a new and sudden challenge (and to only partly understood questions) than to real disagreement about what has transpired.

There is, in fact, near-consensus on two points: first, that family economics have changed from a situation where large numbers of children were no burden, and probably an advantage; and second, that this has been the product of a major transformation of society since the 1940s. Much of the explanation is a "wealth flows" one.[13] At its simplest it is often put in the following form: the parents of fifty years

---

13. J. C. Caldwell, "Toward a Restatement of Demographic Transition Theory," *Population and Development Review* 2, nos. 3–4, (1976):321–66; idem, *Theory of Fertility Decline* (London: Academic Press, 1982).

ago (especially the fathers) were austere, distant, and harsh (often stated with approval); they drove their families hard; children rose early, worked long and hard, and demanded and received little. Subsequently, parents softened or weakened, or demanded less than they should, while children took advantage of this and secured all the concessions they could in terms of less work and more expenditure. Sometimes this is described as the advance of civilization and sometimes as one of the more unsavory aspects of the "Age of Kali."

Many older people, looking back to their childhood, offer an interrelated mass of plausible suggestions for the changes. There is broad agreement that the large family worked best in a subsistence agrarian economy, where land was not particularly scarce or fettered by government regulation, and where a simple, uncomplaining family worked under the ultimate direction of a patriarch who ruled an undivided estate until he died. Most decisions facing the younger generation of married couples were made by the older generation, usually by citing traditional morality and religious prescription, through their undisputed control of their sons. Many informants are willing to concede that this is an "ideal" model, but all believe that the situation before Independence was much closer to this picture than is now the case. In addition, nearly all survivors from that period believe that high fertility was an advantage, at least to the decision-making patriarch.

What happened to this simpler world where males saw no reason for containing the fertility of their wives or daughters-in-law? All explanations emphasize changes that decisively weakened the rigid family system. Some point to the beginnings of these in the wartime economy of the early 1940s, but most regard the decisive change as having arrived with Independence and the drive for economic growth. Most regard economic change as having allowed—rather than forced—social changes which followed imported patterns (usually described as "English" rather than "Western" or "Modern). We now examine the testimony, and attempt to test each section against either external data or quantifiable information.

The fundamental economic change is regarded as the penetration of the monetized economy, often described as "commercialization" or even "inflation." The Indian agrarian economy was surprisingly non-monetized for its complexity. It was consciously kept this way to achieve social stability, with Hindu theological sanction[14] by a series of arrangements for payment in kind for services and labor described

14. D. G. Mandelbaum, *Society in India* (Berkeley: University of California Press, 1970).

as the *jajmani* system. This was broken down by a growing labor market in the towns (which offered cash wages), by an increasing conversion of rural payments from kind to money, by a changeover to dowry with an escalating cash component, and by markets and shops competing ever more in rural areas with older forms of subsistence production.

The evidence is clear that the nonfarming wage sector grew disproportionately during the Second World War[15] and faster still during the implementation of the Five-Year Plans from 1951 onward.[16] The urban labor market in southeast Karnataka was dominated by the city of Bangalore, where the population increased from 0.41 million in 1941 to 2.91 million in 1981. Between 1951 and 1971 the population of Karnataka grew by 51 percent, but male employment outside agriculture increased by 65 percent, and the sectors of manufacturing, construction, transport, trade, and commerce, where most farmers' sons seek nonagricultural employment, almost doubled. In our study area, most agricultural wages are now paid in cash, and in the larger village the *jajmani* payment for services has largely vanished. There is ample evidence that employers have been increasingly tempted to convert to cash payments because of inflation and its promise that real wages could be whittled down by controlling the rise of cash payments. Artisans have moved toward commercial sales because of demands for new goods not specified by the age-old arrangements. By the beginning of 1980, a majority of the work force in the large village was working outside agriculture, compared with under 20 percent a generation earlier. In the small villages, the number of shops doubled between 1980 and 1982.

The social changes identified were broadly classifiable into three categories: schooling, the spread of the urban way of life through contact and the media, and the penetration of the villages by politicians. It is generally agreed that schooling teaches a different message, an "English" one. It is also asserted that town life is different from the village, that all rural-urban migrants, even temporary ones, are to some degree affected, and that the cinema carries, even when dealing with traditional themes, a nontraditional message. The arrival of national politics has sometimes meant a reinforcement of village factionalism, but has in general meant an extra force offering pro-

15. M. Zinkin, "Some Aspects of Change in Indian Society, 1938–60 (A Reminiscence)," in *Changing India*, ed. N. V. Sovani and V. M. Dandekar (Bombay: Asia Publishing House, 1961).

16. G. Rosen, *Democracy and Economic Change in India* (Berkeley: University of California Press, 1967).

tection for dissident social groups and individuals, hence weakening traditional society.

The area acquired its first schools early, the large village in 1934. The last 40 years have witnessed the chance of a child receiving any schooling increasing from one-third to two-thirds. However, the change in some key groups has been spectacular: in the smaller villages in the 1930s, only 3 percent of new brides (or daughters-in-law) had any education, whereas now the figure is 37 percent. The spread of schooling has been central to the concept of an independent India, and not the response to demands from employers. It is an imported concept as is the enshrinement of British law by the Indian Constitution.[17] Because of the mobile tent cinema and buses going to major towns, as well as the propensity of south Indians to go to the pictures, by 1982 three-quarters of the study area population had seen a film in the previous year.

However, the heart of the matter is the interrelation between economic and social changes and the mechanisms by which they have affected the value of children. There is almost total agreement that fathers were able to demand less of their children, especially their sons, once the latter were in a position to go to the town for wage-paying jobs (usually not against the father's wishes, for the augmenting of the family cash income was usually important). However, there is an equally strong belief that parents could demand less from educated children or daughters-in-law, and that husbands treated wives who had been to school differently and listened to them more. The change was compounded once the parents themselves had schooling. We frequently asked why schooling has this impact, but the answers were thought to be obvious, and we were usually told "civilization," "town ways," or "English ways." The older generation intervenes much less often in the medical treatment of children or in the child's age at weaning when the daughter-in-law has been to school, on the grounds that she understands such things. This is, in fact, the second most common advantage quoted for female education.

There is, then, a belief that the family is slowly changing. The testimony placed quite an emphasis on symbolism. Fathers are more apprehensive of being too dominating over a son returned from the town if the latter wears town clothes and an urban-style haircut. To some extent a sexual revolution is taking place, blamed mostly on the

17. Y. Singh, "Legal System, Legitimization and Social Change," in *Aspects of Changing India: Essays in Honour of Professor G. S. Ghurye*, ed. S. Devadas Pillai (Bombay: Popular Prakashan, 1976).

cinema, with town ways and educated attitudes also mentioned. This tends to strengthen the bond between the young husband and his wife at the expense of that between the former and his parents. There are other influences changing the position of the daughter-in-law and therefore her position in the family of her husband. At marriage she is now likely to be older than brides used to be, and her position will probably have been strengthened by bringing a larger dowry (see chap. 4).

Respondents also tended to argue that parents could not obtain as much return from children as used to be the case because of the earlier division of the household and its labor and assets, brought about by the ease with which the son can secure alternative employment, and by his willingness to listen to his wife's urging that they should break from the joint family. In fact, the histories of individual families show that there has been no marked change in the timing of partition (see chap. 5), but this is not wholly relevant because it is precisely the patriarch's knowledge that the younger couple can secede which stays his hand both in demanding more work and in refusing more consumption.

In different senses, both sons and daughters are becoming less of an asset, more of a burden. Because of the possibility of their moving out, sons are trusted less, and even rural families now often say that they are likely to receive more consideration from their daughters in later life than from their sons. Among the middle class of the city, the position is much more extreme because adolescent and young adult males frequently remain unemployed for long periods, fail to give as much help in the house as their sisters, and spend more with their peers as playboys around the town. Even in villages, schools teach children to play, and boys avoid work to play with their companions to a much greater extent than used to be the case. The increasing burden of daughters lies almost solely in the rapid conversion over a few decades of Dravidian India from a limited bride price to an almost unlimited dowry system (see chap. 4).

There are other reasons why children are an increasing burden. There are costs associated with schooling and many other potential expenditures as the villages become commercialized. Clothing is changing, and during periods of food shortage there is more moral pressure than was once the case to buy food. Land reform, although not particularly successful, has raised doubts among larger farmers about their continued prosperity, and many feel that security can be assured only by sending one or more sons to the town, thus often necessitating an investment not only in education but even in securing urban employment. It is now not the number of sons but the per capita investment that matters. Much the same pressures are exerted by land fragmentation arising from inheritance, a phenomenon attested to by the respondents, the recorded family histories, and the literature.[18] Fathers are also more badgered by the members of larger families. Once they ruled through their eldest sons and their wives, whereas now there is a growing tendency for everyone to expect direct access; once there were orders, now there is a movement toward debate.

The key to the changing economic nature of the family and the role of its children is provided by the relationship of the rural family to land. A family's land is its patrimony, and is not sold so as to make better investments, although some of it may be sold in order to raise dowries, escape indebtedness, or allow an entire family to migrate. All outside earnings are regarded as being of the nature of surplus profits, in contrast to the produce of the farmland which is thought of as a "given," and which, in the *ragi*-growing dry land which characterizes the area, seems to have changed little per acre over the decades. These outside earnings are looked upon as being of great value for three reasons: they are a kind of windfall gain above the patrimonial land; they are in cash and not in kind; and they are not subject to seasonal or climatic variation and can provide succor in times of famine or other crisis. As long as the property is not partitioned—and it is frequently less likely to be partitioned if the majority of sons are working in the town than if they are on the farm—money comes back from the family members working in the town for support if needed, for farm improvements, for festivals, and for dowries for the marriage of the household's daughters. Even where the property is not divided, and hence there is a continuing concept of a common family budget, there are, nevertheless, necessarily separate budgets in the town for family members working there, particularly in the case of the married, and especially if they are educated and have middle-class jobs.

The temptation to attempt to secure town jobs for some sons (and town marriages for as many daughters as possible) has increased quite rapidly as a result of three changes. First, there is a growing surplus of male labor on many middle-sized farms, a product of land subdivision, of the greater survival of sons, and, to a lesser extent, of the better health of fathers. Second, there has been a disproportionate increase in the nonfarm labor market. In the towns, it is commonly assumed that many jobs will go to rural-urban migrants, whereas, before the Second World War, urban jobs were mostly filled by townspeople. Third, a

18. E. Parthasarathy and L. Krishnamurty, *Changes in Rural Society* (Madras: Agricultural Research Centre, 1962).

mechanism, in the form of schooling, has come into existence for increasing the likelihood of a farm boy securing a town position. In spite of the stereotype of the towns drawing on the illiterate rural masses for cheap unskilled labor, nearly all families believe that literacy increases their sons' chances of securing any job, and that prolonged schooling is necessary for the situations that most of them long for: positions with a chance of permanency, usually with the government or state corporations, and white-collar or other nonlaboring employment. There was universal agreement that schooling means that children cost more, and a large measure of agreement that, during the years of education, their labor inputs and their earnings are less. It became clear during the research that the strategy of dividing one's sons between farming and nonfarming employment was not regarded as a desperate remedy imposed by land fragmentation but as a challenging and more hopeful way to prosperity. The real bitterness over land is felt not by the small farmer with 2–5 acres (unless he was once a landlord) but by the landless and those with a fraction of an acre. There was also very considerable agreement that educating children for nonfarming jobs was an investment for the future that imposed great strains on all but the rich, and that, during the process of education, a small or medium-sized family suffered less than a large family. The strong desire for a town husband for daughters is harder to explain. Nevertheless, it should be noted that south Indian families have a duty to take their daughters in again if the latter are in distress due to an unsatisfactory marriage or during famine if hungry. It is also true that a well-off daughter can bring gifts home on visits and help in the parents' old age.

An important parallel change is that which is occurring in marriage (see chap. 4). Here the older generation retains full power and marriages are arranged with the emergence of some degree of veto power in the younger generation, although this is largely confined to adult sons. Elopement is often spoken about, but only one example exists from the last three years. Child marriage has virtually disappeared. A series of profound additional changes have occurred. First, whereas male age at first marriage has remained stable at around 25 years all of this century, female age at marriage has continued to climb, now being around 18 or 19 years. This appears to have occurred both because of changing concepts of childhood and dependency, and because of a marriage squeeze arising from declining mortality. There are major social implications: maturer brides; wives closer to their husbands in age and hence more likely to be companions; and the teenage girls of the family more often daughters than daughters-in-law.

Second, there has been a massive movement from token bridewealth to very substantial dowries, affecting Brahmin families from the 1950s, and Vokkaligas and other peasant castes from the mid-1960s. The effect is to make parents more apprehensive of having too many daughters, and hence, beyond a certain point, reluctant to face the outcome of another pregnancy. Third, there has been a swing away from marriage to relatives. The causes have been a more heterogeneous society with greater difficulties in matching spouses, always of the same caste, by background and education; a reluctance by the parents of sons to accept the only nominal dowries paid at the marriage of relatives; and an imported belief in the health risks to children born from related parents.

Family Planning: The Demand and the Role of the Program

There is a fairly widespread apprehension of having too many children. It is not fundamentally a product of the family planning program, although it is clear that many families have articulated that apprehension at an earlier stage than they would otherwise have done because of the public discussion of population. There is also little question that the apprehension would not have arisen if farmers' sons had all continued to become farmers, if agricultural laborers' sons had automatically followed their fathers' work, and if artisanship were inevitably hereditary. Such a picture is not unbelievably static. On the contrary, it is very close to the situation, as we have been able to reconstruct it, that existed until the end of the 1930s.

The change is at least as much one of new opportunities as of worsening conditions. In some ways conditions have worsened. Land holdings have been reduced in size by population growth which has more than doubled the district's population since Independence (although emigration appears now to be creating some kind of equilibrium), and larger farmers are uneasy about the possibility that land reform laws might be regulated more tightly. The growth of a monetary economy has meant more expenditure and consumption, but has also produced a situation where caution about saving and expenditure is much more an aspect of everyday life than was true a few decades ago. Nevertheless, the case against unlimited family growth is primarily one of new temptations.

Despite this, two important points should be made, one demonstrating why the evidence provided above does not guarantee rapid fertility decline, and the other indicating that there is at least one more force propelling a decline. The first is that children still do a great deal of work, and there is widespread awareness that no one can be certain which child will succeed in worldly terms. In addition, the old usually need the help of the younger generation. Indeed, the situation of a widow with no surviving sons can be so bad that one sometimes wonders that any woman would restrict her fertility. Twelve widows live on their own in the study area (5 percent of all widows), some in miserable conditions. Educational levels are fairly low among the older children of the major farming caste (Vokkaligas), and this reflects the fact that working farmers, unlike landlords, with adequate land are more worried about potential family labor shortages than surpluses.

The second point is that a substantial number of women fear the physical impact of an indefinite number of pregnancies, or the problems arising from being pregnant or having infants at peak working times. Indeed, the ability of the south Indian woman to do fieldwork means that she is not necessarily alone in fearing her reduced capacity to work. Her physical problems would have little influence on reproductive decisions in an unaffected patriarchal family, but, as we will see below, some remarkable changes are under way.

The external debate may range as to whether family planning programs (short of coercion) can either initiate or accelerate fertility decline,[19] but most of our interviewees had fairly clear views on the matter. A family planning program would not have worked before the Second World War and would not work now but for the changes that have occurred in family economics. But changes have occurred in most families. In these circumstances the program's advocacy of family planning and its provision of the means (mostly sterilization camps) almost certainly both initiated a somewhat earlier decline and speeded up that decline. In terms of total births so far averted— although the local people use a different terminology, this is certainly what they are saying—a common conclusion is that the shares attributable to socioeconomic change and to the existence of the program are roughly equal (perhaps just an obvious way of affirming that both have had a substantial impact).

Talking of the impact of the program is really a simple way of describing a very complex change. The program has operated in the area for twenty years and now its workers visit every house regularly. Nevertheless, this process has such impact because the policies of the Indian government, and the population debate in the world beyond,

19. P. Demeny, "Observations on Population Policy and Population Programs in Bangladesh," *Population and Development Review* 1, no. 2 (1975):307–21.

have convinced the rural elites that family planning is the necessary and the socially moral way. An investigation of the views of the elites[20] showed that nearly all held this attitude, and many additionally believed that no contrary case should be aired in public. Certainly, we heard the antinatalist case put forward by officials and other important people on public occasions and to school classes, but heard the pronatalist case only in the privacy of the home. All health personnel, including doctors, hold strongly to the family planning case and are undoubtedly more likely to advocate sterilization on health grounds than their predecessors of two decades ago would have been.

The acceptance of family planning can be understood only if the program itself is fully understood. Almost one-third of currently married couples where the wife was of reproductive age were employing some means of fertility control by 1980, but 88 percent of it was by sterilization, largely tubectomy. (Six-sevenths of sterilizations were to wives.) Most villagers believe that they have no other option (and most of the elite believe that the rural poor could cope with nothing else), although, in the large village, some of the Muslim merchants employ condoms that have been purchased elsewhere through commercial channels, and some of the bureaucrats' wives have IUDs fitted by the program.

Nevertheless, most of the population regard the choice as being for or against "the operation." The Hindu case against the operation is not usually put as being one of believing in the value of the large family, nor of being apprehensive of subsequent child death, but of fear of subsequent illness and weakness or of death. Almost the whole rural population believes that prolonged weakness and pain are likely consequences, and nearly half of all tubectomized women and a similar proportion of vasectomized men reported that this had indeed been the consequence. Almost half of the tubectomized women and a majority of vasectomized men state that their ability to have sexual relations was impaired. Such views are widespread in rural India but are rarely reported by the program, partly because of skepticism about their physiological basis. Nevertheless, the important point is that families regard the operation as something that might well injure them. Wives frequently offer to have the operation instead of their husbands on the grounds that the household might not survive the latter's incapacitation or death. In the way in which a certain member of a Hindu household, especially the daughter-in-law, will volunteer or

20. J. C. Caldwell, P. H. Reddy, and P. Caldwell, "The Elites and the Population Question in Rural South India" (in preparation).

agree to be sterilized, there is not only an element of virtue but also one of sacrifice. Frequently, families argue that one spouse is the only healthy one, and hence the risk of sterilization cannot be afforded. It is argued that husbands who work in wet fields or who must use a bicycle cannot be vasectomized. Alternatively, it is often argued that a person is too weak or sick for the operation. The family planning program, aware of the potential impact of publicized disasters, often refuses sterilization on the grounds of illness or weakness, most frequently because of tuberculosis, anemia, or asthma. Women of 35 years or younger frequently say that sterilization is no longer needed, some-times because their stars say that they have reached maximum family size because no one in their family has more than that number of children, but they often also seem to mean that they no longer have sexual relations or that they believe that they have reached meno-pause. In a significant proportion of all vasectomies, the men have had the operation as a fait accompli without telling their wives, but this is not the case for any female sterilization.

On the other hand, there is less fear than we had anticipated that sterilization, together with subsequent child mortality, could result in a dangerously small number of surviving children. The reason appears to be that the death of children after parental sterilization has hap-pened in very few cases, approximately half as often as might have been predicted from the community mortality levels. Certainly there is some apprehension of child death among the sterilized, and this seems to lead them to take more care of their children, tending to substitute maternal for sibling care, and using the health facilities more fre-quently for their children than do nonsterilized parents. This is rein-forced by more frequent visits to the home by health staff for a year after the sterilization, by the family and their children being given access to the doctor at the health center, and by the program offering free medicines for children for up to three years after the operation. Admittedly, those sterilized couples who have subsequently lost chil-dren do feel bitterness toward both fate and the program. The lack of significant differentials within the Hindu community in family plan-ning acceptance is apparently explained by the rather weak position in which two very different groups find themselves with regard to the government program. Even now, the poor are less capable of resisting pressure. During the Emergency the landowners agreed in refusing coolie work to unsterilized persons with three or more children. The elites, even those with large amounts of land, are supposed to be providing social leadership, and both landlords and bureaucrats are deeply troubled if their families continue to grow.

One should be able to discover a great deal about the nature of fertility transition by examining change in birth control decision making. A major problem in the area is the difficulty in separating voluntary decisions taken outside the period of the Emergency from sterilizations carried out during the Emergency, and determining which of the latter were largely coercive and which had a major element of choice. The problem is compounded by some difficulties in exact dating within the year, and the fact that if we identify the Emergency period only by the three calendar years which it overlapped, 1975–77, 54 percent of all sterilizations in the area up to the beginning of 1980 were done during that period, and 31 percent were done earlier and only 15 percent later.[21] Since then, there has been some recovery, and an additional 22 percent have been performed over the last two years. Attitudes toward the Emergency or at least its family planning aspects (for which it is largely remembered), are complex. Many of those forced to be sterilized are bitter, but an almost equal number say that they were bitter at the way it was done but pleased they have had no more children. It is clear that the whole government apparatus was employed and that the village secretary (the representative of government in the village) played a major role. Some of the bitterness comes from persons who say that they agreed to cripple themselves for life because of the operation but that they did this in return for a promise of land or housing which was not delivered. It is also clear that the present universal awareness of the availability and nature of sterilization dates only from the Emergency period, and that most families were largely unaware of the family planning program's activities during the 1960s and first half of the 1970s. It may even be that the existence of a considerable number of sterilized women from that period has made the operation more familiar to the whole society.

If we confine our attention to the years before 1975 and after 1977, we discover that this is a matter in which macrodata are likely to be very misleading (see Appendix). When we carried out a careful survey aimed at showing the contributions of various members of the family to the ultimate decision, defining primary, secondary, and tertiary decision makers, we received answers very largely in terms of husbands and wives, with the former playing the dominant role in 60 percent of the cases. Yet, the work in depth showed in nearly every household a much more complex picture. The husband's parents are

21. All decisions outside the Emergency are treated here as voluntary; the effects of target setting on health workers or of repeated visits on potential acceptors are disregarded.

nearly always consulted, almost inevitably when they live in the same household, and it is rare for the operation to proceed against their wishes. Sometimes the husband's mother tells both her son and his wife that she will arrange his marriage to a second wife if the first is sterilized. The wife's parents are also frequently contacted, especially when the wife has joined them for her delivery. However, the proportion of the older generation who do not choose to exercise a veto power, but instead advise the younger generation that the final decision must be up to them, has increased persistently over the years. The movement that began with the young husband securing some control over the duration of the postnatal abstinence period has subsequently spread to the timing of weaning and to family planning. It is part of a larger change from a situation where the mother-in-law was almost the sole arbiter of behavior and the moral guide for the daughter-in-law. This is not merely a battle that has been fought out separately in each family, for, once some of the old generation abdicate or reduce their area of decisionmaking, then others feel the pressure to do the same— especially as there is an awareness that the new imported moralities favor moves in this direction. There is no simple division, however, between the old who are opposed to sterilization and the young who favor it. At the most, the young are somewhat more favorable to such an innovation, but it should be remembered that the old are talking about the impact upon, and the possibility of education for, their grandchildren. Nor are they the ones who must fear the operation. Yet, there are differences as well as similarities in the cession of power between the generations with regard to sexual abstinence and lactation and with regard to sterilization. The similarities are the secularizing of the behavior in the Hindu community, and the confusion of the older generation; the differences are that the confusion is greater in the case of sterilization because of the complex economic and health issues involved, and because there is governmental (and increasingly a "respectable") view on the matter—a parallel here to medical treatment. Because it is the younger wife who must undergo the tubectomy, her husband and mother-in-law often point out repeatedly that the final decision must be hers, which, accordingly, it ultimately becomes (and may be recorded as such by a survey).

The situation in the villages in now very far from being solely an internal family debate. A participant role is played by the family planning program. Every month or so, a health worker calls at the house, not only advising on family planning, but advocating its employment as a moral good and implying that a family with three children who would resist it must be lost to the virtues. After a year or two, the poor, after ignoring the advice of the better-educated and often higher-caste official perhaps twenty times, just give in. This is probably one reason why one research project found a high proportion of decisions made in a startlingly short time.[22] Another reason is that some families, especially the poorer ones, are suddenly attracted, especially at a time of abnormal need, by the monetary incentives offered for sterilization. Incentives have played a significant role in increasing the number of sterilizations but appear to be less important now than before the Emergency.

The role of the program is even more intrusive. Its workers address themselves to the younger couple to a greater degree than the traditional society would expect. Female health workers, who predominate in the area, talk to the younger wives and about the younger wives to the rest of the family. For those wives who prefer to be sterilized because of unhappiness about the effect upon them of further pregnancies, births, or periods of lactation, or who are apprehensive about such events reducing their earning capacity (for this is south India and the female agricultural laboring wage is a significant fraction of the local economy), the moral alliance with the health worker is a powerful weapon. In the name of virtue, the traditional balance of decisionmaking in the family can be upset. If indeed there are women's issues as well as family economic ones involved in demographic transition,[23] the Indian family planning program can make them surface effectively.

Finally, how do the reasons given for accepting family planning fit in with this picture? Excluding the quarter of families who said that they were coerced and played no part at all in the decision (entirely during the Emergency), 19 percent reported that the reasons were wholly women's issues: health (sometimes with the doctor's advice), fear of more pregnancies and births, or advancing age. A further 4 percent reported solely social reasons, such as the harmony of the uncrowded home, and a further 1 percent said it was to allow sex during the forbidden period after the birth. But 76 percent gave reasons that were predominantly economic, although many argued in highly generalized terms, such as it being clear that the family was already too large. The problem here is merely one of limiting family size, and not the two-fold one that appears to be developing in the Bangalore middle class, where there is an additional need to achieve

22. P. H. Reddy and K. N. M. Raju, "Psycho-social Impact of Sterilization on Rural Acceptors," *Bangalore Population Centre Newsletter* 5, no. 1 (1979).

23. J. C. Caldwell, "The Mechanisms of Demographic Change in Historical Perspective," *Population Studies* 35, no. 1 (1981):5–27.

birth spacing, doubtless a result of earlier weaning. Birth spacing is increasingly being achieved by experimenting with IUDs, condoms, orals, rhythm, abstinence, and induced abortion.

Conclusion

This continuing research project has produced evidence that sustained, and almost certainly irreversible, fertility decline has begun. The reasons for this are known to the participants, and any reported mystery is the product of the nature of large-scale surveys and not of social forces so deep that they are neither noticed nor understood by the actors. The decisive alterations in the society, largely operating over the last 40 years, but with earlier roots, have been economic change (of which economic growth is only one component) and social change arising largely not as a direct product of the economic change, but fueled from external sources, and waiting to exploit the opportunities presented by any destabilization of the old social and economic order. The fundamental element was a basic shift in power, work, and consumption within the family. The family planning program was able to exploit the situation and accelerate fertility decline.

A further matter of fundamental importance to an understanding of demographic transition emerged from the study. The duration of postnatal sexual abstinence began to decline in the generation preceding fertility decline, and the reduction in the period of lactation occurred at much the same time as the onset of fertility decline. One might be tempted to posit some kind of causal chain from underlying social and economic transformation to these intermediate variables, with subsequent fertility control adjustments reacting to the potential for increased fertility arising from diminishing periods of abstinence and lactation. All the evidence in this study, however, suggests that any explanation of this type would be far from the truth. It was economic change, and the intrusion of new social patterns that this change permitted, that weakened the control of the old over the young, allowing the change in the intermediate variables, and altering the intergenerational economic calculus within the family. The reduction in the postnatal sexual abstinence occurred first merely because the tensions here were greater, and there was accordingly more sensitivity to early and relatively slight shifts in the intergenerational power balance. Changes in the deliberate control of marital fertility and in other intermediate variables arose from a common source. It is likely that many demographic transitions are characterized by the onset of fertility and lactational decline at much the same time. The common origins of change in marriage and child mortality are not quite as clear, but they are certainly not absent. The changing balance of intergenerational power is one influence on the timing and conditions of marriage. It has been argued elsewhere that any shift in veneration from the old toward the young has an impact on child mortality.[24] The evidence in this part of India is that this is true here too, although such mortality decline is also abetted directly by social change in that the range of illnesses unequivocally attributed to divine retribution, and hence beyond human intervention, or encouraging lack of intervention, is reduced (see chap. 6).

Finally (and this is an extremely important methodological question), how does one obtain more proof for the arguments put forward here? These are not merely unsubstantiated hypotheses. We regard the mass of individual testimony as important evidence. Data are not merely that which is produced by large-scale surveys, which in fact may not produce real data at all if their questions cannot secure answers in sufficient depth or if the density of questions—the lack of intervening questions on important points—is such that the picture is so incomplete as not to be properly interpretable. Nevertheless, it is important to tighten up the causal and sequential explanations as far as possible. Large-scale surveys, with some concentration on older respondents and on retrospective information, might help to provide a pattern over a larger population. Such surveys, concentrating largely on contemporary fertility differentials between different social groups, seem almost meaningless when it is the whole society that has changed. Our experience to date seems to suggest that change can probably best be explained by a combination of a microapproach (with supporting local censuses, vital rate surveys, and highly focused small surveys) and an attempt by social and economic historians to substantiate, disprove, or modify the testimony from archival economic and social evidence deriving from the period being described. Certainly the explanations must be essentially historical ones, and the search must be for causation and change over time. These are difficult areas for the large-scale cross-sectional survey.

24. J. C. Caldwell, "Education as a Factor in Mortality Decline: An Examination of Nigerian Data," *Population Studies* 33, no. 3 (1979):395–413.

Chapter Three

The Family Planning
Program at the Local Level

In spite of universal pubescent and prepubescent female marriage until the last two decades, the birthrate has probably never been much higher than that found in 1960. One reason is the proscription of widow remarriage in a society where high mortality and a substantial age gap between spouses has meant that many wives are widowed early (although around one-third of widows now remarry). There have traditionally been three major constraints on marital fertility. The first was long postnatal female sexual abstinence, probably around two years in the first decades of the century, but now exceeding 18 months among only one-fifth of the women in the smaller villages and very few in the large village. The second was prolonged breast-feeding, until the last 25 years discontinued only when well into the next pregnancy, except in the case of sickness or a drying-up of the milk. Most women now wean before conception, although lactation still usually exceeds two years. The third was a reduction or cessation of sexual activity within marriage once the husband was in his forties and the wife in her thirties, a practice that is slowly declining but is still widespread. None of this behavior was meant to control fertility. Postnatal sexual abstinence and prolonged lactation was intended to increase the child's chance of survival, whereas low coital frequencies conserved the husband's spermatozoa and hence his strength and resistance to illness.

Other methods of fertility control appear to have had little impact on fertility. No method of traditional contraception was important.

Withdrawal (coitus interruptus) was rarely practiced and is still of little importance even among the urban middle class, apparently because close emotional relations between spouses and a considerable degree of sensuality are needed for its employment. Traditional abortion, mostly employing oral abortifacients, was practiced before the Second World War almost solely to hide conceptions which should not have occurred, before marriage, or, among Hindus, during the first months of marriage before the ceremony permitting the consummation of the union. In the last quarter of a century the demand has slowly increased in order to contain family size and in order to hide extramarital relations in marriages where sexual relations have largely or entirely ceased.

Underlying Social Change

There have been profound changes in family economics over the last third of a century. One complex of causes interconnects declining farm size, the spread of rural schooling, and an increase in the number of town jobs. Most of the population who depend upon agriculture have some land, but the average size of the holding is only about 40 percent of that at the beginning of the century. Most peasant families no longer need more than one son and his wife to join the older couple in cultivating the family property. There is, then, a need to find work for other sons. The preferred occupations are in the towns, where there will be a continuation of income during rural famines. The need is more to gain protection from access to noncyclic incomes than it is to maximize incomes. Most urban employers prefer workers with at least some schooling, and hence there is a growing need to keep sons at school. It is felt to be equally important to obtain sons-in-law with urban jobs. This requires not only a substantial dowry but an educated daughter, for white-collar workers will not have their children raised by an illiterate mother. School children work less and cost more because social pressures compel outlays on school children which are never made on illiterates. Most families explaining the acceptance of sterilization mention the increasing cost of children and make specific reference to the impact of schooling.

Education is not the only reason that children cost more. There is near consensus that large families imposed little economic strain half a century ago, and probably were, in most cases, an asset. This is probably still the case among those agricultural laboring families who resist the pressure to send their children to school, especially if they put them out into bonded labor, which is illegal but widespread. For most

families, a common set of changes has been noted over two generations. Children work less hard because parents do not or cannot
demand such long hours of work. One reason is a growing concept of
dependence which has been promoted by the existence of the schooling system. Another is the fear of fathers that if they push their sons
too hard, they will migrate to the towns. It is widely said that urban
culture, transmitted to the villages by returning migrants from the
town and also by the messages of the cinema, has given children a new
feeling about the limits beyond which they should not be pushed in
terms of work and the minimum levels of needs which should be met.
The satisfaction of child wants has become more expensive as a largely
subsistence agrarian economy has become monetized. During the
three years of our research period the number of retail outlets in the
smaller villages doubled. Thus, children cost more and return less.

In one sense the Hindu population has become more secular. They
still believe in the gods, although increasingly more attention is given
to the Hindu pantheon as enshrined in the great tradition and less is
given to the village goddesses. However, the important changes have
been the transfer of much behavior from the religious to the secular
sphere. Even old, illiterate women no longer feel the same religious
imperative to ensure that their daughters-in-law practice the morally
correct duration of postnatal sexual abstinence or of lactation. The
transition has been speeded up by the increasing likelihood that the
daughter-in-law will have had some schooling and will feel that she has
access to another value system.

These changes would doubtless have impinged also on fertility
control practice at some stage, but the latter has been greatly accelerated by the government family planning program. The Hindu religion has always placed much more emphasis on social behavior as an
expression of purity and righteousness than on other-worldliness, and
civil authority tends to establish new moralities. The family planning
program has approached the young couple, especially the wife, and so
has tended to render inoperative the more traditional family decision-
making processes which controlled sexual morality. There are still
clashes about the appropriate number of children, or the right number
of sons, to have before sterilization, but among the Hindus there is
now little debate about the morality of the operation.

Family Planning Practice

Among married couples in the study area where the wife was under 50
years of age, just over one-third were practicing family planning. It

appears that the practice among the unmarried is negligible. The terms "family planning" and "family planning program" are euphemisms because the program is largely a sterilization campaign. In the eight smaller villages no one has ever been offered any method except sterilization, and the debate within families focuses on whether to have "the operation" or not. In the whole study area, 86 percent of all couples categorized as practicing family planning are sterilized: the wife in 70 percent of cases, the husband in 15 percent ,and both in 1 percent ("Emergency cases"). The *nirodh* or condom is employed by 6 percent of practicing couples, and some form of rhythm by 1 percent.

One-quarter of couples are sterilized by the time the wife is 26 years of age, and one-half by the time she is 36. When measured by the number of live births a similar picture emerges: 36 percent are sterilized by the third birth and 50 percent by the fifth. The users of IUDs are a very special group and are found only in the large village. They are the bureaucracy and some of the more educated large landowners who are their close associates. They are apprehensive of sterilization, although they do not say so publicly. They feel a responsibility for, and almost an ownership of, the health center and are aware that the program can provide IUDs. These they have fitted with little publicity. The other anomalous group are the Muslim merchants. Most of them regard sterilization as outlawed by their religion, yet they are apprehensive of having too many children, if only because their shop sites and business activities mean that they cannot clash with the village *panchayat* (or council). They are the only users of condoms and they obtain them not from the program but through commercial outlets when on business activities in larger towns.

In terms of family planning acceptance, there are no significant socioeconomic differentials. One reason is that although the more educated are more inclined to demand family planning, the poor have had greater pressure placed on them for acceptance. The one major differential is the religious one between Hindus and Muslims. Among the latter, acceptance rates are approximately half of those found among the former. The only significant fertility differential is by religion and is marked only above 30 years of age. It is fully explained by the different pattern of acceptance, and its existence only at older ages can be attributed to the age pattern of sterilization. In this matter the Muslims feel themselves to be an embattled minority, but nevertheless their belief that they are defending religious morality is undoubtedly genuine. They point out that theirs is not a religion of government whim but one set out in a holy book, which, they believe, outlaws sterilization, abortion, and possibly the IUD. There are strong pressures within the community to resist the family planning program, and the leadership is largely identifiable with the religious leadership. Muslims are afraid that if they are sterilized they will not be welcome to enter other Muslim households, to eat with other members of the community, or even to be employed by them. There is some evidence of a greater desire for sterilization among the wives, but both they and the family planning program are apprehensive of the strong negative views of the husbands.

The Family Planning Program

The first sterilization performed by the program was in 1962, but the number of acceptors during the next 13 years grew only slowly. During this period most people knew of the program in a general way, but had no close contact with the operation and were often not at all sure of what is involved.

The position changed dramatically during the period of the Emergency, from June 1975 until March 1977. There is no evidence from our study area that the impact of the Emergency in the field of family planning was less in south India than in the Gangetic Plain. Half of all sterilizations performed during the 18-year period from 1962 until 1980 were performed during 18 months in the Emergency period. There was much bitterness, but it was relatively muted for two reasons. The rural population of Karnataka is gentle, with little tradition of civil disturbance. Moreover, overt opposition was undoubtedly greater when there was a concentration on vasectomies, whereas even during the Emergency three times as many women as men were sterilized in the study area.

Some of the Emergency sterilizations resulted only from much greater publicity and concentration of official efforts on family planning. But most had an element of coercion, and a substantial number involved outright force. People were taken forcibly to the nearest hospital in police or health department vehicles under police escort. The program was organized by the secretary of the panchayat, the chief government official, and all of the bureaucracy participated. Nevertheless, there was little hit-or-miss sterilization. There were a few mistakes, but forcible sterilization was very largely confined to those with three or more children. The overt force impinged more strongly upon the poorest and least educated groups, but the pressures toward sterilization were equally strong among the better-off, except that in their case it was exerted through occupational and other organizational channels. Thus, there was a greater appearance of voluntary acceptance.

One reason that the bureaucracy moved in such a concerted way during the Emergency was that the district council did not receive its full budget unless targets were met. Another reason was that each government department used its own mechanisms for reaching targets, and refused facilities, employment, or payment to those who resisted sterilization. Nor is this the whole explanation. The elites have been convinced that they and the country have much to fear from the unchecked growth of the many and the poor. There was real enthusiasm for a program with such clear aims and such definite leadership from the government. The private sector was deeply involved. Agricultural laborers who refused to accept sterilization were denied employment by landlords who had given them work for years.

The longer-term impact of the Emergency is hard to evaluate. There was much bitterness. Some of it arose from forcible sterilization. At least as much seems to have been caused by a combination of strong pressure toward sterilization together with unmet promises of loans for housing or access to land for farming or housing. It is still unclear whether the officials involved merely made their tasks easier by giving these promises or whether they believed that they would have government backing in delivering them. One aspect of backlash was a majority vote against Congress (I) in 1977. Yet, the vote swung back in 1980, and this was probably a fair measure of attitudes toward the family planning program. There was a small minority who retained their bitterness. There were more who blamed local officials rather than New Delhi. But most regarded it as yet another vicissitude of fate and no longer ascribed responsibility to specific persons.

In the first year after the Emergency, family planning acceptance dropped dramatically, but this appears to have arisen less from political and social reaction, or from a reluctance of the local health personnel to provide health services, than from an exhaustion of the potential demand. Indeed, some of the renewed demand for services in 1981, and especially in 1982, can be ascribed to a greater familiarity of the society with sterilization. It might be noted that had the Emergency continued, and had the target moved to smaller families after all those with three children had been sterilized, India's family planning performance could by now probably be compared with that of China. This did not happen because India is a democracy and because the Emergency's family planning program caused much family distress and social resistance.

The program has never been one based merely on the provision of services, although since the Emergency it has probably been closer to that model than ever before. There were always targets and these were used regularly to evaluate the caliber of program employees. The female health visitors and the more numerous auxiliary nurse mid-wives (now multipurpose health workers) visit each household at least every two months, not only with sales talk but with a message which includes moral imperatives. Given that they have official positions, are more educated, and are often higher in the caste hierarchy, it is frequently surprising that a mother of three or four children resists the suggestion of sterilization during twenty separate visits in a three-year period, especially when these are reinforced by statements from the doctor on visits to the health center. This is why families often suddenly agree to sterilization in a spirit of newly rediscovered moral rectitude, sometimes implying that the daughter-in-law is benefiting the whole family by making a noble sacrifice, a concept very familiar to the Hindu tradition. Accentuating this is the fact that half of all decisions are made while the young couples are still living with the husband's parents.

A major instrument of the program has been the employment of incentives which are now worth Rs 125 or $15. Not even the officials of the program are sure of their significance, and district medical officers vary in ascribing from 10 percent to over 50 percent of all sterilizations to their use. There is some evidence that the role of incentives is very considerably less now than was the case in the 1960s and early 1970s. At that time they were probably responsible for the majority of sterilizations being vasectomies, many of them decided upon by the men involved at very short notice and without consultation with any relatives, even their wives. One reason for a declining belief in incentives is a growing testimony of expenses arising from lost time from work and of subsequent additional medical expenses that eroded most of the incentive.

In recent years, there has been a dramatic move away from vasectomies toward female sterilization. In 1982 the ratio of female to male sterilization in both the study area and the surrounding districts was around 15 to 1. One reason is a growing belief that vasectomies may easily lead to infection and death, or at least to physical impairment that greatly reduces employability. Another is the growing confidence of the medical profession in their ability to perform female sterilizations and an increasing tendency for all family planning personnel to advocate female rather than male sterilization. In 1981 laparoscopy was becoming more popular because of the very small incision required, but by 1982 there was waning enthusiasm because of the embarrassing position that women had to adopt during the procedure.

The family planning program in the study area, and indeed throughout much of India, concentrates much more on sterilization in practice than it is usually inclined to admit when describing its principles and activities. In the study area, most employees of the program state that they would be prepared to offer a variety of methods. But no one in the eight smaller villages, and few in the large village, have ever been offered any method except sterilization. A major reason is that the elites and the officials with a certain arrogance originating in a hierarchical social structure really do not believe that the poor and uneducated can cope with anything else. Nor are they certain that the program itself could successfully handle a continuing distribution system rather than a single medical intervention. There is, throughout the medical profession in India, a suspicion of the effects of oral contraception that is probably unmatched anywhere else in the world. Certainly, the health center has never received any pills, but this may be because they have never ordered any. No woman in the study area has ever employed oral contraception.

Nevertheless, even the investigators have been gradually convinced that the major demand really is still for terminal methods. In the study area, prolonged lactation and substantial periods of postnatal sexual abstinence still provide satisfactorily long periods between births. This situation may well pass for a variety of reasons. One is a continued trend toward shorter lactation periods, with earlier weaning appearing to be largely determined by the duration of education that the mother has received. There are other potential demands for nonterminal methods. The family planning program, apprehensive of being blamed for illness or death, refuses to sterilize a considerable proportion of all women, particularly if they suffer from tuberculosis, bronchitis, asthma, or general feebleness. There are also couples who are apprehensive of sterilization but want no more children either immediately or ever. Another potential source of demand for nonterminal methods arises from the Hindu prohibition on sexual relations during the first months of marriage and the resulting fear felt by the young couples of conceiving during that period.

The situation is changing dramatically among the urban middle class in Bangalore. Among younger couples the duration of breastfeeding has already been reduced to six months when the woman works and to twelve months when she does not. Young couples are faced with a real possibility of having children in rapid succession in the first years of marriage. Accordingly, there is a growing demand for methods which will allow birth spacing. The pill is used, but its use and its value as a contraceptive are severely limited by the negative attitude of many doctors and by the number who will allow only short periods of use, frequently no longer than eight months at a time. The condom is quite widely used, and there is widespread experimentation with rhythm methods, but very little use of withdrawal.

Among Hindus, the decision for or against sterilization is no longer a moral one. The case against sterilization is almost entirely a fear of its impact. A majority of sterilized persons in the study area claim that they have never recovered full health since the operation and that they no longer achieve the same satisfaction from sexual relations. Nearly everyone considering the possibility of sterilization believes that there would be a very considerable chance of their being invalids for the rest of their lives, with much reduced chances of working or earning an income.

Family Planning Decision Making

Among Muslims, questions of religious morality infuse all discussions of family planning, with the usual exception of nonterminal male methods, which, in practice, mean the condom. Decision making is strongly male-dominated.

Among Hindus, the two dominant arguments concern the number of children and their balance by sex and the danger of the operation.

Most families want a minimum of two sons, largely because of the danger of losing one, but also because two are believed to be the minimum size of a male team within the family. Many proverbs are quoted, of which the most common is "One eye is not an eye and one son is not a son." There are also strong emotions about having a daughter. This arises partly because of the relative equality of the sexes in south India, where women's agricultural labor is a major source of income. With increased employment of sons outside agriculture and often outside the village, there is a growing belief that daughters may provide more affection and attention in old age than sons. Nevertheless, there are persistent traditional reasons for needing a daughter. In this part of India, where the local deities are usually female, unmarried daughters are needed for full family participation in many religious ceremonies. Although the husband's parents, and, less frequently, the wife's parents, are now reluctant to intervene to forbid sterilization at all, they show no equivalent reluctance in intervening if they do not believe the family to be of the proper size and balance. Indeed, they have the prime right to make the decision when family residence and property are still not partitioned.

The more complex problems of decision making involve the dangers of sterilization and therefore the preference that the sterilized person should agree that the decision was voluntary and desired. Husbands are apprehensive of vasectomy and mothers are far more fearful of the impact of sterilization on their sons than on their daughters-in-law. Thus, the whole question of sterilization may be discussed or hinted at for a long period before the daughter-in-law appears to make her own decision. In these circumstances, a subsequent survey would probably record that the young wife was the primary decision maker and would give the impression that the decision-making power was much more in the hands of the young and of females than was in fact the case.

Wives do, however, often prefer to be sterilized for one of two reasons. The first is a fear that their husbands will die from being vasectomized. It is widely believed that vasectomies are more dangerous than tubectomies. But the fundamental reason is that the death of a husband will lead to the partition of property and the dissolution of the family in its preexisting condition, often leading to a dramatic decline in the situation of the woman. The second reason, found to be quite widespread, relates to the problems of women with "useless" husbands, that is, husbands who are lazy, unemployable, alcoholic, sick, or given to straying after other women or disappearing for long periods. Women in these circumstances often become apprehensive about continuing to bear children, both because they fear the burden of a large family and because they cannot afford to give up agricultural labor either for wages or on their own land before and after a birth.

The Impact of the Family Planning Program

The family planning program has intruded into a situation where there was little use of the so-called natural methods of fertility control and practically no open-market supply of contraceptives. It still provides nearly all facilities for fertility control.

However, its impact has been much greater than this implies. It has intruded effectively into the decision-making area in two ways.

The first intrusion concerns the reasons for fertility control. The family economic situation is changing quite rapidly and the precedents of only a few years ago may well not apply. In this situation the employees of the program have voiced a conviction about the economic worthwhileness of fertility control that no one else has. Their conviction does carry weight, even though many sterilized couples later comment that they have not received the economic benefit that they anticipated.

The second intrusion is in the area of legitimation of the discussion and practice of family planning. Here they have had a sledgehammer impact. In the large village, a huge, vivid advertisement, covering the largest wall for miles around, pictures a happy man waving a condom about two meters long. In a delicate area involving sexual relations, the program has undoubtedly accelerated by decades the pace of change about what can be discussed.

No one in the study area doubts that the family planning program has vastly speeded up fertility decline. Nearly everyone believes that there has been change in family economics which has allowed the success of the program, but few believe that fertility would have declined decisively for many years without the program. Indeed, in a society which knows little about natural methods, few can understand how fertility control could even be envisaged without periodic sterilization camps.

Given this context, we should finally reemphasize several points made earlier. There has been a substantial decline in fertility, in the study area mostly since the mid-1970s. It can be very largely attributed to the family planning program, with the largest single impact being achieved by the Emergency. However, nearly spontaneous demand is now running at a level which will probably hold the birth rate down to that achieved with a high degree of coercion. If fertility is to be reduced further, other unmet needs will have to be catered to. Nonterminal methods will have to be provided, publicized, and legitimized. Almost certainly, there will be a need for looking more favorably upon oral contraception. The program will also need to demonstrate more tact and finesse, particularly by showing a concern for the health and comfort of those who have been sterilized and for much more investigation of the impact of sterilization and reassurance about its effects. The program has shown adequate concern in one important area, namely, the provision of priority medical attention to the babies of women who have recently accepted sterilization. Among these infants there has been a remarkable drop in the mortality rate compared with the other infants in the study area.

Chapter Four

The Causes of
Marriage Change

In much of the Third World the average age of women at marriage has risen at much the same time as marital fertility has begun to fall,[1] a phenomenon observed in parts of the West during the late nineteenth century.[2] An obvious question is whether the two movements are distinct, or whether marriage delay among women is merely one of the mechanisms employed to reduce total fertility. The Princeton indices,[3] which show fertility as the product of the proportion of women married and their marital fertility, are statistically correct, but have probably encouraged some social scientists to regard a reduction in the time spent within marriage as a mechanism for reducing total fertility.

Persistent rises in women's age at marriage make both India as a whole and Karnataka suitable for such a study, even though the increase began from a younger age and Indian women still marry earlier than, for instance, in Southeast and East Asia. In the search for a baseline it is better to ignore the census of 1931, as the recorded

1. See Gavin W. Jones, "Marriage Trends: Determinants and Implications," in *Social Science Research on Development in South-East and East-Asia: A Review and Search for Directions,* report of the International Review Group of Social Science Research on Population and Development (Mexico City: el Colegio de Mexico, 1978), app. 3, chap. 3, 19–24.
2. E.g., United States, Australia, Ireland.
3. Ansley J. Coale, "Factors Associated with the Development of Low Fertility: An Historic Summary," in *World Population Conference, 1965,* (New York: United Nations, 1967), 2:205–13.

proportion of very young married women was usually large, because of the rush by parents during the late 1920s to marry off their daughters before the passing of the Child Marriage Act (generally known as the Sarda Act), which attempted to prevent girls marrying before the age of 14 and men before the age of 18 years.[4] Comparing the first quarter of the century with 1971, the mean age of women at marriage in India rose from around 13 to 17 years and in Karnataka from 15 to 18 years.[5] The fastest rise occurred during the 1960s, and this is believed to have persisted, or even accelerated, through the 1970s, although no statistics on marital status by age are yet available from the census of 1981. The later marriage pattern of Karnataka was typical of south India, although in Kerala mean age at marriage was 21 years by 1971, whereas in its progressive core, Travancore, it was 17.5 years by the beginning of the century. Between the beginning of the century and 1971 the mean age at marriage of men in India had climbed slowly from 20 to 22 years, but in Karnataka had risen hardly at all, perhaps by half a year from 24.3 to 24.8 years. There is some evidence that after 1961 it may have begun to decline slowly. Part of the explanation probably lay in the great age gap between husbands and wives in Karnataka, ten years in 1891, and still, in 1971, at seven years, the largest in India.

In the Seventh Round of the National Sample Survey,[6] only slight differences in marriage age were found between the two major religious groups (the only two represented in our study area), Muslim women marrying almost a year later than Hindu women, with the difference for men being 1.5 years. In the 1951–52 Mysore Population Study, the difference was in the same direction but half the size for each sex in the towns and for men in the city of Bangalore, whereas in the city Hindu women married slightly later than Muslim women.[7]

---

4. L. S. S. O'Malley, "The Hindu Social System," in *Modern India and the West: A Study of the Interaction of their Civilizations*, ed. L. S. S. O'Malley (Oxford: Oxford University Press, 1941), 360–61. The act was passed in 1929 and came into force in 1930.

5. Except where otherwise noted, the national and state statistical data in the remainder of this section are derived from Asok Mitra, *India's Population: Aspects of Quality and Control* (New Delhi: Abhinav Publications for the Family Planning Foundation, 1978), 1:294–370. In this part of his work Mitra draws most heavily on S. N. Agarwala, *India's Population Problems* (Bombay: Tata McGraw-Hill, 1972); R. P. Goyal, "Shifts in Age at Marriage in India and Different States During 1961–71" (Delhi: Institute of Economic Growth, 1975), mimeograph; and *Reports* of the National Sample Survey.

6. Carried out in 1953–54.

7. United Nations, Department of Economic and Social Affairs, *The Mysore Population Study*, Population Studies no. 34 (New York: United Nations, 1961), 96.

This reversal of the pattern among urban women has been confirmed in an analysis by the Registrar General's Office, although the margins are small.[8] Differences by caste in the National Sample Survey were negligible,[9] but Driver recorded a faster move toward higher marriage ages among Brahmins in central India.[10] By 1971, marriages for each sex in India occurred about 2.5 years later in urban than rural areas, whereas in Karnataka the margin was 2.2 years for women and 1.6 years for men. In the rural plains (where our study area is located) insignificant differentials in marriage age by occupational status of the household were found in the Mysore study,[11] but in the city and towns (where 30 years ago most of the educated were living) women's mean age at marriage was one year higher for those who attended middle school and a further three years higher for those with high school education.[12] The important point is that most differences are not large, and that the move toward later marriage among women has been general and not primarily a feature of only one sector of society.

Karnataka has been characterized more by very early marriage of women than by child marriage. Even during the early decades of the present century, in the overwhelmingly rural district in which the study area is located, one 1 percent of 5 to 9-year-olds were married, and the numbers have been insignificant since the 1940s. The proportion of 10 to 14-year-old girls who were married fell from 25 percent in 1901 to 20 percent in 1921 and stabilized at around 5 percent from 1951.[13] In the Mysore Population Study, 42 percent of women born between 1893 and 1902 had married before 13 years of age in the rural plains, compared with 18 percent of those born between 1928 and 1932, whereas the analogous figures before 16 years of age were 83 and 72 percent respectively.[14]

By 1980, in our study area only 1 percent of 10 to 14-year-old girls were married, 31 percent of those aged 15–19 (somewhat understated because of a tendency for young married women to round their age to 20 years), and 82 percent of those aged 20–24. Even in the smaller villages, which made up half the population, the proportions were 1,

8. The Registrar General, *Fertility Differentials in India, 1972* (New Delhi, 1977), 17.

9. Seventh Round, 1953–54, employing broad categories.

10. Edwin D. Driver, *Differential Fertility in Central India* (Princeton: Princeton University Press, 1965), 65.

11. United Nations, *The Mysore Population Study*, 102.

12. Ibid., 99.

13. *Census of India*, Mysore State volumes, 1901–61.

14. United Nations, *The Mysore Population Study*, 93.

36, and 92 percent respectively. For the first time, households were beginning to experience the presence of unmarried daughters in late adolescence, and, in the larger village, even of young adult single females.

The Changing Nature of Marriage

Among Hindus, marriage is a sacrament of transcendental importance. Traditionally, it has been assumed that marriages were not only arranged by families, but that there was an element of divine guidance. Widows were not supposed to remarry because their marriage might well be reconstituted with the same husband in the next life, as it might have been in past lives. Widow remarriage is still relatively less common than the remarriage of widowers. This difference between the sexes has an important bearing on the marriage market, as will be discussed later.

That market has not been conditioned by the impulses of young men and women to marry, but largely by family decisions as to when to bring a new daughter-in-law into the household and when to change a son's status by allowing him to marry. In many societies a young bride is preferred, so that her personality can be molded by both her husband and his parents. This is important in India, too, but traditionally it has not provided the main motivation for early marriage of women in the study area. That motivation was provided by divine sanctions against girls who failed to marry before menarche, and against the family that erred in this way. An English observer, reporting on Mysore society at the end of the eighteenth century, wrote of the Brahmins, "Unless a woman marries before the signs of puberty appear, she is ever afterwards considered impure,"[15] and, of a merchant caste, that a girl "must be married before any signs of puberty appear, for afterwards she is considered as being deflowered and incapable of marriage".[16] However, it was clear even then that some of the service castes were not greatly disturbed by breaking these rules. Child marriage provided an insurance against even precocious puberty.

15. Francis Hamilton Buchanan, *A Journey from Madras through the Countries of Mysore, Canara and Malabar Performed under the Orders of the Most Noble the Marquis Wellesley Governor General of India for the Express Purpose of Investigating the State of Agriculture, Arts and Commerce: Religion, Manners and Customs; the History Natural and Civil and Antiquities in the Dominions of the Rajah of Mysore and the Countries Acquired by the Honorable East India Company* (London: T. Cadell and W. Davies, 1807), 1:52.
16. Ibid., 259–60.

Even now, a major control over the age at marriage of women is provided by the fact that many families feel deep disquiet and guilt over the presence of an unmarried menstruating daughter in the household, an emotion that may be fueled by an apprehension lest she become pregnant and unmarriageable, but which cannot be wholly explained in this way. The age of marriage of men has largely been determined by the commitment of families to provide daughters with a marriage (and, eventually, sons with land and other property). In rural Karnataka this was usually taken to mean that sons must remain single and work with their fathers to provide their sisters with the wherewithal for marriage until even the youngest sister had married (see chap. 5).

Two major changes are under way throughout most of south India. One is from a bridewealth to a dowry system, and the other is reduction in the proportion of all marriages between close relatives. Both have implications for age at marriage.

Bridewealth and dowry are not antithetical. Both are forms of marriage payment which imply the making of arrangements and the provision of payments by persons other than the future spouses, with the almost inevitable consequence of a high degree of influence over the young couple after marriage. The true antithesis to both is the absence of both payments and arrangement by the older generation. The position is made more complex in India because gifts from the family of one of the partners generate reciprocal gifts from the other side, and alternating gifts may continue for a considerable period. Where dowry is paid, distinctions can be drawn between that which goes to the bride and that which is destined for her husband's family, but, when she is entering a joint family,[17] in the normal circumstances where her husband has much control over her property and where he forms part of a larger economic unit, such distinctions may mean little in practice. Even in north India, most marriage payments appear on balance to have been bridewealth, with dowry being an ideal type paid in royal marriages and by some devout Brahmins. However, an intensification of the practice of hypergamy (i.e., wives marrying socioeconomically upward, usually in the same caste but sometimes between subcastes, into richer or more esteemed families who require compensation for what would otherwise be a misalliance) during the eighteenth and nineteenth centuries led to an inflation in dowries in north India, especially among the twice-born (the Calcutta Brahmins

17. See chap. 5, this volume, for the demonstration that this usually happens, at least at first, in the study area.

of Rabindranath Tagore's short stories of the 1890s worry a great deal about the cost of marrying daughters).

In south India there was no hypergamy, partly because of the high incidence of marriages between relatives, perhaps because of greater socioeconomic homogeneity within castes, and possibly, as Dumont argues,[18] because of an emphasis on the need for alliances. There are reports of the payment of considerable dowries (i.e., above the level of the ritually expected gold and saris to accompany the bride into marriage) by Brahmins in the city of Madras as early as the mid-1930s (perhaps influenced by the issue of paper currency), but elsewhere in the region we cannot find the practice reported until after Independence. During the 1950s it began to appear in Bangalore, and by the early 1960s dowries of some magnitude were reported in provincial towns and among the largest rival Brahmin landlords. In the study area the first dowry paid by a Vokkaliga (the major peasant caste) was in 1965. By 1980 most Harijans had ceased paying bridewealth and assumed that dowries would appear as the decade progressed.

The authors of two important studies have failed to realize that the important change in south India is the rapid move from bridewealth to dowry which may be encountered at different stages according to the village or caste examined.[19]

In the study area there is a large measure of agreement about the reasons for the surge of dowry through the community. Its coming is widely deplored and no one suggests that its practice is spiritually or socially uplifting, a form of Sanskritization.[20] Instead, two reasons are given, usually both by each respondent.

The first is the affirmation that the marriage market has changed

18. Louis Dumont, *Hierarchy and Marriage Alliance in South Indian Kinship*, Royal Anthropological Institute Occasional Papers no. 12 (London, 1957), and "Marriage in India: The Present State of the Question," *Contributions to Indian Sociology* (Paris: Mouton), vol. 5 (1961), vol. 7 (1964), and vol. 9 (1966). See also S. J. Tambiah, "Dowry and Bridewealth, and the Property Rights of Women in South Asia," in *Bridewealth and Dowry*, ed. Jack Goody and S. J. Tambiah, Cambridge Papers in Social Anthropology no. 7 (Cambridge: Cambridge University Press, 1973), 100–110.

19. Tambiah, "Dowry and Bridewealth," 100–10; Barbara D. Miller, *The Endangered Sex: Neglect of Female Children in Rural North India* (Ithaca: Cornell University Press, 1981). In spite of its title, the latter work devotes considerable attention to South India.

20. I.e., adopting Brahmin ways, a term first employed in M. N. Srinivas, *Religion and Society among the Coorgs of South India* (Oxford: Clarendon Press, 1952), 30. The turn toward dowry in south India is described as Sanskritization in T. Scarlett Epstein, *South India: Yesterday, Today and Tomorrow* (London: Macmillan, 1973), 193.

over a few decades from a surplus of potential husbands to a surplus of potential wives. We will examine this proposition later, but stress here that its truth is generally accepted in the study area and that there has been a reversal from a situation where the boy's family actively sought a bride for him by going from house to house, to one where the girl's family does this. In fact, among the younger marriages in the study area, the girl's parents seem to have made the first approaches in only about half of all cases, but this is a considerably higher proportion than among the older marriages.

The second, affirmed by nearly everyone, can be considered a form of hypergamy (although not even anthropologists employ the term to describe what has happened in south India). Parents desire their daughters to marry educated men with urban jobs, because such men have higher and more certain incomes which are not subject to climatic cycles and which are paid monthly, and because the wives of such men will be freed from the drudgery of rural work[21] and will usually live apart from their parents-in law. In a sellers' market, created by relative scarcity, there was no alternative but to offer a dowry with one's daughter. The lead was given by the upper castes (who, some say, learned the practice from the north) because they produced the first significant numbers of educated young men. Others add that with increasing monetization and a growing desire for investment, it was inevitable that superior sons-in-law should be thought of as the best investment (even though, as shown below, there is debate about the extent to which there are returns from sons-in-law).

Traditionally, marriages to relatives have been preferred, and to a very considerable extent the parents of either the boy or the girl could insist on such a marriage taking place. The preferred marriage was that of a man to his sister's daughter (i.e., his niece), but nieces of a suitable age have often not been available. In fact, only 30 percent of husbands and wives in the study area have been sufficiently closely related before marriage (one-third among Hindus and one-quarter among Muslims) for it to be possible to define the exact relationship. However, the proportion fell quite steeply as the ages of the spouses declined, showing clearly that the practice was becoming less common. In recent marriages (where the wife was less than 30 years or the husband less than 35 years old) only 20 percent of marriages have been of this type.[22] Half of all marriages between relatives were to first cousins

21. Thorner's term for the Russian employed by Chayanov in *The Theory of the Peasant Economy*, ed. Daniel Thorner, Basile Kerblay, and R. E. F. Smith, (Homewood, Ill.: Richard Irwin, 1966), 6.

22. Although a further 38 percent believe there was a distant relationship

(cross-cousin among Hindus and parallel-cousin among Muslims), but only 6 percent were between uncle and niece.

Three reasons were given for the decline in marriage between relatives. The most common was the rise of dowry, with the temptation for the boy's parents to seek a marriage outside the family, for the tradition persists that the cost of marriage between relatives must be small. The second was the same as the explanation given for the rise in village exogamy: a more heterogeneous society in terms of both education and wealth means that it is now more difficult to arrange an appropriate match and it is necessary to search through a larger population. The third is a growing belief that such marriages might produce sickly children, clearly a cultural import (probably affected both by north Indian and Western attitudes). Although marriages within the village are not frowned upon in south India (in spite of a lurking feeling that a daughter-in-law should not find it too easy to carry tales home and thus increase tensions between the two families), the wider search for potential spouses now proceeds much more often than not beyond the village, frequently, in the case of smaller castes, for 10 or 15 kilometers, to the nearest villages populated by the same caste. It is said in the study area, and our statistics confirm the point, that marriage between relatives usually occurred at younger ages than that between nonrelatives, partly because it had long been assumed and hence there were no delays, and partly because there was no apprehension about sending young girls off to alien households.

Finally, the age at marriage should be seen in the perspective of marriage decision making. A point that must be emphasized is that marriages are still arranged. In the study area, 50 marriages have taken place over the last two years, but in only one have the spouses made the decision on their own. Elopement is still a cause of scandal, and, to the young, of excitement. Many parents now aver that they consult their children before a final decision. In the case of daughters, this means little more than informing them, with one exception: a girl still at school, and who has not reached menarche, may occasionally object that her education would be halted and may find some support within the family. Parents arranging the marriage of a son in his mid-twenties are increasingly likely to give him some veto power, especially if he has secondary school education or they lack property to act as a lever.

The extent to which the situation is misunderstood by outsiders is shown by the use of the English term, "arranged." Parents are not primarily choosing a wife for their son, with the added qualification

---

(sometimes merely because the family had obtained more than one wife from the same village).

that she should suit them. They are primarily acting as the principals in selecting their daughter-in-law, the next female generation of the stem household, and it is that role which will determine the timing of the marriage and the characteristics of the girl. The most common reason given in the study area for the timing of the marriage of a son is that some change in the household, such as the mother becoming ill, meant that more women to assist were urgently needed. It is nowadays also increasingly hoped that as they grow older, the young spouses will be found to suit each other. Over half a century, the older couple have moved increasingly toward regarding the frequency of sexual relations between the younger couple, the time at which their daughter-in-law weans her children, and whether the younger couple practice birth control, as areas from which they should at least partly abdicate from power (see chap. 2). There is also a growing concept that their grand-children are foremost their children's children. Among the educated urban middle class, similar attitudes are beginning to emerge with regard to marriage, but in the villages there is, as yet, little abdication of authority in this area.

This, then, is the context within which the rising age at women's marriage must be studied. Over a quarter of a century, the circum-stances of rural marriage have been changed by two major transitions: that from bridewealth to dowry, which has been rapid and traumatic, and that toward marriage with nonrelatives, which has been slower and caused much less concern.

The Passing of Child Marriage

The virtual disappearance of marriage of girls before puberty and the lengthening gap between puberty and marriage appear, in the study area, to be two distinct phenomena and will be treated as such in the analysis. One reason for maintaining the distinction, at least from the viewpoint of a demographer interested in fertility, is that sexual rela-tions between marriage and menarche cannot result in a conception. Another is that nearly every respondent in the study area maintains that such relations do not occur and never have. In this sense, child marriage is a marriage contract rather than a marriage, and sexual relations are prohibited until after a second ceremony following men-arche (*sobana* which allows *prastha* or consummation).[23] Some doubt is thrown on whether this really has been the case by the determination

23. Socially it is a marriage, and remarriage after widowhood preceding men-arche is discouraged (hence Gandhi's concern with virgin widows).

of reformers to legislate for an age of consent, first set at 10 years by the Vidyasagar Act in 1860 and later raised.[24] Even when a Hindu girl has reached menarche before marriage, consummation of the marriage is not supposed to take place for several months until an auspicious time marked by a further ceremony (again the *sobana* or *prastha*). There is much apprehension about the possibility of giving birth earlier than a full year after marriage, for only a period of twelve months provides clinching evidence that she was a virgin at marriage. In the study area, 95 percent of Muslim marriages were consummated within 24 hours, but among Hindus the median delay was three months, with only 25 percent of couples having sexual relations within the first month.

Although child marriage has never been universal in south India, there have been strong supports for it. From the viewpoint of the bride's parents it ensures marriage before menarche, which once insured against divine disapproval and now insures against paying the dowry increases which mount from menarche onward (itself a sign that an unwed girl who has attained puberty can already be classed as damaged goods). From the viewpoint of the boy's parents it means that the daughter-in-law is still young and pliable, and that their son is no longer restless because no thought has been given to his marriage. When the marriage was one between relatives, especially one arranged by parents who had lived in the same joint household, the marriage had probably been envisaged for years and it was a relief to all involved to have the matter finally settled.

Yet, child marriage over the last decade or two has almost disappeared in the study area. One reason—the obverse of the advantage cited above—is the smaller number of marriages between relatives. Others are connected with the payment of dowry, the fact that the search for a suitable spouse is now undertaken by the girl's rather than the boy's family, and by the increasing frequency of the need to obtain a degree of consent from the boy. Given that the latter is likely to be a young man well in his twenties, and that he may have visited the cinema several times (the situation in the study area for such young men)[25] it is increasingly difficult to get him to accept a girl of immature appearance and the inevitability of waiting for years to consummate his marriage.

24. O'Malley, "The Hindu Social System," 359–60.
25. In 1982, of young men of marriageable age in the study area, half had seen the cinema in the previous month (half at places outside the local area where there was a "tent" cinema), while half of the marriageable young women (over 15 years of age) had been to the cinema within the previous six months.

However, there are other forces—unrelated to these specifically south Indian changes, and hence operating right across the country—which militate against child marriage, and, in some cases, against marriage at menarche as well.

Child marriages were more important when mortality was higher and hence more capricious at all ages. Parents felt strongly that they should have fixed all their children's marriages before death, and also that they should have seen their grandchildren. A rise in expectation of life at birth of perhaps twenty years in Karnataka over the last forty years has reduced this pressure. Child marriages were also most important, given that a family would usually try to marry its daughters before arranging the marriages of its sons, when women bore children from menarche to close to menopause—even when daughters married at 12 years of age, a daughter born to a woman 44 years old might preclude her son born when she was 18 from marrying before he was 38 years old, or alternatively involve an undesirable decision that he should marry before one or more of his sisters. The family planning program (nearly half the women in the study area are now sterilized by their 35th birthday) is increasingly reducing this pressure. The century-old legislative fight against child marriage hardly had an immediate effect in the village, but there has undoubtedly been a cumulative effect, especially in convincing influential people who tend to proffer advice (especially as many people of this kind appear now to include the move against child marriage as one of the aims of the struggle for Independence).

However, all these changes now tend to be subsumed into the single attitude that premenarchic girls are immature. They are unsatisfactory as wives and daughters-in-law. They are ignorant not only because of their tender years, but also because their early marriage will have disrupted any schooling. There is also an awareness that society has changed. Because of schooling (and the majority of girls now receive some schooling) and the only partially related spread of concepts of child-dependency, child wives are unlikely to be worked as hard as was once the case, and, in alternations between their home of origin and their marital home, they are likely to spend a greater proportion of their life before menarche in the former.

The Proper Time to Marry

Of the younger married persons (men under 35 years of age and women under 30), the median ages at marriage were 24 for men and 18 for women (depressed somewhat by the truncation effect that not all marriages in the cohort have yet taken place)—not dissimilar from the figures for the rural population of the whole state. There are some differences in age at marriage by caste and socioeconomic status (closely related in the study area). Median ages for recent women's marriages are 15 for Harijans, 17 for Vokkaligas (the main peasant caste), 18 for Jains and Muslims, and over 20 for Brahmins. Among men the ages are around 23 or 24 years for Harijans, Vokkaligas, and Muslims, 25 for Lingayats and Jains, and 28 for Brahmins. However, all the differences among women and most among men can be explained by education. When asked what was the best age to marry, men gave a median age of 25 (60 percent actually said 25). One-sixth of women said soon after menarche, and the remainder gave a median age of 18 years (three-quarters providing an age slightly older than that at which they had actually married). Among those in the same age range not yet married—younger on the whole but with somewhat higher levels of schooling—men still opted for 25 years but women for 20 years. It is clear that there are no substantial pressures from the younger generation to change men's age at marriage, but that there are upward pressures on women's.

The attitude toward the proper age and circumstances of women's marriage varies little by generation. There is no longer much evidence of any feeling of religious or moral transgression in failing to marry a girl by menarche. There are still strong feelings about the disaster that would befall the girl and her family if she were to become premaritally pregnant, and a related belief that it is irresponsible not to begin marriage arrangements at menarche, and highly irresponsible to leave a girl who has reached puberty at school. Parents with daughters at secondary school are keen that they should attain the SSLC (Secondary School Leaving Certificate, awarded after three years of secondary schooling, and two years before the university entrance examination) and increasingly apprehensive that menarche will occur before the examination—if that does happen, girls are usually removed from school even within days before the examination (exceptions being the Brahmin and certain other educated families).

Nevertheless, there is a keen awareness that the arrangement of a woman's marriage takes time and that the difficulties and the resulting prolongation of the unmarried state after menarche increase each year. It is abundantly clear that as long as the girl is kept at home and efforts toward match-making are under way, neither her parents nor those of prospective grooms are much disturbed by this delay. The reasons include those which have led to the abolition of child marriage. Girls aged 14 or 15 years are immature as daughters-in-law and as wives.

They often lack responsibility and may lack strength. Young adult men are now often reluctant to agree to marriage with such a bride. However, there are two additional arguments that are now voiced most frequently. First, giving birth to a child at such an age may hurt both child and mother, and may make it difficult or impossible to bear any more children. Second, such young mothers are often unsuited to rearing the household's children. The latter complaint is itself a sign of change: that the mother-in-law has at least partially abdicated from a position of absolute female authority.

This does not mean that the older generation who are responsible for the arrangements are usually ready as yet to think in terms of waiting until the girl is 19 or 20 years of age before taking action. To some extent they are deterred by the prospect of rising dowry, but their overwhelming fear is that no husband may be found at all. They also fear the possibility that their daughters will not remain virgins, and both they and their daughters fear gossip on this point, whether true or not. Such gossip may badly damage the chances of a good marriage not only for a girl but also for her sisters. There is also a related economic problem. A girl who has reached menarche is usually withdrawn from agricultural field work, especially paid work for other households which is so important for the lower castes, and cannot resume such activities until after marriage.

In the case of men, there is a mechanical case against their marrying younger, namely, that their parents are usually anxious to marry off all their sisters first (not strictly adhered to if the age gaps are too great). But there are other arguments. Most families feel that a man who marries much before his 25th birthday will be sexually immature and that such early drains on his sexual strength will have permanent effects on his physical strength. One of the reasons most commonly put forward for a large age gap between spouses is that this is a necessary mechanism for giving husbands sufficient dominance to resist their wives' sexual demands. Most also feel that he will make an immature husband, unsuited to heading a nuclear family (or a segment of this kind within a larger family), and, as brides' ages increase, likely to be too close to his spouse's age to keep her under control or to always defer to his mother's wishes against those of his wife.

The arguments against older marriage for men are not felt as strongly as any of the other situations but include two that most families make. First, men's sexual powers begin to wane after about 30 years of age and steeply after 35. As a man becomes older, too much sexual activity drains him physically, affecting his other activities, whereas women have much greater capacity for sexual activity.[26] It might be noted that widowers are not expected to bring such youthful vigor to their marriages. Second, such an old age at marriage carries a risk that the parents will die either before the marriage can take place or before the grandchildren are born. There is also some fear among parents that their son will become morally dissolute, and some apprehension among aging but single young men that people will begin to tease them for not having really reached a man's estate.[27]

Ideas in the community about what is happening to ages at marriage are fairly clear, namely, that there has been a long, persistent, and continuing rise in women's age at marriage, and that men's marriage ages displayed an upward trend that has probably halted, and may even have reversed, during the last decade or two. There is evidence, referred to above, from census analysis, that in Karnataka men's mean age at marriage may have peaked around 1961 and have since fallen slightly.

The reason given widely for the peaking of men's age at marriage is that sons, by their mid-twenties, are growing restless to attain a man's full estate by marrying. It is also quite frequently added that in the past young men did not grumble about being denied marital sexual relations, but that the cinema and other urban or external influences are changing this position and that parents are beginning to take such complaints into account. The continued rise of the women's age at marriage is explained by the increasing difficulty of finding suitable grooms. However, many respondents also mention the impact of education. They tend to take it for granted that girls who have been to school for any length of time should marry later, but find it hard to explain why. In fact, in the study area, primary schooling delayed women's marriage by one year and secondary schooling by a further two years. Until menarche, the main reason is that schoolgirls are not likely to be withdrawn in order to marry; beyond menarche, when most girls have been withdrawn from school, the chief cause is probably the delay arising from a greater difficulty in deciding upon an

---

26. See also David G. Mandelbaum, *Society in India: Continuity and Change* (Berkeley: University of California Press, 1970), 77; Gerald D. Berreman, *Hindus of the Himalayas* (Berkeley: University of California Press, 1963), 170; Alan R. Beals and Bernard J. Siegal, *Divisiveness and Social Conflict: An Anthropological Approach* (Stanford: Stanford University Press, 1966), 43–46; Bruce Elliott Tapper, "Widows and Goddesses: Female Roles in Deity Symbolism in a South Indian Village," *Contributions to Indian Sociology*, New Series 13, no. 1 (1979):7–8.

27. Srinivas, *Religion and Society*.

appropriate match for a girl of such qualifications. Secondary or tertiary, but not primary, education delays men's marriage, partly again because of the problem of matching, but partly so that such educated young men can become established.

Is There a Marriage Squeeze?

In the study area it is believed by everyone that potential wives were once scarce and are now in surplus. In fact, among the population as a whole the sex ratio is 105 males per 100 females, slightly above the ratio that has characterized Karnataka for most of the last 100 years and typical of the whole country.[28] However, such ratios are an appropriate test only when men and women marry at the same age. When women marry at younger ages, a surplus of potentially marriageable young women is added to otherwise reasonably equal numbers; in fact, this is the mechanism that allows a substantial level of polygyny in many societies.[29] Furthermore, in a growing population, where each age group is larger than the preceding older one, this surplus can be considerable, rising with the rate of growth of the population. In the study area, if we compare the numbers of single women over 15 years of age with those of single men over 22 years old (assuming the current seven-year age gap between spouses), there is a surplus of women amounting to 29 percent. This ratio tends to exaggerate the problem, because more single men emigrate than women. Such emigrants, even in the city, remain members of the rural marriage market (as our urban interviews confirmed), because the parents who arrange the marriages remain in the countryside. For this reason, the statistics for larger areas, such as the whole state or country, provide better measures of the extent of the marriage squeeze.

This situation has developed over a few decades. The ratio in Karnataka (Mysore) of never-married men aged 15–24 to never-married women aged 10–44 (the upper limits of the age ranges are of little significance because of near-universal marriage) was 1.38 in 1931, similar to the position at the beginning of the century, but by 1961 it had dropped to 1.19 and by 1971 to 1.01. In India as a whole, for those three dates, the ratios were 1.25, 1.12, and 0.93 respectively. Even in

---

28. Mitra, *India's Population: Aspects* 1:376.

29. See John C. Caldwell, "Marriage, the Family and Fertility in sub-Saharan Africa with Special Reference to Research Programmes in Ghana and Nigeria," in *Family and Marriage in Some African and Asiatic Countries*, ed. S. A. Huzayyin and G. T. Acsadi, Research Monograph no. 6 (Cairo: Cairo Demographic Centre, 1979), 359–71.

Karnataka, if we adopt a more realistic age gap between spouses for that state (seven years), there was a surplus of marriageable women already by 1971. This surplus is slightly increased by including widowed and divorced women and assuming a remarriage rate of 33 percent (in the study area the remarriage rate for both men and women had been similar during a limited period preceding the study), and increases still further if we employ estimates (calculated for all India) of remarriage rates among the widowed of 33 percent for women and 66 percent for men.[30]

The situation is that of a classic marriage squeeze. During the last half-century the expectation of life at birth has approximately doubled, with a resultant broadening of the base of the age pyramid. Comparing the censuses of 1931 and 1971 for the whole country,[31] the number of females aged 10–19 (the group containing most brides) was ten percent larger than that of males aged 20–29 (the group containing most grooms) in 1931, but 30 percent larger in 1971. Comparing the total number of females over 10 years of age with that of males over 15 years of age (the all-India age gap between spouses is smaller than that of Karnataka), there was a surplus of 12 million females in 1931 compared with 20 million in 1971. The key to the situation is that these populations contained a surplus of widows who had not remarried over widowers who had not done so, a margin which was around 16 million both in 1931 and 1971 (a stability that attests to declining mortality). If we subtract this number from our previous surpluses, we find that a deficit of 4 million females in 1931 was converted to a surplus of 4 million in 1971.

There is, then, much truth in the popular belief that potential brides were in short supply a generation or two ago, and that this situation has reversed relatively quickly to yield a surplus. This is the result of declining mortality during a period when the birth rate remained relatively high and the age gap between spouses considerable, and of a substantial surplus of unmarried widows over unmarried widowers. The latter is a product of three factors: greater discour-

30. P. N. Mari Bhat and Ramesh Kanbargi, "A Preliminary Note on Levels, Trends and Differentials in Widow and Widower Remarriage in India in the Twentieth Century" (Bangalore: Population Research Centre, Institute for Social and Economic Change, 1981), mimeograph, 29ff. For 1971, the authors estimated the absolute number of remarried widows as 12 million and remarried widowers as 14 million with an average age at remarriage of 29 and 40 years respectively. Of widow remarriages, 60 percent were levirate marriages to relatives.

31. I.e., prepartition and postpartition India, but this makes a negligible difference to this type of analysis.

agement of remarriage for widows, slightly higher mortality among women, and, most significant, the age gap between spouses, which results in women being widowed earlier than men on the average.

Putting off Marriage beyond Menarche

A generation ago the major problem in investigating the rising age at marriage of women would have been the passing of child marriage and the number of girls whose marriages were delayed until near or at menarche. This is no longer the case. Nearly all families in the study area believe that attempts to marry daughters should begin at menarche and should be successful as soon as possible. Therefore, the explanation of the continuing rise in women's age at marriage (now on average at least four years beyond menarche) must lie in the time taken in achieving that success. We now possess detailed information about that process for half the families in the nine-village area. We discussed the subject separately with married children and their parents, and discovered that there were few differences between them about the facts of each case. We shall examine the assessment of the general situation in the community, the specific comparison of the reasons for differing marriage gaps between daughters and their mothers, and the extent of delay in the marriages of the younger generation.

In terms of community attitudes, a point of great significance is that the proper time for a girl to marry is slowly rising above the age of menarche. It is often expressed in the form of relief that it took a year or two to arrange the marriage, and that no attempt was begun until menarche. The reason given is the girl's immaturity, but people admit that the age regarded as the threshold of maturity is slowly rising. Half of all reasons given relate to the dangers of having children immediately after menarche, mostly to both the mother's health and that of the child, the danger in the former case often being cited as the possibility of death or the inability to bear more children. Other reasons given are that a very young wife can neither work sufficiently hard nor responsibly enough as a daughter-in-law, nor adequately care for her husband or children. There is a subtle change in these latter concerns, because once the mother-in-law managed all these matters absolutely. Such changes in attitude are not likely to lead to a radical rise in women's age at marriage. Nearly everyone reports fears that a much longer delay might mean that no suitable husband, and sometimes no husband at all, could be found, and many point out that they could be found only by paying higher dowries. This is reported to be a relatively new but increasing problem. The supplementary reasons are fear of sexual immorality, and an even greater fear of gossip suggesting it, whether well founded or not. There is also some belief in declining fecundity.

Nevertheless, when discussing specific marriages in the community, around nine-tenths of all explanations are mechanical rather than social ones. There is almost equal stress on the admittedly interrelated problems of surplus females and the difficulty of finding husbands and on rising dowries and the trouble in marshaling resources. Some also argue that girls with substantial schooling usually do—and should—marry later, although, of the 177 brides of the last decade where the history of the marriage was examined in detail, only 16 continued schooling until menarche; 12 left immediately and in only three of the remaining four cases was their continuation at school said to have postponed their marriage. In about one-tenth of cases marriage postponement was explained by children's protests about either marriage at that time or the chosen husband. A small minority talked of changed attitudes toward dependence and the concept of childhood—mostly parents with some education. A few blamed the cinema, but most said it was new ideas, essentially beneficial ones, from the outside world.

However, when we sought explanations of beliefs in each family where a daughter married at a later age than her mother why this had happened, the role of schooling and increased dependence was mentioned in about 30 percent of all cases, although only 4 percent explained it mechanically in terms of the girl still being at school. The single most important cause given was the problem of finding an acceptable level of dowry and raising the money for it in 35 percent of households, and that of finding a husband, given the shortage of potential bridegrooms, in the other 35 percent although most maintained that the two issues could hardly be separated.

In the marriages of all wives still under 30 years of age, we examined the reasons for postponement. The reason why the search for a husband began later than had been anticipated was usually later menarche. Once the search had begun, the first serious attempt at negotiations led to marriage in three-fifths of all cases, although not always immediately. In most cases of failure the reason was the inability to agree about dowry payments, although daughters' views on the match were crucial in two cases and adverse information about the boy's character in another. Dowry is higher, and often marriages cannot be arranged at all, if there have been sexual indiscretions among any female members of the girl's family, any criminal or socially disapproved behavior in the family, or if the girl's complexion is dark. In one-fifth of marriages four or more possible husbands had been considered. Although it is now part of the folklore of the area that once the boy's families scoured the countryside seeking scarce wives while the situation is now reversed, the first formal approach was made by the boy's side in 60 percent of all cases, although it is clear that this figure is much lower than it was a quarter of a century earlier. The go-betweens were nearly always relatives, although parents were the major actors in only two-thirds of all cases.

Change in Men's Age at Marriage

The community is well aware that there has been no radical change in men's marriage age. Most parents oppose any significant downward change in the age at which their sons marry on the grounds that they would then be too immature to be a husband or father—again, an interesting view if the new couple is to be embedded, as is usual,[32] in a joint family—and that premature regular sexual activity would reduce the amount of work they could do and endanger their health. On the other hand, they are apprehensive of delaying their sons' marriages into their late twenties because the community will begin to regard them as immature and the right bride and the desired dowry will be harder to secure. There is a remarkable consensus that a man should marry at about 25 years. Nevertheless, many specific marriages were delayed: some because of problems in completing education or training or becoming established in a nonagricultural job; in a small but growing number because the sons demurred at their parents' first choice; and in most because of problems encountered by the prospective bride's family in raising money for dowry and wedding expenses. Nevertheless, the average age of men at marriage in both this community and in the state of Karnataka has probably been falling slowly for twenty years. The reason given in most cases for a slightly premature marriage is that a good opportunity occurred. A greater selection of potential wives is now available than a generation ago, and dowries offered, in contrast to the earlier period, can be very tempting. Some parents also seize the opportunity because they feel their sons are becoming sexually restless—often alleged to be caused by new social influences, especially the cinema—and fear that they will acquire reputations as rakes.

32. See chap. 5 for a discussion of the determinants of family structure.

The Dynamics of Marriage Change

We now have most of the evidence in hand to explain the marriage trends noted at the beginning of this chapter, and the explanation is almost certainly valid for most of mainland South Asia.

First, some of the rise in average age of women's marriage is statistical rather than biological. Hindu marriage with child brides was not consummated—according to religious fiat, and probably mostly in practice at least during the present century—until menarche. Strictly, sexual relations are delayed until a ceremony which occurs about three months after menarche, or, in the case of postmenarcheal marriages, three months after marriage (*sobana* or *prastha*). Child marriage has all but vanished as a result of imported social disapprobation related largely to concepts of dependency and childhood (as the pejorative term "child" marriage indicates) and of radical changes in the nature of marriage itself.

The underlying causes of these radical changes are demographic rather than social, although the exact form taken by subsequent developments did depend on the available social models. Before the persistent mortality decline following World War II, the expectation of life at birth was low (under 30 years in 1931), as was the rate of population growth (under 1 percent per year during the 1920s and somewhat over 1 percent during the 1930s), with a resulting age pyramid with steeper sides and more similarity between the numbers in adjoining age groups (at least in the age range 5–34 years) than during the last quarter of a century. Even so, a marked age difference between spouses at the time of first marriage would, before the Second World War, have provided an excess of potential brides but for two factors. The first reason is India's well known high sex ratio: 105 males per 100 females recorded in the census of 1881, varying little until the census of 1951 when a figure of 106 was recorded, and thereafter slowly deteriorating until 1971 when the value was 107. In Karnataka (Mysore), as in the rest of the south, the situation was better until 1951, with ratios of 102 in 1881 and 103 from 1921 until 1951; thereafter the ratio, as in every other southern state except Kerala, began to rise, reaching 105 in 1971.[33] The second reason is the large number of unmarriageable widows, a product of a substantial age

33. The provisional results of the 1981 census indicate that this trend may have been arrested, and provide a ratio of 104. B. K. Das, Director of Census Operations, Karnataka, *Census of India, 1981: Series–9, Karnataka, Provisional Population Totals: Paper 2 of 1981* (Bangalore: Government Press, n.d.).

gap between spouses, high mortality, and discouragement of widow remarriage.

The smaller number of females in the population has long been a matter of interest and concern. In every census during the last hundred years (especially that of 1901) attention has been drawn to this, and reasons suggested. Interest mounted with the detailed work undertaken by Pravin Visaria on the census of 1961.[34] The disparity in numbers arises from higher mortality of women, and in various studies it was shown that females were relatively neglected (together, in north India, with infanticide of girls at an earlier period in some social groups).[35] The neglect was related to the nature of marriage, and sex ratios were highest precisely in those areas where hypergamy (marrying women to men higher in the social scale by providing large compensatory dowries) was commonest.[36]

During the last 30 years the deficit of potential brides has turned into a surplus in India as a whole, and also in Karnataka. From the point of view of parents of marriageable daughters, a sellers' market quite literally became a buyers' market. The response was a transition from bridewealth to dowry, a change rendered easy by the models provided of Brahmanical and royal marriages in ancient literature[37] and by the earlier move to widespread dowry in north India. Indeed, the movement to dowry has been described for another area in southern Karnataka and has been attributed solely to cultural change, to Sanskritization.[38] The evidence from the present study is very different. In nine villages we have not found a single case of parents of daughters praising the change or explaining it in any way other than necessity; they haggle for the minimum dowry required to obtain the son-in-law upon whom they have set their eye. Subsequently, they are,

34. Pravin M. Vasaria, *The Sex Ratio of the Population of India*, 1961 Census of India, vol. 1, monograph 10 (New Delhi: Office of the Registrar General, 1961); idem, "The Sex Ratio of the Population of India and Pakistan and Regional Variations During 1901–1961," in *Patterns of Population Change in India, 1951–1961*, ed. Ashish Bose (New York: Allied Publishers, 1967), 334–71.

35. India, Ministry of Information and Broadcasting, *The Gazetteer of India* (Nasik: Government of India Press, 1965), 1:330–32; Kumudini Dandekar, "Why Has the Proportion of Women in India's Population Been Declining?" *Economic and Political Weekly* 10, no. 4 (1975):1663–67; Mitra, *India's Population: Aspects* 1:371–97; David E. Sopher, "The Geographical Patterning of Culture in India," in *An Exploration of India: Geographical Perspectives on Society and Culture*, ed. David E. Sopher (London: Longman, 1980), 296–300; Miller, *The Endangered Sex*.

36. Kshatriya castes of Rajasthan, Uttar Pradesh, Punjab, and Haryana.

37. Tambiah, "Dowry and Bridewealth," 68ff.

38. Epstein, *South India: Yesterday, Today and Tomorrow*.

of course, proud of their daughter's new husband and of the fact that they managed to put together such an impressive dowry and to provide such a lavish marriage. The only Sanskritic touch may be the way the change occurred over time—from the higher to the lower castes. But this may well be largely explained by the order in which the decline of mortality occurred, by the relative levels of education and wealth needed to identify new solutions and to adopt them, by the danger of socially innovating unless the way had been shown by those at higher levels in society, by the order in which considerable numbers of educated young men in each caste became available, and by the strength of the feeling that their daughters should not be subject to agricultural drudgery. The educated are well aware that all morality does not favor high dowries and lavish weddings; the government of independent India disapproves of both and has proscribed the former and attempted to limit the latter.

The situation is not simple. The size of the dowry moves steeply with the desirable qualities of the son-in-law in a way that bride price did not for daughters-in-law. Furthermore, desirable qualities are defined to an astonishing degree by the extent of modern education and the access of the bridegroom to an urban occupation (Westernization rather than Sanskritization), as well as the amount of property owned. The problem is that the rise in modern education occurred at about the same time as declining mortality began to have a real impact on the marriage market. Many—but not most—of the families ascribe greater importance to the growth in availability of prospective bridegrooms who were not illiterate farmers or agricultural laborers than to the change in the balance of the sexes when explaining the rise of dowry. Education is almost certainly not the fundamental source of change, as is shown by the fact that peasants' sons who have had little or no education can demand considerable dowries, although this is a relatively recent phenomenon. Nevertheless, education is largely the way of ordering the new marriage market.

There are questions which are difficult to resolve with regard to the marriage market. Families who do not seem to be particularly oriented toward children, and certainly not toward daughters, will borrow impoverishing sums, or sell vitally needed land to secure superior husbands for their daughters. They go still further. They are giving their daughters more schooling, as is shown by the declining sex differentials at every level of education, even though such investments cannot be offset against the amount of dowry. Rather, the schooling is explained as the minimum qualification for securing an educated husband and as a necessity for helping children with *their* schooling, being an efficient wife and housekeeper, and looking after the whole family's health. The parents are adamant that they secure little from their daughter's marriage, only the knowledge that she will not toil as her mother did, and that, if she has an urban husband, she will be spared farm work and the vicious seasonal cycle and alternation from wet to drought years that rural life entails, as well as securing a regular monthly income. They almost certainly understate their gains. Probably the two largest ones are negative. First, if they were not to borrow to the limit—and some do not—they would lose social esteem, which, in settled rural societies where most pleasures are social relations, is all-important. A good marriage, a large dowry, and a fine wedding are talked about by the parents for the rest of their lives. Second, south Indian parents guarantee the economic well-being of their daughters even after marriage. If a married daughter's husband fails to support her adequately, then her parents must supply food grains or a milch buffalo or cow so that she can sell milk. Such a situation is not only an economic burden but also the source of much social embarrassment and is to be avoided at all costs. Yet it seems likely that there are greater positive advantages than are usually admitted. A family's social horizons are broadened by the link, even through a daughter, with the exciting urban world; one needs connections just to be able to participate at all in such nontraditional life. Younger children may be sent to the urban household for further education. However unorthodox help from married daughters may be, it is probably given on a larger scale than most families will readily admit—periodic visits home (including those for the birth of children) provide one avenue. Educated sons-in-law can give advice and may help in dealings with bureaucrats or in private negotiations. They may also give assistance to their wives' parents if the latter are clearly in need during old age.

What effect has the growth of dowry had on the society and on the position of women?

Perhaps the first point to make is that dowry and wedding expenses are not a revolving fund, little more than a book entry. Such a situation is found among pastoral peoples of the African savanna, where a single bridewealth payment can take the form of a herd of cattle, sometimes equivalent to a century's income per head, and where lineages, large enough to have a similar number of young men and women, pay a young man's bridewealth expenditure with the cattle they have just received from the marriage of a young woman of the lineage. Most of the expenditure in India now comes from the girl's side, but half of it may not be dowry but wedding costs where the expenditure is dispersed among the merchants and service castes of the community. The dowry is not a simple transfer from the parents of the girl to those of the boy. Much of it is retained by the younger couple, although more traditional parents of bridegrooms can demand a share and the existence of stem and stem-joint families can result in an upward leakage. Furthermore, dowry is not offset by the payment of marriage expenses—the changing marriage market has seen to that. Thirty years ago the bridewealth, and the much more expensive wedding costs, in the study area were very largely paid by the bridegroom's family, the wedding being held in their house; now by far the greater share is borne by the bride's family and the locale of the wedding has moved to their house. That dowry is not seen as a revolving fund, and does not act as one, is evidenced by the determination of the family not to marry children of the opposite sex alternately, but to marry all the girls first. Already families in which all children are daughters are being relatively impoverished compared with those in which all are sons—they sell more land and borrow greater amounts for marriages. At a time when all children are beginning to be something of an economic burden, the transition is occurring more rapidly in the case of daughters. It is probably no accident that, even in south India, changes in the sex ratio showed a deteriorating situation as regards females between 1951 and 1971: by 3 percent in Tamil Nadu, and by 1 percent in Karnataka and Kerala. Boys were being fed and cared for relatively better than girls, not because of a negative emotion, such as hatred of daughters, but because of the more positive awareness of where the family's safety and priorities lay.

The second point is that a massive readjustment process to the marriage squeeze is already under way. The change in sex ratios, even though they are occurring somewhat more rapidly among the young than among the whole population, will make only a marginal difference. However, the narrowing of the age gap between spouses will make a very great difference. It is probable that the gap in Karnataka is already being closed by at least one year per decade and that this process will continue for the rest of the century. The reason is that brides' ages are being raised, and that the most important cause is the difficulties encountered in marrying them: the shortage of husbands, the increasing delays in agreeing to ever-mounting dowries and finding means of meeting them, and the increasing educational and occupational heterogeneity in the society, which means greater problems in arriving at a suitable match. At the same time, bridegrooms' ages are not rising. One reason is that there is a ceiling beyond which young men are unwilling to remain without a wife and without being head of a family, even if at first only a segment of a larger family. This is being

reinforced by social change with a growing emphasis on marital sexuality and a weakening of parents' absolute control of sons' marriage
ages (see chap. 2). It is also reinforced by a reluctance of the older
generation to postpone the birth of grandchildren, especially the establishment of a continuing male line. Nevertheless, the main reason is
almost certainly the temptation to secure an advantageous marriage in
terms of the quality of the bride and the size of the dowry when this is
offered. These temptations are occurring ever more frequently as the
surplus of potential brides builds up. Thus, dowry provides a powerful
mechanism in South Asia, unlike the rest of the Third World, for
mitigating the impact of the marriage squeeze. Nevertheless, the non-
demographic effects are likely to be very great, tending toward a nega-
tion of every one of the benefits believed to accrue from the substantial
age gap. Where brides are older and closer to the bridegroom in age,
they will probably fit less readily into the extended family, and their
emotional bonds with their husbands will probably compete more
with the bonds between husbands and their mothers. Wives and husbands will probably move further toward joint decision making.

The third point is that fertility in the study area has been declining
slowly for two decades, as has been the case generally in south India,
and perhaps later and less generally in north India. This change is
probably already helping to reduce the dimensions of the marriage
squeeze, but it may be decades before its impact is more important
than the reduction in the age gap between spouses.

Marriage Delay and Fertility Decline

We now return to the original question. Is it a coincidence that fertility
decline and the deferment of women's age at marriage are occurring at
the same time, or is the deferment of marriage just one more device,
paralleling the deliberate control of marital fertility and perhaps at
first being more acceptable to a traditional society, for controlling
overall fertility?

The latter question is the easiest to dispose of. In an examination
of a decade's marriages among a population of 5,000 persons, marriages largely characterized by brides marrying later than their
mothers did, we did not find a single case of the marriage being
explained or justified in terms of a smaller final family size, or even of
young parents having fewer children on their hands while they were
establishing themselves. Indeed, it is widely felt that a woman who
marries two or three years after menarche will probably be more

fecund because her reproductive powers will not be impaired by early damage.

The delay of women's marriage has been brought about by a marriage squeeze caused by a decline in mortality that steepened after the Second World War. In contrast, the fertility decline resulted from a reduction in the net value of children and was accelerated by a family planning program that provided a mechanism which allowed a quick response to these changed circumstances.[39] Indeed, the decline in fertility will ultimately be one mechanism for reducing the pressure on women to marry later.

Nevertheless, the two processes are far from being unrelated. Mortality decline is partly a product of imported medical technology that has been instrumental in the elimination or reduction of a number of infectious diseases. It is also the product of economic growth and complex social and political changes. Since Independence in 1947, Indian governments have placed an emphasis on rural health services. They have placed even more emphasis on schooling, and the evidence in the study area is that the education of mothers has been a more important determinant of child survival than has access to health services (a finding which is not unique to India).[40] In an area where the impact of parents' income on child mortality is relatively slight, mothers with no schooling lose 20 percent of their children within five years of the child's birth, compared with 13 percent for mothers with elementary schooling, and 11 percent for those with secondary schooling. Social and political changes have produced greater equality within the family, and this, together with increasing commercialization, has made it more likely that in times of food shortage the rationed household food stores will be supplemented by additional supplies from the market. These are exactly the changes in the family economy which have made fertility decline inevitable, and they are central elements in the mortality decline.

The declines in mortality and fertility are the products of profound, worldwide changes during the last half century. One could even plausibly argue that the leap forward in medical technology, and even

39. Chap. 2 provides a detailed analysis of fertility decline in the study area.

40. John C. Caldwell, "Education as a Factor in Mortality Decline: An Examination of Nigerian Data," *Population Studies* 33, no. 3 (1979):395–413; John C. Caldwell and Peter F. McDonald, "Influence of Maternal Education on Infant Mortality: Levels and Causes," in *International Population Conference Manila 1981, Solicited Papers*, International Union for the Scientific Study of Population, vol. 2 (Liège: IUSSP, 1981), 79–96.

more the means and will to distribute the new technology to rural populations of the Third World, were part of the same process of creating a global economy and society as that which made the independence of India inevitable. The synchronous movements are very far from accidental.

Each change sets in movement new changes. The steep rise in dowry, as well as the educational costs and the withdrawal from labor imposed by the need to make girls suitable wives for the scarcer husbands, especially those with the desirable qualities produced by the growth of nonagricultural employment,[41] has rendered the birth of girls much less economically advantageous than used to be the case in south India. Stronger emotional links between husbands and wives, partly a product of shrinking age gaps, and the increasing threat that they will withdraw from stem or stem-joint families, render sons, too, less economically advantageous to patriarchs. Thus, the marriage squeeze will certainly contribute to sustaining fertility decline. The later marriage of daughters makes it more difficult to keep the joint family together with the sons unmarried, until all the girls are safely placed in marriage (see chap. 5). Ultimately, the family planning program, by placing an upper limit on women's age at reproduction of perhaps less than 30 years, will do something to solve this problem. In the meantime, it will become increasingly necessary to marry sons before all their sisters are married.

Thus, the postponement of women's marriage is not a mechanism at the individual family, or social level, either consciously or unconsciously, for controlling fertility. Rather, the postponement of marriage and the control of fertility are products of the same complex of changes. Nevertheless, the fertility transition will ultimately be one of the forces reducing the pressure toward rising women's ages at marriage and rising dowries. As yet, the increase in women's age at marriage has done little in rural areas to reduce fertility levels. However, marriages have now been delayed to the point where further delays will almost certainly result in reducing fertility and in providing daughters with greater veto powers over their marriage arrangements (thus, perhaps, delaying marriage even further). Furthermore, wives are now becoming sufficiently old to play a more important role in making decisions about fertility control, a significant point, as there is an element of the position of women as well as the cost of children in some of these decisions. Of even greater demographic and social

41. John C. Caldwell, "A Theory of Fertility Decline: From High Plateau to Destabilization," *Population and Development Review* 4, no. 4 (1978):570.

significance is the fact that the squeeze has proceeded to the point in the study area, and doubtless elsewhere, where some of the single women may not marry at all. One-sixth of the women aged 20–24, and 3 percent of those aged 25–29, are still not married. Parents have talked for years of the fear that their daughters might not marry, but now it is likely that families and societies will have to accommodate themselves to a spinster class, as, almost certainly prior to the transition period of the present century, they accommodated themselves to bachelors.[42]

The rise in women's age at marriage is almost certainly self-sustaining in that as the society becomes more accustomed to unmarried girls beyond the age of menarche, there will be less concern about the situation. One result will be a greater likelihood of girls staying on at school, which will itself be a further force for raising the age of marriage. The reduced age gap between spouses is already producing, at least in the context of rural India, a somewhat more companionate marriage, and that change too will not be easily reversible.

42. The 1911 Census showed 5 percent of males over 40 years in the district as never married.

Chapter Five

The Determinants of Family Structure

With regard to a range of agrarian societies, there has been substantial debate on two related points: whether the large joint or extended family is giving way to the conjugal or nuclear family, and whether this is an inevitable result of economic modernization and indeed an important index of it.

Nowhere has the debate been greater or longer than in India, and nowhere are there more data on family types. The decennial census has played a major role in this debate, which was first really joined by E. A. Gait when writing his report on the taking of the 1911 census. He held that the census showed the joint family to be disintegrating, as evidenced by the substantial proportion of nuclear families and by an average household size not very different from that found in England.[1] Nevertheless, he felt that family transition was occurring at only a slow rate. Implicitly, both views continued to be held in all census reports up to and including that of 1951.

The correlation between development or modernization and family type had been argued globally in terms of fertility transition by Kingsley Davis[2] and from a more cyclic point of view by Nimkoff and

1. E. A. Gait, *Census of India, 1911* (Calcutta: Superintendent of Government Printing, 1913), 239.
2. K. Davis, "Institutional Patterns Favoring High Fertility in Underdeveloped Areas," *Eugenics Quarterly* 2 (1955):33–39.

Middleton,[3] who identified suitably small and independent families existing in hunting and industrial societies in contrast to the large family of peasant agriculture. This concept of the right family fit to the mode of production was carried further by William Goode although he did concede that the evidence of change in India was not compelling.[4] However, anthropological studies carried out in India in the 1950s and early 1960s did tend to maintain that, insofar as there was economic change, family structures were under compelling pressure to alter. Kathleen Gough reported of a village in Tamil Nadu that joint families were breaking up as mercantilism replaced feudal land practices.[5] In Karnataka itself, Scarlett Epstein asked how one could have joint families without joint estates, and averred that cash cropping tends to break up estates because families are much more likely to dispute the allocation of the expenditure of money than of the distribution of grain and other kind.[6] Just to the north of Dravidian India, in Orissa, F. G. Bailey argued that the large rural family could not withstand the creation of the outside job market with the younger married males of the family frequently refusing to put all their external earnings into a common family budget.[7]

The attack on the economic determinism of the Manchester school of anthropology came in 1958—at first mainly with African evidence—from Cambridge with the publication of Jack Goody's *The Developmental Cycle in Domestic Groups*,[8] especially from Meyer Fortes's introduction. Here it was argued that even if a whole society strives toward its ideal of joint families, there will inevitably be a very considerable proportion of simpler families at transitional stages in a demographic cycle because of deaths among the older generation, the departure from the joint family of surplus married brothers, and other factors. Hence, even a considerable proportion of nuclear families in a population is evidence neither of change nor of the favoring of that type of family. Support for this argument in terms of the Indian experi-

3. M. F. Nimkoff and R. Middleton, "Types of Family and Types of Economy," *American Journal of Sociology* 66, no. 3 (1960):215–25.

4. W. J. Goode, *World Revolution and Family Patterns* (Glencoe, Ill.: Free Press, 1963), 14, 238–47.

5. E. K. Gough, "Brahmin Kinship in a Tamil Village," *American Anthropologist* 58 (1956):832.

6. T. Scarlett Epstein, *Economic Development and Social Change in South India* (Manchester: Manchester University Press, 1962), 177–78.

7. F. G. Bailey, *Caste and the Economic Frontier* (Manchester: Manchester University Press, 1957), 92.

8. Jack Goody, *The Developmental Cycle in Domestic Groups*, Cambridge Papers in Social Anthropology no. 1 (Cambridge: Cambridge University Press, 1958).

ence was not long in coming, as can be seen in Harold Gould's work.[9] Indeed, the assumed relationship between a largely subsistence-oriented, unchanged agrarian society and the joint family has been attacked by A. M. Shah,[10] who argues that in Gujarat at least, the town has been more characterized by such families than has the village.

Curiously, both sides of the debate have taken the clinching proof to be the statistical distribution of family types in the whole society. The developmentalists have assumed that a significant proportion of nuclear families signified some demand for their existence and movement in that direction from a time when there was little demand. The adherents of the developmental cycle have been more inclined to point to demographic levels, to construct models incorporating them, and to relate these models to census or survey evidence.[11] The difficulty—often greater than admitted—is specifying the model, because of a range of difficult questions about social practice. Does partition of a joint family depend only on the death of the older generation, or can age also play a role? If death, then of one or both partners? If the joint family is the aim, is it nevertheless the aim for any number of married sons or only up to some maximum? How does migration, long an aspect of Indian society, affect the situation?

There is an alternative methodological approach, although there does not seem to be any evidence that it has been attempted. That approach is to investigate the genesis of existing families and to attempt to formulate a set of rules for family formation and family partition. Such work is well suited to the micro type of demographic investigation we have been undertaking in rural south India, and accordingly we made it one of our focuses. In fact, it was necessary to investigate family change in order to be able to explain other aspects of demographic change.

This chapter, then, reports on research with a central aim of describing the existing pattern of family types. It subsequently employs these data, together with case studies of how these families have come into existence and retrospective information on the family situation throughout this century, to attempt to deduce whether there is

9. H. A. Gould, "Time-Dimension and Structural Change in an Indian Kinship System," in *Structure and Change in Indian Society*, ed. M. Singer and B. S. Cohn (Chicago: Aldine Publishing Company, 1968), 413–21.

10. A. M. Shah, *The Household Dimension of the Family in India: A Field Study in a Gujarat Village and a Review of Other Studies* (Berkeley: University of California Press, 1974).

11. E.g., K. W. Wachter, E. A. Hammel, and P. Laslett, *Statistical Studies of Historical Social Structure* (New York: Academic Press, 1978).

evidence of change or stability in family structure. If there is little structural change, then are other significant but internal changes occurring within the family? It will be necessary to decide the conditions of family partition and whether these conditions are altering because of socioeconomic change.

Family Patterns

The study of nuclear and more complex types of family is beset by definitional problems, and variation in terms used by writers explains the looseness in the terminology so far employed. Hereafter, the term *nuclear family*[12] will mean a conjugal couple with their unmarried children. A *stem family* will describe two married couples in different generations—in our area almost invariably where the older couple are the parents of the younger husband. A *joint family* refers to married siblings living together—in our area almost always brothers; and a *joint-stem family* is the classical full pyramid where the older couple have with them more than one of their married children and usually grandchildren as well. Any of these types can be *extended* if other persons, usually relatives, live with them. Note should also be taken of *eroded families*, sometimes indistinguishable in censuses: for instance, if a widowed mother lives with a younger couple because both couples shared residence before the death of the widow's husband, this is an eroded stem family; but if the widow joined the younger couple for support only after the death of her husband, this could be regarded as an extended nuclear family. In this chapter any family structure more complex than a nuclear family will be called a *large family*, irrespective of relative numbers of members.

In India, family or household partition or division is not merely something defined for analytical purposes by the social scientist. It is one of the central facts of social life, observed and discussed by all. There is little in the way of an intermediate or blurred situation: when partition occurs, division, somewhat ceremoniously and usually without rancor, is effected in eating arrangements, the family budget, land (if any), and residential arrangements. The latter may mean the acquisition of one or more separate houses or the building of a partition in an existing house or just the imaginary drawing of a line in an existing

12. As employed in J. C. Caldwell, G. Immerwahr, and L. T. Ruzicka, *Family Structure and Fertility: Illustrative Analysis* (London: World Fertility Survey, 1982) an adaption from F. Le Play, *Les ouvriers européens* (Paris: L'Imprimerie Imperiale, 1855).

house or hut. Some agricultural tools may still be shared, and farming labor may be exchanged, although from now on some kind of notional accounting will begin to emerge. Relatives and others will help to accomplish a fair division, especially in terms of type of land. However, if any sisters still remain unmarried, there will probably be a clear acceptance of joint, continuing obligations to meet the marriage costs. The only blurring occurs when there is an informal division preceding the financial settlements of a formal division or when the division has been made to appear more formal than it really is in order to escape the land-reform legislation.

One point should be strongly made. Our more anthropological work, participant observation, and discussion have shown that most people believe that families are changing even when their structure is not. All our evidence confirms George Conklin's[13] findings in Dharwar (further north in Karnataka) that conjugal couples in stem and joint families are acquiring new roles and developing new relations and that these changes are closely related to education, urbanization, and the possibility of acquiring nonfarming jobs.

Many of our respondents believe that joint families are breaking up earlier than was the case in the past. Two matters are important. First, with declining mortality,[14] division would have to occur earlier —in the sense of more prematurely or longer before the patriarch's death or enfeeblement—merely to sustain the existing distribution of family types and not to prolong the period after marriage before a couple could control their own destinies. Second, the fact of education among the young or their increasing ability to secure work elsewhere poses a continued threat of partition, at least as seen by the patriarch; this has meant a reduction in the pyramidal control structure of the classical joint-stem or stem family, which in this qualitative sense is being transformed. That transformation may save it in a residential sense.

Three aspects of the region's society help to mold and to set limits on the possible family structures. Two are concerned with marriage and are dealt with more fully in chapter 4.

The first is marriage between relatives. In marriages of this type, Hindus (78 percent of the population) most commonly marry cross-

13. G. H. Conklin, "Emerging Conjugal Role Patterns in a Joint Family System: Correlates of Social Change in Dharwar, India," *Journal of Marriage and the Family* 35, no. 4 (1973):742–48.

14. On some effects of declining mortality, see T. G. Kessinger, *Vilyatpur 1848–1968: Social and Economic Change in a North Indian Village* (Berkeley: University of California Press, 1974).

cousins, although the preferred marriage is of a man to his elder sister's daughter. In contrast, Muslims (21 percent) frequently marry parallel cousins.[15] Most of our respondents claim that such marriages make joint families easier to establish and less likely to disintegrate, because the young wife already knows the family she is entering and will be expected by joint relatives of herself and her husband to live in this family. Indeed, when she is her husband's niece, she will be joining a household that her mother lived in before marriage; and her mother-in-law, usually a largely unknown quantity and the cause of apprehension, will also be her grandmother. When a Hindu girl marries her father's sister's son, her mother-in-law will also be her aunt and will have lived in her own household before marriage. When she marries her mother's brother's son, she will be joining a household in which her mother lived before marriage and which she has subsequently visited with her mother; and her father-in-law will be her uncle, and her mother-in-law will be her aunt by marriage. When a Muslim girl marries her father's brother's son, she will not even change residence if it is a joint family.

However, marriage between relatives is declining because (a) greater socioeconomic and educational heterogeneity in the community means a wider search to obtain a suitably matched couple, and (b) the rise of a dowry system, with concessional or negligible dowries from the parents of a related bride, means that a boy's parents are increasingly likely to seek a bride among nonrelatives. Peasant castes and Muslims are most likely to arrange marriages between relatives; Brahmins, Harijans, and the service castes are least likely to do so. With the exception of the Brahmins, for whom there are religious considerations, these data support the view that among Hindus a major pressure toward marriage between relatives is the desire to keep wealth within the family.

The second aspect is a slow but persistent increase in the average age of brides, which has two effects: (a) a new type of family is emerging, with unmarried postpubescent girls living at home; (b) if boys' ages at marriage have also risen (i.e., if the age gap between spouses has not declined as fast as the age of brides has risen), the daughters-in-law will tend to be with the families for a shorter time before the old couples are parted by death (if declining mortality does not fully compensate for this effect).[16]

15. A cross-cousin marriage is that between the children of a brother and sister; a parallel-cousin marriage is that between the children of two brothers.
16. Statistics on the increasing age of female marriage in India in this century imply a greater change in the timing of entrance to the husband's household than has

The third aspect is a predilection in the community for stem rather than joint-stem families, which has always been the case even among the oldest persons.

Table 5.1 presents a condensation of the original full census tabulation of 70 family types (the original full theoretical classification listed 433 categories, but 363 had no examples in the cells for such reasons as anticipating linkages by female instead of male relatives). It is divided by village size because of meaningful differences between the largest village—with considerable service functions and a relatively high level of education—and the smaller, more purely agricultural villages.

The census of the research area (reported in table 5.1, somewhat corrected from the subsequent participant observation) demonstrates the essential patterns. In the whole research area, 59 percent of households are nuclear. However, the social impact of nuclear families on the community is less than this figure might imply. First, only half the population live in such families, the explanation being their smaller average size. Second, intact nuclear households make up only 48 percent of all households, the discrepancy between this and the earlier figure largely being explained by the death of one parent. It might be noted that families are largely formed by marriage and reproduction. Extension by the addition of outsiders, whether relatives or nonkin, occurs in only one of nineteen households, and is common only in the larger village for reasons that will be explored later.

The typical large family is the stem family, forming almost five-sixths of all stem, joint, and joint-stem families. The large joint-stem families make up only one-twentieth of all families and their proportion may never have been much larger.[17] Even the older people regard the joint-stem families either as rare examples of families that found that they could work together successfully or as transitional families that will soon divide, rather than as the archetypal family. Most joint families, composed of brothers and their families, were found to be representatives of a transitional stage in which the father had not died long before and the partition would soon take place. Some joint-stem families were also transitional, having recently been formed from a

---

actually been the case, because child brides usually stayed with their own families until puberty.

17. P. H. Reddy, "Family Structure and Fertility," *Social Change* 8, no. 1 (1978), 24–32. A study of 5,200 households throughout Karnataka state, conducted in 1975 by the Bangalore Population Centre, recorded the percentage of different types of household as follows: nuclear 57.3, stem 30.8, joint 4.7, and joint-stem 3.4.

stem family by the marriage of another son, and now awaiting a decision as to which younger couple would seek residence elsewhere; or alternatively, they were waiting for a still single sister to marry.

Unexpectedly, polygamy, although rare, was found to be more common among Hindus than Muslims. Older people believed that polygamy had been more common in the past, especially among the Muslims. Four-fifths of those in single-person households are women, mostly elderly widows without surviving sons, although there is also a significant proportion of separated wives.

Clearly, there are several significant points with regard to structure and change. In terms of structure, the existence of stem families, which include only one married son with his family, necessitates a considerable proportion of nuclear families. In terms of change, there is some evidence of slow secular change toward nuclear families, provided by the higher proportion of nuclear families and lower proportion of stem families in the large village.

However, there is one change of considerable portent. One-quarter of the nuclear families now contain unmarried postpubescent girls. Female adolescence is beginning to be a significant aspect of family life in a way that could not be provided by young daughters-in-law. In the large village there are now, for the first time, young unmarried adult women in some households. The explanation is later marriage, and statistically the difference in this regard between the large and the smaller villages is almost wholly explained by higher educational levels (see chap. 4). Nevertheless, this change must alter the nature of the household, the position of the mother in the household, and the situation into which new daughters-in-law come. Given the fondness and respect that often develop between an Indian father and his unmarried adolescent daughter, especially if she is more educated than her mother, this may well do something to reduce the authoritarian and patriarchal nature of the family.

Some Evidence Bearing on Change

The following analysis is based on the investigation during the years 1970–71 of half (actually 46 percent, because of the dropping of one of the small villages) of all households and the investigation of the histories of a sample of households in much greater depth. The sample was a systematic one of every second household and was carried out this way so as to secure a representation of even the smallest caste groups in a society where each caste is residentially segregated.

However, we should first note that from the original census, and

Table 5.1. Household Structure, Rural Karnataka, 1981

	Percentage Distribution of Households					
	Large Village[a]		Eight Smaller Villages[a]		All Villages[a]	
Type of household	Not extended	Extended	Not extended	Extended	Not extended	Extended
A. Full classification						
Intact nuclear:						
Only unmarried daughters under 15 years	39	2	33	1	36	2
At least one married daughter 15–19 years	9	(0.2)	10	(0.0)	10	(0.1)
At least one unmarried daughter 20+ years	3	(0.2)	1	(0.0)	2	(0.1)
At least one separated/divorced daughter returned home	(0.2)	(0.0)	(0.3)	(0.0)	(0.3)	(0.0)
Residual nuclear[b]	10	1	9	(0.3)	9	1
Intact stem:[c]	9	1	11	1	10	1
Residual stem:[d]						
Widow in older generation	10	1	14	1	12	1
Widower in older generation	1	(0.2)	4	(0.0)	2	(0.1)
Other	1	(0.0)	1	(0.0)	1	(0.0)
Intact joint:[e]	1	(0.2)	1	(0.0)	1	(0.1)
Residual joint[f]	(0.0)	(0.0)	(0.3)	(0.0)	(0.1)	(0.0)
Intact joint-stem	2	(0.2)	4	(0.0)	3	(0.1)
Residual joint-stem	2	(0.5)	2	(0.3)	2	(0.4)
Polygamous:						
One married man	1	(0.0)	1	(0.0)	1	(0.0)
More than one married man[g]	1	(0.0)	1	(0.3)	1	(0.0)

Single person	2	—	3	—	3	—
Nonfamily[h]	1	—	(0.3)	—	1	—
Complex[i]	1	7	1	4	1	5
Totals	93		96		95	
B. Summary						
Nuclear	61	3	53	1	57	2
Stem	21	2	30	2	25	2
Joint	1	—	1	—	1	—
Joint-stem	4	1	6	—	5	1
Polygamous	2	—	2	—	2	—
Other	4	—	4	—	5	5
Totals	93	7	96	4	95	5
N	413		373		786	

[a] The large village consisted of 413 households with 2,557 residents; the eight smaller villages ranged in size from 13 to 100 households (totalling 373), with from 62 to 543 residents (totalling 2,216).

[b] Widows or widowers or separated/divorced parents with one or more children; couples without children in the house.

[c] Two or three generations in which the oldest couple are the parents of one or the other spouse (husband in all but one case) in the single couple of the next generation. There also may be a couple in the third generation (no case among intact stem families, but one case among residual ones).

[d] One of the couples broken, almost always by death. "Other" means widowhood in the younger generation.

[e] Two or more siblings with spouses (in all cases the siblings were brothers).

[f] At least one couple broken (in all cases by death).

[g] Joint families with one polygamous marriage and one case of a stem family with one polygamous marriage.

[h] Not a family but everyone related (e.g., a woman and her niece).

[i] Even more complex, and not being merely an extended form.

subsequent adjustments, there is little evidence that the present situation, in which half the population lives in nuclear families, does not provide the protection and labor of a large family for older couples. Table 5.2 presents the information on all older persons who do not live in a real family situation from the village viewpoint.

Thus, about 6 percent of all households and 12 percent of all older individuals are in an unusual family situation. Nevertheless, the proportion who are in a distressing situation or who regard themselves as being in an unusual one are fewer than those who appear in table 5.2. The major reason is that some of the couples and two-thirds of the widowers are living close to relatives and are content to live in the accommodation they have always occupied. This was ascertained both by interviewing and by observing the continuity of contacts. Because caste members are residentially found together (except in the case of two new government-sponsored *janata* housing settlements), it is unusual for anyone to live further from relatives in the same center than one hundred yards in the smaller villages and two hundred yards in the large village. The real problem is provided by the 8 percent of older persons who either never had any children or no longer have any surviving children.[18] Furthermore, it should be noted that this section of the population had borne their children prior to the beginning of fertility decline, and hence had not been caught by a decision to restrict their families' size.

The important point is that none of these situations is new. Indeed, in higher mortality conditions the proportions of older per-

Table 5.2. Older Persons Outside Family Situation

Grouping	Situation	Percentage of all households	Percentage of all persons over 50
Couples:	All children have died or have left home	0.6	1.8
	Did not have children	2.3	6.3
Subtotals		2.9	8.1
Single persons:	Widow	1.5	2.1
	Divorced or separated female	0.4	0.5
	Never-married female	0.1	0.2
	Widower	0.4	0.5
	Divorced or separated male	0.4	0.5
Subtotals		2.8	3.8
Totals		5.7	11.9
N		786	570

18. This proportion is not directly ascertainable from table 5.2 because the first section of the table amalgamates them with couples whose children have emigrated and the second section does not identify them separately.

sons in these residential conditions may well have been greater. Local people do not explain these problems in terms of transition from joint-stem to stem or from stem to nuclear families. Indeed, they point out that stem families, broken by the death or migration of the younger couple, are sometimes re-formed by the movement of another married son to join the older couple, or, more commonly, by the older couple moving. When there is land, much depends on where that land is situated. Not even an average household size of only six persons demonstrates change, for this is the situation that the Indian census has been recording for a century.

Neither single-person nor lone-couple households were determined as much by caste as we had anticipated. Harijans and service castes were twice as likely to produce single-person households but contributed only one-third of such households, whereas lone couples were often better educated and richer, so that they were commonest among Brahmins and Jains.

The Partition

The formation of households of different types usually depends on the partitioning of an existing household in terms of property, budget, feeding arrangements, and, to a considerable extent, decision making. It is an event of supreme importance, and its details are remembered. Those details are recorded in tables 5.3 and 5.4 for the households within the 46 percent sample that had been formed by division.

When interpreting table 5.3 it should be remembered that the great majority of the partitions that took place did not leave either the old couple or the survivor on their own, but most commonly split a nuclear family off, leaving them in a stem family. There is also evidence of how transitional joint families are formed. Some of the sons who reported receiving a larger share are in effect farming their own share, and that of the old parents or a surviving parent, until further mortality makes another adjustment necessary.

The comparison of the situation of the smaller, and more traditional, villages with that of the large village does support the oral evidence of a persistent move toward an earlier partition, often long before the patriarch's death. It also shows that his death is rarely marred by a rush to partition. In spire of the Hindu Succession Act of 1956 legislating for the equal division of property among children,[19]

19. According to the Hindu Succession Act (Act 30 of 1956), sons and daughters are entitled to an equal share in parents' property. See G. D. Sontheimer, *The Joint Hindu Family: Its Evolution as a Legal Institution* (New Delhi: Munshiram Mano-harlal Publications, 1977), 218ff.

Table 5.3. The Mechanics of Household Partition

	Percentage distribution of households		
	Large village	8 smaller villages	All villages
A. The timing of division			
When father was still alive	54	36	41
When father was dead:			
At death	7	3	4
Later, but mother still alive	12	21	19
At mother's death	22	5	9
Later still, after existence of a joint family for some period	5	35	27
B. How land was divided			
Equally between brother and sisters	10	7	7
Equally between brothers	64	59	61
Equally between brothers still farming	6	21	18
Unequally between brothers	10	4	5
All to single son to keep farm intact	10	9	9
C. Who acquired the house			
Stem or joint family	43	44	43
Son with whom parents were living	4	4	3
Widow in her own right	0	1	1
Daughter with whom parents were living	0	1	1
Only son	11	16	15
Older son or sons	15	11	12
Younger son or sons	15	11	12
Other sons	6	2	3
Compensating arrangements with other payments, or building or providing other house, or providing equal value of land	6	10	9
D. Who was believed to have benefited most[a]			
No one more than anyone else (or arrangement was just)	58	55	56
Widow	0	4	2
Children of first wife	26	8	16
Eldest son	11	8	9
Youngest son	5	8	5
Other sons	0	17	12

Note: Data are from 8 villages (one small village omitted) and cover every second household (i.e., 359 households or 46 percent of all households in the 9 villages). For subsections of the table, each was not applicable to all households, so *ns* vary.

[a]Excludes those in continuing stem or joint families.

the beneficiaries are still usually only the sons, as has been the case traditionally. The division is usually among all sons, but there is now some tendency toward reducing the inheritance of those working outside agriculture, especially if there already has been an investment in educating them or securing work for them. A similar argument, especially now that considerable dowries are paid, is often put forward to explain why daughters usually get no land (but the same informants cannot easily handle questions as to why daughters did not obtain equal shares a generation ago, before dowries became common in south India [see chap. 4]). The widow receives practically nothing in her own right, although legislation providing otherwise, the Hindu Women's Right to Property Act, came into force as long ago as 1937.[20] In reality her inheritance is the responsibility placed upon sons to care for her, in keeping with the ancient view that a woman's rights lay in the responsibility of the family to provide her with adequate maintenance and care. The main grievance arises from charges that the children of successive wives, when a man has married again after widowhood, are treated unequally.

The Establishment of the Stem Family

When we began to demonstrate that the usual form of the large family in the area was the stem family, we assumed that there was also a commonly accepted way of forming it—either the first married brother continued to live with the parents, or the marriage of each brother led to the splitting off of a married elder brother from the parents' house. Surprisingly, in our discussions we found only doubt and denial about firm patterns. The emphasis was on the characteristics of different sons and the opportunities available.

Accordingly, we carried out a survey so that we could base further discussions on the information obtained. This survey tended to confirm what we had been told. Sometimes a new marriage resulted in an older married sibling leaving at once or shortly before the marriage, and sometimes it was the newly married couple who ultimately went to a new residence.[21] The latter is frowned upon because there may be

20. The Hindu Women's Right to Property Act (Act 10 of 1937) provided that marriage made a woman a co-parcener to joint family property and hence conferred the right of inheritance limited by the provision that the *stridhana* (wealth in the form of gold or jewelry passed from females of one generation to those of the next) already received should be taken into account. See Sontheimer, *The Joint Hindu Family*, 214ff.

21. One study of adjacent rural Tamil Nadu also reported that the decision about partition was forced by the marriage of the second son to marry, although

insufficient opportunity for the mother-in-law to train her daughter-in-law, but the younger couple eventually leaves in half of all cases, largely because the elder brother is already settled in with the parents who are often dependent upon him for both advice and physical assistance. Frequently, there is a considerable period of joint residence before either brother leaves, a period that is longer when it is the younger brother who is to go.

There is what appears at first to be an anomaly. At each marriage there seems to be a somewhat greater chance of the eldest brother staying, but ultimately a small majority of parents live with the youngest son. This situation arises from the fact that if the eldest son, for instance, has a 60 percent chance of staying with each successive marriage, his chance of remaining for two subsequent marriages is only 36 percent and only 22 percent for three. Furthermore, if he grows ever older and his parents continue to live, his wife might well suggest that he and she be replaced by a younger married couple whose children are not yet approaching marriageable age.

There are a few cases where old parents live apart, each with a different married child, and a handful where they rotate together between their children's households.

Finally, it is necessary to emphasize that not all stem families are formed by the partition of joint-stem families, even transient ones. There are two other ways of explaining some of the predominance of stem families among the large families. First, they may be formed from a nuclear family by the marriage of the first son, before the next marries. Second, they may be formed from a nuclear family by the arrival of old parents who have been living alone or with another son. The latter may have migrated or died, or there may have been a dispute. These two causes appear to explain 15 percent and 10 percent, respectively, of all stem families found at any one time in the research area.

The Triggering of Partition

Partitioning may usually be inevitable, but reasons can often be given for why it occurred at a specific time or why one couple and their children left instead of another. Table 5.4 provides an analysis of the partitions that were investigated.

---

partition might at first be informal. See J. P. Mencher, *Agriculture and Social Structure in Tamil Nadu: Past Origins, Present Transformations and Future Prospects* (Bombay: Allied Publishers, 1978), 217.

Table 5.4. Immediate Causes of Household Partition According to the Participants

	Percentage distribution of responses				Percentage distribution of responses
Type	Large village	Other villages	All villages	Subtype	All villages
Life cycle	32	56	48	Death	31
				Marriage	17
Problems	44	28	34	Female discord	20
				Male discord	12
				Too many people	2
Mobility	24	16	18	Migration for work	14
				Migration for land on wife's side	4

Note: As for table 5.3.

The separation of the causes of partition is clear neither in this table nor in the minds of those involved. The clearest causes are related to the life cycle, especially in the smaller villages where there remains a stronger concept of the effect of a certain cause. Yet, there are choices here, too, between whether with the death of the patriarch a joint-stem family will split or will remain a joint one.

At first sight the proportion attributed to marriage appears to be astonishingly low. The reason is that the marriage is merely taken to be a background variable. The timing of the partition, and the couple who will go, are determined by the existing problems. Female discord includes conflict between daughters-in-law and mothers-in-law and between daughters-in-law themselves. It cannot be completely separated from male discord because frequently the women are arguing for the fairer treatment of their husbands and children. Often it is necessary for the women to be regarded as the major actors in a dispute, because after partition the men usually have to maintain cooperation with regard to farming and many other matters. Frequently, they are the major disputants because the daughters-in-law are the essential foreigners in the household and because a very painful transition is under way from a situation in which women's main relationship is with their mothers-in-law, who train and direct them, to one in which the main relationship is with their husbands. Male disputes tend to be between brothers rather than between sons and fathers, although they may originate in suspicions of unequal paternal treatment and favors.

There are signs of change. There always has been some migration for access to land and other property and quite a tradition of going to the wife's home area if her parents have no surviving sons or none willing to live in the area. However, 21 percent of partitions in the large village and 11 percent even in the smaller villages are now caused by younger couples leaving to seek work elsewhere, often in Bangalore. All testimony reports that this proportion has been rising constantly. The higher proportion of problems reported in the large village is also a sign of change. This is not necessarily evidence of any rise in tension or bitterness but a greater willingness of young couples to argue such difficulties and to press for partition, as well as a greater willingness of older couples to accept this is a case for division. Certainly, the case studies of the causes of partition appeared to show that conditions that were tolerated without partition only a generation ago are much less likely to be tolerated now. Sometimes the conflict arises directly from the pressure for partition. It is a greater acceptance that peaceful agreement to partition might be a good thing, together with higher levels of emigration (partly arising in turn from higher levels of education), that explains the somewhat greater proportion of nuclear families in the large village.

The Experience of the Large Family

Even though half the population are found in nuclear families at any given time, nearly all have very considerable experience of living with parents or parents-in-law. The married men investigated had averaged 28 years of married life, of which 57 percent had been lived with parents (while their wives had lived with parents-in-law). Only one in eleven had not lived at all with parents, and only one in eight had lived for less than five years with them. Few marriages that start with parents result in separation from them during the first five years. Even the decision that one married brother must leave usually occurs after this time. Indeed, of those who live at any time with their parents, the average period together is 15 years. Nor are there significant differences in this regard between the large and the smaller villages. This period is, of course, an average of brothers who are the mainstay of the stem family and stay very long with their parents and those who leave five or six years after marriage. The proportions are also higher than the earlier discussion might have suggested because, in one-fifth of all families, two or more sons did not survive to adulthood and marriage.

Thus, large families still dominate early married life, and with fertility falling, the period when most conceptions take place and contraceptive decisions are usually first made. Even after partition most younger couples still live very close to the husband's parents, although it might be noted that the society assumes a lesser level of influence over the younger couple's decision making after partition.

The Extended Family

Beyond the normal structure of either the nuclear or the large family, only 8.1 percent of households have any other residents, 14 percent in the large village and 6 percent in the smaller ones. In this sense the household is very much a family castle. Indeed, few outsiders ever penetrate it beyond the attached cow shed which serves as a meeting place, and in Hindu households fewer still reach and thereby defile the kitchen. This is particularly the case when persons from other castes are concerned.

Rural households do not take in boarders, nor, with the passing of legislation against bonded labor, full-time, live-in adult laborers. In the small villages there are still some bonded children. In the whole study area, nonrelatives are found in only one house in sixty and constitute less than one-quarter of the outsiders found in the extended family.

Of the remainder, the majority are the unmarried siblings of the spouses, those of the husband being twice as frequently found as those of the wife, and, in the case of the husband, brothers predominate over sisters. In the smaller villages, as was probably the case in all villages until recently, these siblings are almost the only persons outside the pyramidal kinship system. Most feel they have as much right to be in the household as anyone else, and they are, in fact, the residue of an earlier and now extinct pyramid. They are the equivalent of the Victorian maiden aunt, and their situation often seems similar. In the large village but not in the smaller ones, a few houses now have taken in nephews and nieces.

The latter have arrived for one reason: to gain access to the educational facilities of the large village. Sometimes it is anticipated, or already agreed, that in the future they will marry one of the children of the household. When asked whether their presence was economically advantageous or disadvantageous, most families said it was disadvantageous. The unmarried siblings undertake the same duties as other adult members of the household and are not thought of as an economic burden, although there is some apprehension about the provision of dowries for the females' later marriages.

Discussion

What appears at first sight to be a somewhat motley array of families of different types, and evidence of some kind of transitional situation, begins to make sense once their functions are explored. It is no longer nearly as certain that persistent change is under way. Furthermore, it becomes clear that no analysis that merely employs a dichotomy between the nuclear and the large family will make sense.

Only 7 percent of all households are joint-stem or joint, and only 11 percent (13 percent if polygamous families are included) of the area's residents live in them at any one time. However, several times that proportion have lived in such families at some time during their lives, and they play a key role in the local developmental cycle. Our informants have no doubt about the indispensability of that role. They argue that the joint-stem family serves two essential purposes.

The first—and there is no question that this is where their priority lies—is to act as an engine for marrying off the daughters of the family. By definition, there is a single household budget, the product of all members' labor, which indisputably can be used by the patriarch to provide dowries and other marriage expenses. None of the patriarch's sons can question this use or the amount, let alone opt out from financial responsibility, while he is a member of the household. One reason for the existence of some joint families is that they are residual joint-stem families, in which the patriarch died before all his daughters were married and in which the brothers have decided to retain the undivided budget until their sisters are provided for.

The second reason is to provide a training institution for a new daughter-in-law. Admittedly, this does not necessitate a joint-stem family. In fact, the first daughter-in-law is usually to be found in a stem family, and it is only when the second son marries that a joint-stem family is formed. Even if there are no longer daughters to be married from the household, the joint-stem family may be allowed to persist for a considerable period, for two reasons: first, so that the marriage should not be seen as the cause of one family unit being ejected from the larger family; second, so that the senior daughter-in-law can help in the training of the junior daughter-in-law, especially if the mother-in-law is becoming older. In arranging marriages, families have had in the past as their central concern the choice of the right daughter-in-law rather than the right wife for a son, and this situation has by no means entirely passed.[22]

However, the joint-stem family has not been the typical kind of family for a number of reasons. One is that the pressure placed on sons to stay together until their sisters are married, and, even if they are becoming older, to forgo the joys of being a household head in their own right, means that some relaxation of the pressure is inevitable

22. See chap. 4 for a detailed discussion of the causes of marriage change in the research area.

after the marriage of the last daughter. Another is a lack of much enthusiasm for the four-generation family (only 1 percent of all families were of this type). There is a quite deep-seated feeling that by the time a man is arranging the marriage of his children, he should be the head of his own household; and even with the contemporary situation, in which daughters are unlikely to marry before puberty, this may well mean a marriage only 16 years after his own and the first arrangements several years earlier than that. A third reason is a real feeling that a family can be too large, that there can be too many people around and too much responsibility. An old couple can get on very well with one younger couple, but an aging father wants neither to be the cause of disputes between two resident married sons nor the arbiter of such disputes. His aging wife also may feel this way about two daughters-in-law, but this was less commonly expressed to us.

One other point should be noted: there is little feeling that family arrangements, once made, are immutable. Parents, living with one of two married sons, do not work out the chance of one dying or moving to the town, because if something like this happens, they can usually arrange to live with the other son. At the worst they can arrange to depend more heavily upon him; for, in a small village where everyone lives close to each other, distance poses few problems. A married daughter and her husband may also be persuaded by the parents to join them, particularly if they own land and may pass it on.

The classic demographer's question about family types is whether they affect fertility.[23] There are no significant fertility differentials by family type in the research area, for reasons which may apply in many other societies as well. Only 9 percent of wives had not started their married lives in a large family, and, given the limited population, statistical significance in fertility differentials is hard to achieve. Furthermore, the data suggest that it might not be achievable even with larger populations because, unless further subdivision were undertaken, those few who started married life on their own are made up of three distinct groups: the most educated who sometimes take jobs elsewhere; the least educated who have no land and no dowry obligations to sisters and hence have little to hold them together; and those who by chance (e.g., only sons with dead parents) find themselves in this situation. In addition, the family planning program is equally intrusive into families of all types and does much to nullify the different systems of advice and control—at least with regard to antinatal practices—which presumably used to exist in families of dif-

23. Caldwell, Immerwahr, and Ruzicka, *Family Structure and Fertility*.

ferent types (see chap. 10). Now that over one-third of village women
are having no more than three children and these during the first
decade of marriage, the chances are that at least two of these conceptions, and probably the first decisions about fertility control, will take
place while they are living with their parents-in-law (see chap. 10). In
these circumstances, it matters very little what type of family one
subsequently lives in when a researcher collecting cross-sectional survey evidence ascertains the type of family, the number of children, and
the nature of birth control practice.[24]

The classic family sociologist's question is about stability and
change in family type. The fundamental system in the region is one
whereby a couple, separated earlier from a large family, forms a stem
family by marrying one son and a joint-stem family by marrying a
second, finally dissolving the latter when all daughters are married. In
fact, this usually occurs before all the sons are married because daughters, who on average used to marry ten years younger than sons and
still marry seven years younger, are often already married. It is this
substantial difference between female and male age at marriage that
has made it relatively easy to keep the sons at home until their sisters
are married and that has rendered joint-stem families rare. The case
studies show that when joint-stem families split, the parents usually
stay with the younger-generation couple who feel the need for separation less urgently. Because of the productive efficiency of the larger
household, there may be some economic inducement for the younger
couple who remain with the parents; but, as we have seen, no inducement in terms of a greater share of the inheritance is offered—as
appears to have been the case in Ireland and elsewhere.

Because the stem families form the balance or reservoir beyond
the nuclear families that exist when the first child is married and the
joint families that follow until all daughters are married, the system
has proved remarkably resilient to change. With the fall in mortality
during much of this century and the increase in the number of surviving children, the duration of the joint-stem family may well have risen
(but could have been qualified by a relative numerical decline in the
segment of society—usually the largest Brahmin landowners—in
which such families persist until the patriarch's death). Now that
fertility decline is commencing to affect the number of persons of

24. A larger study in the Bangalore division found marital general fertility rates
of 269, 243, 208, and 198 in joint-stem, stem, nuclear, and joint families respectively,
but concluded that the differences arose largely from age structure and differential
access between urban and rural families to housing, employment, etc. See Reddy,
"Family Structure and Fertility."

marriageable age, the period spent in joint-stem families, and hence the proportion of all families that these families constitute, may begin to fall. Ultimately, the ratio of stem to nuclear families should rise as the typical family moves from having two or three sons to one or two.

Similarly, the balance between joint-stem and nuclear families has proven capable of coping well with social and economic change. There always has been a sufficiently large reservoir of nuclear families—necessitated by the aging parents' preference for living in stem rather than joint-stem families—to make it easily possible for some young couples to migrate for employment, or, if they wish, to live separately in the village.

Given that the old have usually been cared for in stem families, and that there are still few old people living without younger relatives, there is little evidence of fundamental change in family structure. One will be able to identify such change only when and if the considerable number of nuclear families are paralleled by a substantial proportion of old persons and couples living on their own. Admittedly, declining fertility, together with an increasing penchant of the young to migrate, could conceivably bring about this situation.

Finally, this chapter has said very little about social and economic differences in family structure. One major difference has been widely noted and was found in the present study. Among those with no land at all, 71 percent are found in nuclear families; with land up to one acre, 65 percent; with land from one to four acres, 58 percent; and with over four acres, 46 percent. With more resources and a need for more labor, there is more point in keeping a larger family together. Now this is even more the case because of legislation that threatens to give ten-anted or leased land to those who till it.[25] There is also some tendency for larger merchants to keep their families together in a similar way. Other apparent differentials, by education or occupation, turn out to be merely reflections of this relation between resources and family structure, while the caste evidence is surprising and clearly does not provide the underlying explanation for the relation between land and family structure. As can be seen from table 5.5, Harijans and peasant castes are less likely to live in nuclear families, although the somewhat lower proportion found among the latter is derived partly from the fact of residence in smaller villages. The significant contrast arises from social and religious attitudes which dichotomize the two landlord groups, so that no Jain family is joint-stem, whereas one-seventh of the

---

25. Karnataka Land Reforms Act, 1961 (Karnataka Act 10 of 1962), and the Karnataka Land Reforms Rules, 1974.

Table 5.5. Household Structure by Caste Group (Percentage distribution)

			Caste Groups			
Household structure	Jain	Brahmin	Service castes	Peasant castes	Harijans	Muslims
Joint-stem	0	14	4	4	5	6
Joint	0	0	0	1	3	1
Stem	32	22	21	33	28	27
Nuclear	64	64	63	55	54	64
Polygamous	0	0	2	2	3	1
Other[a]	4	0	10	5	7	1
All households	100	100	100	100	100	100

[a]Single person households; households comprising nonrelatives, etc.

Brahmin families (containing over one-third of all Brahmins) are of this type. There is a little evidence that the son with the more educated wife may opt to be the one to move when the joint-stem family splits, but there are almost as many exceptions to the rule as families that follow it.

Yet the situation is not as simple as mere land resources. The possession of a larger land holding is closely associated with the possession of a larger house, an almost inevitable result of being richer and living according to one's means and station in life, and often dictated by the need to have a structure large enough to include a cattle shed and storage room for grain. Where families stay together, they tend to explain the decision more in terms of the number of rooms in the house than in terms of their ability to exploit the land. The tendency for the landless, almost invariably possessing one-room houses, to establish nuclear residential families has been accentuated by the government provision of loans for the building of cheap additional houses in the form of *janata* or "people's" housing.[26]

For at least this part of India, the evidence is clear and supports the *developmental cycle* argument. There is no evidence of change in the pattern of family structure during the past several generations and no real evidence that the present situation has not persisted almost indefinitely. The society cares for its aged by means of a stem-family system which hitherto has meant a larger number of nuclear than stem families, although with much the same number of people living in each. Now that there is a real possibility that the society will be

26. For parallels in rural Tamil Nadu, see Mencher, *Agriculture and Social Structure*, 217–20.

characterized by low fertility (see chap. 10), the balance might well shift toward a greater number of stem families. Except among the Brahmin families, where the large joint-stem family is felt to have a religious justification, both joint-stem and joint families are transitional forms following such life-cycle developments as marriage or death. They are, nevertheless, of social importance, especially in the early training of daughters-in-law. There are not—and have not been in living memory—fixed rules for when partition should take place and which married son should leave. Perhaps the most surprising discovery was the similarity in behavior between different caste and socioeconomic groups, a similarity that has allowed us to present most of our findings for the whole society with little qualification.

Finally, to echo Conklin[27] once again, families are likely to change much faster in terms of internal relationships (and in the likelihood of *wealth flows* reversing)[28] than they are in external structure. One reason is the growing concept of dependency, clearly shown by analyses both of the reasons for allowing children to go to school and the reasons provided in marriage case studies for parents not being upset by the increasing delay of marriage until well after menarche (see chap. 10). Another reason follows from the delay of female marriage, namely, the increasing tendency for adolescent girls within village households to be daughters rather than daughters-in-law.

27. Conklin, "Emerging Conjugal Role Patterns."
28. J. C. Caldwell, *Theory of Fertility Decline* (London: Academic Press, 1982).

Chapter Six

The Social Component of Mortality Decline

It has previously been reported that mother's education exerts an influence on infant and child mortality that is independent both of the level of medical technology found in the society and of the family's access to it.[1] This finding suggests that social change may have played an important role in the mortality transition and that social factors may explain the failure of health services to be more effective. Clearly, an adequate investigation of this proposition means a study not only of mortality but of preexisting morbidity, an area in which there has been only a limited development of research methodology.

Our research area was well suited to a study of mortality decline. Modern (or allopathic) medicines arrived in the large village in 1929 when the Maharajah of Mysore ordered that a health center be provided. Since then, a medical practitioner has been stationed there almost continuously and in 1983 a second practitioner (female, as planned) and a small hospital were to be added. In addition, in 1977, the son of a local family of landowners set up in private practice,

1. I. O. Orubuloye and J. C. Caldwell, "The Impact of Public Health Services on Mortality: A Study of Mortality Differentials in a Rural Area in Nigeria," *Population Studies* 29, no. 2 (1975):259–72; J. C. Caldwell, "Education as a Factor in Mortality Decline: An Examination of Nigerian Data," *Population Studies* 33, no. 3 (1979): 395–413; J. C. Caldwell and P. F. McDonald, "Influence of Maternal Education on Infant and Child Mortality: Levels and Causes," *Health Policy and Education* 2 (1982):251–67.

although his clientele is still very small, being largely confined to relatives and the family's friends and employees. By 1981 a Muslim cloth merchant judged the demand for modern medicines, mostly patent medicines, to have reached the point where he was justified in stocking most of his premises with pharmaceuticals and employing a trained pharmacist for dispensing. The residents of the large village visit the health center during its official hours of opening on any day of the week, but the majority of people from the smaller villages who come for treatment do so only on Tuesdays when the market is held. The private practitioner now visits the two most populous of the smaller villages once a week, and the government multipurpose health workers (until recently known as auxiliary nurse-midwives or ANMs) visit each family in all but the smallest village every other month, although, admittedly, their main concern is family planning.

In spite of some uncertainty about exact levels and trends, the overall picture of mortality decline in both India and Karnataka is reasonably clear.[2] In the whole country the expectation of life at birth was certainly lower than 25 years at the beginning of the century, probably over 30 years by 1941, close to 35 years by 1951 and 40 years by 1961, and is probably now at least 50 years. Until the Second World War the gains in life expectation had been only about one-quarter of a year for every elapsed year; subsequently the increases have been twice as fast. In Karnataka, expectations of life at birth have tended, at least since 1941, to be between two and four years higher and may now be close to 55 years. However, in the rural study area, the level is still about 50 years, perhaps 52 years in the large village and 48 years in the eight smaller villages. The infant mortality rate in the study area in 1981 was around 115 per thousand live births[3] compared with perhaps 100 in the whole state.

These figures suggest a simple explanation. The smaller villages

2. For calculations from child survival levels in the Indian censuses since 1951 for the whole country and for Karnataka (Mysore) since 1941, cf. United Nations, *The Mysore Population Study*, Population Studies no. 34 (New York, 1961); the Karnataka Dual Record System, 1977 (P. H. Reddy, A. Shariff, M. Guruswamy, and A. V. Diwakar, *Dual Record System* [Bangalore: Population Centre, 1980]); and material from Asok Mitra, *India's Population: Aspects of Quality and Control* (New Delhi: Abhinav Publications for the Family Planning Foundation, 1978), 22–127.

3. A longitudinal study of infant mortality carried out two years earlier by research workers in the Bangalore Population Centre in the rural areas of five districts, including that of the study area, yielded an infant mortality rate of 102. See V. S. Badari, Y. S. Gopal, and S. C. Devaramani, "Infant Mortality in Rural Karnataka: Findings from a Longitudinal Study," *News Letter* 5 (Bangalore: Population Centre, 1979):1–11.

have less access to Western medicine than the large village, whereas the latter compares unfavorably with the average for the whole state, which contains urban as well as rural areas; mortality decline is proportional to the penetration of modern medicine. This explanation is far from sufficient. The death rates in the smaller villages, with only very limited access to modern medicine, have fallen by two-thirds since the beginning of the century (when the expectation of life at birth was two-fifths of its present level). Some of the difference can be explained by the success of campaigns against epidemic disease (bubonic plague, smallpox, and cholera) during the first two-thirds of the century, and the partial success against malaria,[4] but no estimate of their earlier incidence will explain the whole margin. Nor will these explanations suffice for the gain of perhaps ten years in expectation of life over the past 20 years at a time when the major epidemics had already been brought under control. In addition, it is also necessary to explain why modern health facilities in rural areas have had only limited, but increasing, success in attracting patients. Given the levels of sickness and size of the population, the queues at health centers are a fraction of the length that might be anticipated from the experience of countries with lower mortality. Furthermore, the young and the very old are underrepresented among the patients.

These are the questions to be answered. Increasingly we have found that the answers are not fundamentally connected with the condition of the medical arts and delivery systems, but with profound changes in the nature of the society. Hence, the preexisting society, and its very substantial survivals, are treated here at some length. Earlier[5] we have suggested that social institutions play a major role in determining the degree of success achieved by the application of medical technology, but the investigation is carried much further here. We have also previously suggested the existence of a clash between the beliefs relating to health of members of the more traditional sectors of society and those who have made greater contact with external influences through schooling, but we have not presented a detailed examination of the traditional beliefs to show why resistance to treatment by modern medicine can be so effective for such a long period.

4. By the mid-1960s malaria had apparently disappeared in the study area, as in most of the rest of India. Its incidence is now relatively high, with, however, little direct mortality. For most of the period, plague, smallpox, and cholera were the only notifiable diseases, and hence their trends are best known. There is little evidence to suggest that tuberculosis is declining.

5. Cf. references in footnote 1.

The Research Approach: Failures and Some Success

In many health surveys in developing countries, there are unwitting major errors because of the nature of the underlying assumptions. For instance, in South Asia it may be—and frequently is—assumed that all treatment is undertaken either by allopathic practitioners or their counterparts in the Ayurvedic or other great traditions of medicine.[6] In other studies, treatment that is not given by practitioners but employs remedies given in the home or by neighbors is disregarded.[7] Such surveys are not self-correcting because interviewees and interviewers alike assume that it is this essentially practitioner-oriented behavior that is being investigated. Much of the sickness that does occur is not reported because it is thought to be imbalance, error, or sin, for which the appropriate treatment is very different from the matters investigated in the survey. Respondents identify the survey and its interviewers with the modern world—with government, the health center, medical practitioners, and the ethos of bureaucrats and schools, limiting their responses to matters that are appropriate to such persons and institutions.

The survey approach provided usable information on deaths, if not always on their timing. Unlike African society, where the discussion of death or the dead may bring ill-fortune upon the living,[8] and where mortality is, therefore, inevitably understated, rural Indians are prepared to cooperate painstakingly in constructing a record of deaths, provided that the discussions occur at a propitious time, when the sun is high in the sky, and not at night.

In contrast, different definitions of illness meant that the survey approach failed miserably when we employed it to measure morbidity. Repeatedly, cooperative but clearly sick persons denied that there was any illness in the house. However, the information in the survey on attendance at the health center or treatment by the private practitioner tallied with the medical records. The information on how long it took them to seek treatment, the forms of treatment first attempted, and the extent to which they persisted with the prescribed treatment could be

6. E.g. A. Ramesh and B. Hyma, "Traditional Medicine in an Indian City," *World Health Forum* 2, no. 4 (1981):495–99.

7. Cf. P. Claquin, "Private Health Care Providers in Bangladesh," *Social Science and Medicine* 15B (1981):153–57.

8. J. C. Caldwell, *The Study of Fertility and Fertility Change in Tropical Africa*, Occasional Paper no. 7 (London: World Fertility Survey, 1974), 18.

shown both by observation and by the records and conclusions of the staff at the health center to be very much less trustworthy. By using a mixture of the survey and the case-study approach, we obtained useful information on the persons who first noted a child's illness and on the authorization of treatment.

For much of the rest of our investigation, there was no satisfactory alternative but to employ a micro approach, selecting and modifying anthropological techniques. Much of the information could never have been obtained but for the fact that we were well known in the area, and some of the more significant points would have been overlooked if we and our assistants[9] had not discussed continually where our leads were taking us. The statements from informants had to be treated with caution: for instance, Brahmins (inevitably the source of much advice) persistently understated to us (and doubtless to themselves) the role of sacrifices and the employment of non-Brahmin priests. A case-study approach was necessary to record the changing behavioral pattern relating to the purchase of food when home stocks were failing. Participant observation yielded information about the intrusive role of schools in insisting on the treatment of sick pupils, and about the use of *mantras* and *yantras*[10] and the role of specialized temples. Only organized periods and methods of observation yielded satisfactory information about the physical treatment of children, the likelihood of their being spared from work when sick, and the distribution of food within the family. The theory behind disease and its treatment—necessary knowledge, if many disorders and their treatments are to be fully noted—can be obtained only from long, probing, largely unstructured interviews in depth.

Once work of such a micro type is carried out within a society, some aspects of it can be investigated in larger populations by means of a survey. Nevertheless, when the investigation goes beyond mortality to include morbidity as well, the survey will always tend to be superficial. The method is insufficient to study the whole family or neighborhood because of the atomizing effect of sampling and even of individual questionnaires. It will yield something less than the truth, because of an insufficient density of questions on any particular matter. It will obtain an apparent spread of answers from people with the

9. Staff of the Population Centre and other persons with graduate degrees in the social sciences who had been trained for the project and who progressively accumulated experience within it.
10. Chants and charms described in greater detail below.

same experience and views, because short answers mean that some people begin reporting the same experience from one aspect and others from another. It will almost inevitably lose intellectual coherence, because the final analyst will not have played a first-hand role at every level of the investigation. It will contain many questions inherited from previous surveys, unless it is linked to microstudies for the generation of new hypotheses and hence new questions and new focuses of research. Nevertheless, it may well establish patterns and associations among variables that will provide some support for those hypotheses, and some evidence that detected behavioral patterns exist over a larger population.

The following report on morbidity and mortality is based upon work in the nine villages since 1979, using 100 percent censuses of households and certain surveys, 50 percent sampling for intensive surveys employing in-depth questions and a case-study approach, repeated in-depth knowledge and reporting on 25 percent of households (although we came to know many other households almost as well), plus residence in the area and prolonged acquaintance with it. The report attempts to substantiate its findings for a broader population by citing confirmatory or opposed evidence from the literature on social science and health on India.

Sickness, Its Cause and Treatment

The reporting of mortality presented fewer difficulties than had been anticipated, although there is a greater reluctance to reveal all deaths during an interview held at night than during one conducted in daylight. More serious is a reluctance to report or discuss certain types of sickness. This is particularly the case when the illness is of a kind which is not only caused by a deity, but where the sickness itself is believed to be a manifestation of the responsible goddess still being within the person. This is striking in the case of children with chickenpox, as it has been in the past with smallpox. It also happens when a disorder is regarded as a divine punishment, as in the case of leprosy or skin complaints, and hence not as a sickness at all. There is clearly underreporting of current morbidity, and almost certainly of past morbidity as well, even though less danger would be involved in such reporting. It is frequently denied that persons being studied are sick, when quite obviously they are very ill.

Much of the reporting in the literature of the treatment of illness implies that healing has been carried out by one of the great traditions in medicine, either by those schools indigenous to India (Ayurvedic, Unani, or Sidha) or by the opposed modern (or allopathic) medicine.[11]

These implications are often present in surveys,[12] and attention is thus concentrated almost exclusively not only on these methods of treatment, but in any particular region on the disorders in which they specialize. Research in the study area showed that this approach is almost inevitably very misleading. Ayurvedic medicine has changed a great deal during this century because, on nationalistic grounds, the independence movement espoused it and established training colleges which concentrated on medicines and aspects of treatment converging on modern medicine, thus broadening the gap between the great tradition and the local religious, magical, and herbal treatments that we have called the little tradition in healing. Both the medical officer in the study area and his counterpart in the neighboring district had received more training in Ayurvedic than in allopathic medicine, but, although praising the cultural benefits they had received from the former, they practiced only the latter because they saw themselves as part of a government or modern system and because the government health services provided them solely with drugs belonging to the allopathic system. As Ayurvedic medicine loses its magico-religious elements, those choosing between it and allopathic medicine are likely to opt for the latter in even larger numbers as being associated with the more powerful materialist tradition. We discovered that the indigenous great tradition was of little importance in the study area. There were no Unani practitioners, and the only Ayurvedic practitioner was in the largest village but had few patients; the nearest Ayurvedic pharmacy was 30 to 40 kilometers distant. Consequently, the situation reported in this chapter is largely the continuing contest between modern medicine and the little tradition.

What success either Western or Ayurvedic practitioners have is conditioned to a very considerable extent by the way they are seen as fitting into older systems. More than any other culture, India, even Hindu India alone, is characterized by *pluralism*, and this extends to healing. The rural areas contain not only government and private practitioners but a range of other persons who play healing roles: local

11. The terms *great tradition* and *little tradition,* as used first by anthropologists of the Chicago school, referred to the variants of the culture and its religion found on the one hand among the learned, in the towns and in the written records, and on the other among simple villagers. In this sense, Western (allopathic), Ayurvedic (Hindu), Unani (Moslem, deriving from Ionian or Galenic medicine) and Sidha (Dravidian) practitioners are in great traditions.

12. Ramesh and Hyma, "Traditional Medicine."

authorities on healing and herbs, both unpaid and paid; priests and saints; those who cast horoscopes or have other astrological knowledge; and midwives. Pluralism extends to trying many systems. A description of a rural area in north India will serve also for many of the people in our study area: "In the lives of most villagers, clinics serve as momentary stopping places on the sick man's pilgrimage from one indigenous practitioner to another."[13] Undoubtedly, more people in the study area have faith in Western medicine than in practitioners trained in Western medicine. Where modern medicine succeeds, it often does so because it assumes the same certainty felt by those other practitioners who interpret the divine intention and will. There is still much that is relevant in Carstairs's observation, made a quarter of a century ago and 2,000 kilometers further north, that patients do not give a history of their complaints because they assume that a healer must know,[14] and in his description of traditional practice: "When their healers say, 'He will recover,' they are not expressing a personal opinion but are speaking with the authority of the supernatural power which is the real agent of their cure."[15] Traditional healers always specify the time that recovery will take; the failure of modern practitioners to do this gives rise to great doubts about their powers. Villagers have traditionally known their healers, who have been in some way part of their personal and family networks, recommended and known by the decision makers within the family. Most are reluctant to consult strangers outside the area, be they modern or traditional healers, unless the cure is to be effected by a famous saint or at a temple well known for its cures of this complaint or for its general power. In the study area, those with disorders sometimes made long pilgrimages to two temples, one in Andhra Pradesh (Sri Venkateswara) and the other in Kerala (Ayyappan). Hindus may make shorter trips even to the tomb of a Muslim saint.

Simpler disorders have always been believed to have arisen either from an accident or from some kind of physiological imbalance caused by the wrong kind of diet or way of life. In these cases, there is no argument but that herbs or pharmaceuticals or medicines of any kind can help with the cure, given only that change in diet is probably always necessitated. There is a clear field here for modern medicines

13. M. Marriot, "Western Medicine in a Village of Northern India," in *Health, Culture and Community*, ed. B. J. Paul (New York: Russel Sage Foundation, 1955), 241.

14. G. M. Carstairs, "Medicine and Faith in Rural Rajasthan," in Paul, *Health, Culture and Community*, 130.

15. Ibid., 112.

(as well as Ayurvedic medicines). Where the Western practitioner often fails is by not suggesting changes in diet as well as other treatment. The community have readily accepted aspirin and Vick's Vapour Rub.

The imbalances can be those of diet, behavior, or sexual indulgence. Basic to the Indian concept of simple illnesses and their cures is the division of foods into "hot" and "cold," which has little to do with temperatures. Although some kind of balance is important, cold foods tend to be better for the person, but they also tend to be more expensive and to be eaten by the better-off. For instance, milk, curds, and most greens are cold, whereas meat, chilies, and other spices are hot. There is also a relation with caste: Brahmins say that they eat predominantly cold food in order to achieve calmness, whereas the hot foods of the lower castes partly account for their base passions and hot tempers.[16] Too much spice can lead to fever, and an excess of cold foods can give rise to influenza. Good health comes from the right kind of life, which involves daily bathing, regular elimination, and sexual moderation. Gandhi was very much in the central Indian tradition. Diarrhea can be caused by too much heat in the body which is likely to arise from eating a disproportionate amount of hot food, or from displacement of the navel which calls for massage as a treatment. Headaches are normally the product of immoderate behavior. Excessive sexual indulgence weakens a man and can lead to a range of diseases, including tuberculosis. The good health of some older men is explained by their adoption of sexual abstinence, and of others by the fact that they eat sufficient cold food to replenish their semen. The eating of meat is injurious because of the heat (*ushna*) it produces. Even disorders as serious as rheumatism can be put down (perhaps correctly) to bodily imbalance: in the study area one man who knew the forest well supplied roots for the treatment of this complaint. Sometimes, illness results from an imbalance of the stars, which can be explained by local astrologers who also offer solutions.

It is in the case of more serious diseases that the traditional culture is very much at odds with the explanations and cures of modern medicine. In south Indian villages the deities that impinge most directly on the lives of most people except the Brahmins are local goddesses, both those of the village and also more regional goddesses

16. There is in fact a concept of a division of diet into three types by *varna* division (Brahmins, Kshatriyas and Vaisyas, Shudras and Harijans); see R. Lannoy, *The Speaking Tree: A Study of Indian Culture and Society* (Oxford: Oxford University Press, 1971), 150–51.

concerned specifically with epidemic diseases.[17] With Aryanization, these female deities have come to be explained as being intermediaries between the villagers and the great gods,[18] and in the study area as forms of Parvati (the wife of Siva), although elsewhere they are reported as sometimes being the younger sisters of Hanumantha (the monkey god).[19] These goddesses can cause a range of troubles through their curse (*dosha*): in human beings, plague, smallpox, chickenpox, cholera, and typhoid fever; in the fields, plant disease and drought.[20] However, they are not essentially malevolent. They are always female and given to strong emotions and likely to cause adversity if misunderstood, or even if just present. Their essential nature and ancient origin is shown by how closely their names usually approximate to the word for mother. Thus, they are not only the source of disease but also its cure. Disease comes from the goddess being in the house and in the person. Nevertheless, it is always an aspect of the goddess, her devil (*devva*), as in *Kaliammana devva* or Kali's devil. Therefore, one can prevent infection by using various devices to deflect the goddess from the house (for instance, by putting pots of water on the roof, or by writing "*naleba*" or "come tomorrow" on the door and leaving it there indefinitely), and one can effect a cure by persuading her to leave the body. This may be done by religious ceremonies at a temple and by sacrifices, usually of goats. The temples of the great tradition take only vegetable offerings, in contrast to those of the little tradition for which expensive animals are often needed.[21] Most members of the village attend her annual festival or special ceremonies at the time of an epidemic. Vaccination against smallpox is permissible if it is thought of as a way of discouraging the goddess from the body, which is quite plausible given the disfiguring vaccination mark in a society which

17. See H. Whitehead, *The Village Gods of India* (Calcutta: Association Press, 1921), 17; B. Elliot Tapper, "Widows and Goddesses: Female Roles in Deity Symbolism in a South Indian Village," *Contributions to Indian Sociology*, New Series 13, no. 1 (1979):11.

18. Carstairs, "Medicine and Faith."

19. A. R. Beals, "Strategies of Resort to Curers in South India," in *Asian Medical Systems: A Comparative Study*, ed. C. Leslie (Berkeley: University of California Press, 1976), 187. One manifestation of Parvati, who in south India exhibits the characteristics of a regional goddess but who has been incorporated into the Hindu pantheon, is Kali.

20. On the suffering of crops and human beings from common divine sources cf. K. N. Venkataravappa, "A Study of Customs in Rural Mysore," *Sociological Bulletin* (Indian Sociological Society) 11, nos. 1–2 (1962):211–15.

21. Cf. A. R. Beals, *Gopalpur: A South Indian Village* (Stanford: Stanford University Press, 1962), 47–49.

regularly marks bodies to repel evil spirits. Where conflicts did develop, it was usually because there was already smallpox in the village and the vaccinators did not understand the fear that a displeased goddess already within the body might react by killing the person. For the same reasons, villagers have always banned certain foods and treatments of sickness while epidemic disease existed in the area. In this part of India, goddesses causing epidemic diseases can be led out of a village by means of a series of pots which are moved onward along the road by most of the populace each night[22] and which are accompanied by a wooden figure. When an epidemic like cholera, smallpox, or whooping cough breaks out in a village, it is not regarded as a sign of the sinfulness of an individual or a family, but of the whole community. Therefore everyone must be involved in finding a solution. It is believed that epidemics break out when many members of a community indulge in immoral behavior, or neglect to worship the gods at regular intervals. As a forceful reminder the gods spread epidemics, usually through the mediation of a local deity, in the community. Then the whole community reviews the behavior of its members, and undertakes certain rituals for appeasing the gods and eradicating the epidemics. It might be noted that most villagers do not realize that smallpox is now extinct, and Mariamma, the goddess of the disease, is still treated with great respect. One reason is the lack of distinction usually made between smallpox and chickenpox, and the other is that although goddesses may be quiescent for long periods, they do not die.

A specific type of local god is the snake god, who may jealously guard certain areas. Snake bites are fairly common, partly because of the phallic symbolism of both snakes and termite mounds (clearly associated with Siva) and the incautious approach of worshipers to the shrines constituted by snakes living in old termite mounds. Snake bite is invariably regarded as a matter beyond earthly resources, and not a single case has even been brought to the study area health center for treatment. There is a local herbalist who employs the bark of a bush which mongooses eat, if bitten by snakes, for curative purposes. Nevertheless, most sufferers regard this treatment as impious and ineffective and employ *mantras* or chants (see below), deciding on the verse by the coloring under the snake's head and the number of stripes. If this fails, they may visit the snake temple to seek, amid living snakes, the help of the god and his intermediary, the priest.

There is another range of disorders which are not the result of accidental or capricious invasion by a deity, but instead are a planned

22. Cf. Whitehead, "Village Gods of India."

form of divine punishment for sins and transgressions in this life or in previous lives. Examples of this group are leprosy, skin cancer, and tetanus. Those diseases specifically caused by the snake god include dermatitis, impetigo, and other skin complaints. Because these disorders are planned punishments rather than capricious happenings, there is much less likelihood that they will be brought to modern practitioners for treatment. There is also a sense of shame, which means that such ailments are little talked about and often hidden. Leprosy may be the penalty exacted for failing to adhere rigidly to the laws segregating the castes. The main function of the snake temple is to alleviate these diseases as well as blisters upon the skin and infertility of women.

As sickness becomes more protracted or severe, it is likely to change in classification from the capricious act of a deity to intended divine retribution. In terms of the total impact on mortality, this is most significantly the case with regard to a range of childhood disorders in the area of extended diarrhea and resultant dehydration and the whole complex of malnutrition which leads to distended abdomens. At first, diarrhea can be treated as an imbalance of hot and cold food or some similar error, and children can be brought to the health center or given home remedies. But, as the complaint worsens, it is recognized as being one of the group resulting from the retribution of the gods. In Karnataka, it is known as *balagraha*, literally meaning a divine visitation to a child. Necessarily, such complaints must be treated by reconciling the gods. Priests or other local practitioners can perform *mantras* by chanting religious verses, and they can make *yantras* by writing verses or the number of verses on paper, blowing the name of the person upon it, after which the paper is folded, wrapped in string, and tied around the neck. The *yantra* may also be metallic, in which case, before placing it around the neck, it may be placed in water which is subsequently drunk. Probably the greatest single failure of modern medicine is to convince the populace that *balagraha* can be treated by medical practitioners. However, it might be noted that some of the healers who employ *mantras* give Ayurvedic or herbal concoctions at the same time. In the study area the sap of certain trees is sometimes employed. It is, of course, true that the local health center can do little about malnutrition arising essentially from the poverty of the family.

In general, as complaints become more prolonged or the symptoms more serious, or the person appears to be suffering from wasting, the diagnosis is likely to shift from accident or whim to punishment for sin. This is true of a range of surprisingly common liver complaints.

Among children, malnutrition appears capable of damaging the liver, and the hardened liver and abdomen are described as one manifestation of *balagraha*; among poor adults, usually of lower castes, liver disorders can arise from the practice of going to bed hungry and stilling the pain with a drink of highly spirituous local arrack. It is possible that as much as one-tenth of all deaths are due to liver complaints.[23] Where no transgression is known to explain a disease, it is assumed to have happened in another life; it is reported from elsewhere that worms in wounds indicate incest in previous life, necessitating purification ceremonies for that sin.[24]

The supernatural world is not merely one of gods but also of demons, evil spirits, and ghosts. Children are particularly susceptible to spirit invasion, and this explains much of the apparent low level of infant care. Both a casualness about the conditions of birth and a lack of intensive care during infancy denote, in fact, a high degree of concern. Any obvious trouble about the child or any precautions against sickness would invite the jealousy of demons and might well result in the death of the child. Precautions include burning spots on the infant's abdomen with the heated ends of broken glass bangles, the placing of black spots (with the soot from the end of a burnt stick), on the forehead—especially in the case of a handsome young boy—and the wearing of various cords and pieces of copper around the neck or a knotted black thread around the neck or waist. Spirit possession is relatively common, particularly in the case of young daughters-in-law who may even scream at their mothers-in-law and the rest of the household. A beating by a stick tied with fresh green leaves (*peepul*) or a branch retaining leaves may drive the spirit out, but if this fails the girl will have to be taken to a temple for treatment by the priest. Magicians may also understand and control evil spirits; sometimes they come from relatively low castes who, as hunters, have had more contact with wild and magical places.

23. This estimate is from a government medical officer in the neighboring district who had specialized in liver disease. See A. Singh, S. S. Jolly, and Leela Kumar, "Indian Childhood Cirrhosis," *Lancet* 1 (1961):591, for the conclusion that childhood cirrhosis "apparently rises from genetic inheritance coupled with malnutrition," and L. E. Glynn and H. P. Himsworth, "Massive Acute Necrosis of the Liver: Its Significance and Experimental Production," *Journal of Pathology and Bacteriology* 56 (1944):297, on the clearer relationship between adult liver complaints and malnutrition.

24. S. Fuchs, "Magic Healing Techniques Among the Balahis in Central India," in *Magic, Faith and Healing: Studies in Primitive Psychiatry Today*, ed. A. Kiev (London: Collier-MacMillan, Free Press, 1964), 126–27.

Closely related are the problems caused by ghosts. These are unsatisfied souls who cannot reach the other world and must stay in the air, from which they keep returning to the land of the living because of a range of grievances such as having been murdered, having drowned or committed suicide, or not being accorded proper ceremonial respect after death. They usually trouble their relatives. However, persons carrying meat or traveling alone at night, usually if they look back, can be injured or killed by ghosts haunting the place where they died.

There is also a danger, especially to children, from the *evil eye* (*drushti*). This is an ancient concept found across much of Africa, the Middle East, and South Asia (and older Europe). In India, the possessor of the evil eye has come into its possession by accident, usually because of early severe pollution (such as eating of feces when a baby).[25] The evil eye can cause sickness or death, usually when its owner feels jealousy or greed. This is a major reason for doing little about a pregnancy and making few preparations for a birth of arrangements for postnatal care.

There are also other dangers deriving from hostile persons. Magic, especially if a magician is employed, can be used to harm or kill, and may be countered by a range of measures, including those devised by another magician. When adults are sick, especially if vomiting takes place, poisoning by enemies is suspected, and much effort is expended on recollecting what food was given by others or taken at another's house (especially if secret enemies are feared). By this time the poison is believed to have solidified in the stomach and the appropriate herbalist or magician is approached to secure its removal.[26]

Plurality and Change in Treatment

In spite of the traditional explanations and cures for disease, most households in the study area now use the health center. However, it is clear that they are more likely to do so for some complaints rather than others, and the maladies omitted include some of the most important causes of death. Furthermore, the visit to the health center is usually only one of the stratagems employed and it may come late, frequently

25. L. Minturn and J. T. Hitchcock, *The Rajputs of Khalapur, India* (New York: John Wiley and Sons, 1966), 76.
26. Parallels with many of the findings reported here can be found in R. S. Khare, "Folk Medicine in a North Indian Village," *Human Organization* 22, no. 1 (1963):36–40.

too late, in the series of steps taken. Partly because of this plurality of methods, not all the treatment recommended by the physician may be employed. More seriously, villages contain substantial numbers of people who clearly require medical attention, but who are not treated because neither they nor their relatives see their problem as medical, sometimes merely because they are old and there are signs indicating the decision that this life has run its course. This is true even when they are identified by the local multipurpose health worker and told to go for treatment.

The greater and more efficient use of Western medical facilities is essentially a process of secularizing Hindu society. It is not seen as a turning of the back on the gods or the ghosts, but everywhere there is a slow movement of attitudes to the treatment of specific complaints which transfer marginal cases from the area where Western medicine cannot help to where it may be of some value.

There is no point in transfer taking place too rapidly as the facilities are not available to meet the full potential demand. Karnataka still has only one Western medicine practitioner (including those with only one or two years' training in modern medicine plus Ayurvedic training) per 10,000 persons and one nurse per 13,000 persons.[27] The relative shortage of nurses is an India-wide phenomenon, arising from the reluctance of parents to have their daughters working away from home and working in an occupation whose members are believed to be immoral and who work in circumstances where ritual pollution is likely.[28] There is still a considerable dependence on Christian nurses from Kerala.

Treatment may cost more in practice than in theory, partly because practitioners recompense themselves for outlays in obtaining their positions, and partly because patients offer money believing that a practitioner who is paid and who gives services outside normal hours will try harder. More basic is the concept of an exchange of a gift (*dakshina*) for any kind of service and a deep-seated belief that healers,

27. *Statistical Abstract of Karnataka 1976–77* (Bangalore: Government of Karnataka, Bureau of Economics and Statistics, 1978), 191.

28. Nurses were forced until recently to resign from their profession on marriage, and hence it was widely held that many preferred to retain their income by remaining unmarried but having sexual relations with boy friends (see Y. B. Damle, "Auxiliary Nurse Midwives: A Study in Institutional Change," *Bulletin of the Deccan College Research Institute* 19, nos. 3/4 (1959):237–79). Some parents, probably more frequently in north than in south India, were also averse to their daughters being in close contact with human waste, after-birth, and corpses, all of which are ritually polluting. The situation is rapidly changing and there is an increasing demand for places in training centers for nurses.

teachers, and priests must be paid. Much of the cost arises from time taken off work, traveling expenses, and buying food while undergoing treatment. Ayurvedic medicine is usually cheaper and local healers much cheaper still. There is much that the health centers cannot do. They do not, in fact, carry antivenom to counter snake bites or vaccines against rabies, and there is little they can do about the basic causes of malnutrition (although iron and folic acid tablets for treating anemia are now frequently given).

In the move toward Western treatment, one important aspect has been the greater degree of Westernization and extent of schooling among the younger generation. The position is more complex than this because these same influences have led to a slow transfer of authority over the treatment of illnesses from the older generation to those of intermediate age. Grandparents have in the past felt very resentful if parents took much initiative at all in caring for the children or even in paying them much attention. Successive treatments are still decided upon by the most authoritative persons in the family network. However, they were once the very old, whereas now they are quite likely to be the most educated.

There is increasing discussion as to the extent to which that power is employed to provide differentials in treatments to members of the household. Twice as many boys as girls are brought to the health center in the study area, and there seems to be some evidence that oldest sons are likely predominate among the boys.[29] However, somewhat surprisingly, the center treats twice as many women as men. The latter may be evidence of another form of discrimination, because the excess of women among adult patients is entirely explained by much higher levels of anemia and other nutritional deficiency diseases among women (although menstruation and childbirth are undoubtedly aggravating factors). Although differential treatment, amounting to infanticide, has been reported for another part of Karnataka,[30] we found no evidence for this.

The Reduction of Contamination and Infection

Probably more than any other society, India has deep and ancient concepts of contamination and pollution. Such concepts have usually

29. Cf. Beals, "Strategies of Resort to Curers," 193, where he shows that 73 percent of money spent on medical treatment during critical illness of sons is on the eldest, who make up only 32 percent of all sons, 90 percent on the two eldest sons (62 percent of all sons), and 100 percent on the three eldest sons (80 percent of all sons).

30. Beals, "Gopalpur: A South Indian Village," 81.

operated to allow infection rather than reduce it because of concentration on a different order of priorities.

Pollution is caused by association with persons of lower castes, especially by allowing them contact with one's cooked food or drinking water. It has been pointed out that drinking in tea or coffee shops can be polluting, not because of the possibility of sharing inadequately washed cups but because of the association with people of lower castes, with the resultant reduction of production of semen in the body and hence of strength and health.[31] The greatest pollution of all is not contact with infectious disease or with germ-ridden filth but with menstrual blood, fetal remains, or the presence of miscarriage or death.

Proximity to any death endangers one from forces of the supernatural, and funerary ceremonies are mainly aimed at reducing pollution.[32] For everyday pollution, bathing is the most common means of restoring a reasonable degree of purity.

Bathing is undoubtedly cleansing. Yet the avoidance of pollution, such as ignoring feces and the corpses of animals until such time as the ritually impure may remove them, must have an adverse effect on community health. Some of the better-off people in the villages have latrines but they are often in an appalling condition, obviously a possible source of disease, because fear of pollution means that the family cannot do much about the matter and should not even let their thoughts dwell upon it. Similarly, the insistence that the Hindu kitchen must be protected from defilement by lower castes means that most village cooking is done in an interior, windowless room, filled with smoke even though there are usually some holes in the roof. This apparently does lead to a high level of respiratory complaints among women, in contrast to the situation found in most tropical societies where food can be cooked and eaten out of doors. The use of village streets as drains and the presence of animals in houses adds to the impression of unsanitariness.

Bacterial pollution has undoubtedly been reduced by the improvement of village water supplies. Where water is still drawn from ponds, there is little evidence that the infrequent testing and treatment of the water has been of much avail. There are now some treated and piped rural water supplies, and in the large village in the study area this facility was available. However, the major improvement has been the

31. Carstairs, "Medicine and Faith," 125.
32. In Gujarat, villagers use the same word for both pollution and mourning. D. F. Pocock, *Kanbi and Patidar: A Study of the Patidar Community of Gujarat* (Oxford: Clarendon Press, 1972), 119.

provision of tube wells drawing water from sufficient depths for it to be uncontaminated (although in one of the villages the tube well water has been shown to be impure and dangerous). In all the smaller villages there are now publicly provided tube wells, although the well may be out of action for considerable periods due to mechanical breakdown. Most tube wells can be used by all castes, in contrast to the situation with wells, because the tube well produces a free jet of water into each person's bucket, so preventing the bucket from ritually polluting the supply as happens in the case of wells or ponds. The government has attempted to ensure Harijan access to tube wells by placing them near or in Harijan settlements. In one village in our study area the non-Harijans still go to an inconvenient, distant, and clearly impure pond, rather than share the biologically purer water in a ritually less pure area from the only tube well adjacent to the Harijan settlement. Non-contaminated water supplies do not mean that water is necessarily still uninfected when it is drunk, especially in circumstances where the pollution of drinking water is judged by whose hands touch the outside of the vessel rather than whether the inside has been scalded or dis-infected. The evidence on the extent to which originally noncontam-inated water is likely to remain in that condition is far from reas-suring.[33] A major source of contamination is probably the insistence on washing everything when preparing meals. Clean plates or cups, and peeled vegetables or fruit, must be washed again, often with water that is clearly far from pure in that it is cold, without soap, and stirred by dirty hands. The lack of cleanliness in washing is partly unavoid-able, but also arises from the fact that the washing is at least partly ritual.

The Role of Education

Differences in infant and child mortality in the study area are surpris-ingly small. When other factors are controlled, there are only minor differences by economic status, father's occupation, and religion. One of the reasons why Harijan children are not at greater risk is that they are mostly found in the larger village, in which there are a major tank, some irrigated land, Brahmin landlords, and hence agricultural lab-orers. Thus, the Harijans live not only in the village with the health center but, because that center and the government colony for officials

---

33. See the Gandhigram Institute of Rural Health and Family Planning Bulletin, *Research Activities, 1964–76: Major Findings and Implications* (1977), 84–85; similar findings have also been reported from the Matlab research area in Bangladesh.

were deliberately built close to the Harijan colony, they and their illnesses have a high degree of visibility.

On the other hand, one powerful determinant of infant and child mortality is the education of the children's mother.[34] In the study area as a whole, where the mother has not been to school, infant mortality rates are close to 130. Where she has had primary schooling, the rate is around 80, and where she has had some secondary schooling it is 70.[35] The difference is clearly recognized by the community. The single most important reason given by both the educated and the uneducated for sending girls to school is that they will be able to look after the health of their families.

It is clear how they do this. First, by dint of their education, or superior education, they are much more likely to be ceded decision-making rights by their parents-in-law. Both the medical officer at the health center and the private practitioner in the large village report that they are much more likely to bring their children for treatment and do so earlier before attempting older methods of cure. Furthermore, both maintain that educated mothers are much more likely to persist with the recommended treatment and to return if the sickness persists, rather than try alternative cures. Educated mothers are also likely to share food more equally between the generations and between the sexes.

These changes do not arise primarily from the acceptance of school instructions, but rather from a feeling that the school has enrolled them in a different society, not necessarily wholly Western but certainly transitionally so. They are aware that the health center, the medical practitioner, immunization of children against disease, and taking early action about infant diarrhea all belong to the same system as their school, the officials, the government, and themselves.

Nutrition

It is very doubtful whether food supplies per head have increased during this century. In fact, most people in the study area believe that the opposite has occurred. However, the important point may be that fewer persons suffer from debilitating periods of extreme crises. At the

34. This has been reported as widespread elsewhere. See Caldwell, "Education as a Factor in Mortality Decline"; Caldwell and McDonald, "Influence of Maternal Education."

35. Similar differentials were obtained but not published in a Bangalore Population Centre project in rural Karnataka; for a description of the project, see Badari, Gopal, and Devaramani, "Infant Mortality."

level of the whole community this is explained by better communications and improved government famine-relief schemes.

However, there is evidence that an equally important change has taken place at the family level and arises not only from attitudinal changes, but also from the penetration of the countryside by commerce and the related monetization of transactions. The famine years and the period immediately before the harvest in any year have traditionally been regarded as times of inevitable want, when belts were tightened and the weak occasionally succumbed. It is ever more likely that family income will be used during these periods to buy food from the market, and this is now coming to be regarded as a normal procedure even by farming families who usually grow and store most of their major varieties of food.

Undoubtedly, other changes within the family are also tending to protect the weakest. Women still usually eat last, and daughters-in-law politely serve their mothers-in-law before themselves. The young wife traditionally could not play a role in allocating how much food her husband was to have because, for years after her marriage, it was the husband's mother's task to serve him. Differential feeding was as much a matter of poor communication as of deliberate intent, and men usually did not know what the younger women ate. There have been continuing changes in internal family relations, including a strengthening of the bond between the young husband and his wife. Such changes have almost certainly meant a better internal distribution of food within the family. The internal maldistribution of food within the family has undoubtedly been a major reason for the higher mortality of females in India.[36] However, the greater influence of the young wife may protect her children more than herself, as is indicated by a deteriorating sex differential in mortality.

We made use of responses to direct questions and the research team's observations to try to piece together an adequate picture. The work was not easy, because the direction of our probing was clear and met with some resistance. This is itself important information, for it demonstrates the existence of some belief in equitable distribution, at least among children. Nevertheless, in households where there were both boys and girls, one-third of the families believed that the boys obtained a disproportionate share of the food, while the research team put the proportion at one-half or higher. We investigated two mechan-

36. Cf. *The Gazetteer of India* (Nasik: Government of India Press, 1965), 330–32; Barbara D. Miller, *The Endangered Sex: Neglect of Female Children in Rural North India* (Ithaca: Cornell University Press, 1981).

isms, that which follows from eating separately and in succession, and that which arises from unequal shares, irrespective of eating arrangements.

In half of all households, the male household head and any other adult males eat first. In one-fortieth of these cases the wife of the household head also eats with them. In one-seventh of households everyone usually eats at the same time, although the women may stand in the background. In the remainder, eating occurs more capriciously and is determine by who is around when the meal is ready for eating. Eating at the same time is more common in smaller households, or in those where everyone goes to the field together, and is rare in large stem or joint households with more segregation of tasks. In most households boys tend to join any group eating, usually those taking food first. In the case of girls, this is true only for the very young, and at various ages from six to twelve years (peaking at nine years) they join the women. As food tends to run low during the hungrier time of the year, there is certainly a mechanism here whereby many boys tend to receive more food than their sisters.

However, the major mechanism of differential feeding appears to be boys obtaining more, even when both brothers and sisters are eating together. Boys are mostly given somewhat larger shares, usually justified on the grounds that boys need more or are more active. However, another mechanism is to show greater favor to aggression by boys than by girls, so that boys are much more likely to demand extra food than their sisters, and are much more likely to get it once the demand is made. In addition, boys do pick up wild foods or obtain something from other houses more commonly than do girls.

It is sometimes suggested that females have more access to food both before and after meals than males, and accordingly we made considerable efforts to investigate this matter. In only one-fifth of households was there any evidence that food was ever eaten during preparation. In 40 percent of these households it was said that this nibbling of food was done by whoever prepared it (many were nuclear families). It was done by mothers-in-law in 38 percent of cases, by daughters-in-law in 5 percent, and by both in 17 percent. We also investigated the fate of leftovers, which are found reasonably often in only one-sixth of households, and these the better-off where most members are reasonably fed. These remainders are eaten by the women and children in 40 percent of cases, often as bribes given to the children to do tasks, by the family at the next meal in 25 percent, and by the cattle in some cases.

Treatment at the Time of the Study

We found that middle-class or urban Indians, let alone foreigners, cannot be disassociated in the minds of villagers from the modern world, its medical practitioners, and its hospitals. It is possible to convince rural respondents that one is reasonably neutral with regard to evaluating the kind of activities that the family planning program should undertake. It is much harder to convince them of genuine empathy in the struggle to appease ghosts and to ward off demons. The survey document itself is so much part of the modern world. Rural respondents felt that what we, like many officials, really wanted to evaluate was the efficiency of modern services and they attempted to help us in this task. We attempted to counter this by probing for conditions and symptoms rather than joining the debate on whether these constituted illness.

Yet this is not the whole problem. A more basic difficulty is that we inevitably asked about sickness, and accordingly were told little about disorders arising from imbalance in the diet, environment, or the stars, and much less still about punishments for deliberately or inadvertently transgressing against the divine order. It is practically impossible to obtain an estimate of the full extent of *balagraha* in a survey, even though it is probably the single greatest killer. Many infants were reported as having died without being sick. When asked when they were last sick, some clearly very ill respondents peered into the past and reported that they had never been sick in their lives.[37]

Given this problem, it is still of very considerable interest to note that the median time reported by adults as having elapsed since the last case of sickness in the household was two months for women, four months for men, and six months for children. This accords well both with the statistics for attendance at the health center and the recognition of disorders as illnesses. There is general agreement that invasion by supernatural powers is much more likely for persons under ten years of age, and hence children's illnesses are more likely to be classified as such and therefore to not warrant attendance at the health center. Nevertheless, the survey did confirm that the great majority of families now believe that modern medicine can be effective for a

---

37. Government health workers, when undertaking surveys, frequently report an overstatement of ill health, sometimes as a way of complaining about the lack of facilities. We avoided this partly because we were not so identified and partly because we sought symptoms.

considerable range of disorders, and in these cases they are willing to use modern health facilities.

The survey also confirmed that the authorization of health treatment is one of those areas of decision making where there has been fairly rapid transition during the last 20 or 30 years in terms of the oldest generation ceding power to the younger married generation, with regard not only to the latter's own health but also that of their children. Thus, the effective decision to take children to the health center was made in almost two-thirds of all cases by parents—who were subsequently overridden by grandparents in only one-tenth of all households. Decision making in south India is rendered more complex by the fact that grandparents are commonly in charge of the children, while their parents are in the field. Men appear to make decisions about themselves in about three-quarters of all cases, being mostly strongly prodded in the rest of the families by either wives or mothers. On the other hand, women are twice as likely to be sent by their husbands as to make the major decision themselves. Nevertheless, women, especially those with schooling, appear to be attaining a greater role in decision making about treatment. This change is explained by most people in terms of strengthening of the conjugal emotional bond between younger couples.

Our examination of individual cases of sickness showed why the passing of more power for noting illness and suggesting treatment is so important. In the case of children's illness, parents first noticed it seven times more often than did grandparents, and mothers ten times more frequently than fathers. However, it should be noted that even now, mothers suggest the possibility of treatment no more often than do fathers, and make decisions about treatment considerably less than half as often as fathers. Wives identify sickness in their husbands and urge that something should be done about it twice as commonly as husbands do for their wives. When children were sick, our assessment was that mothers were really distressed far more than any other relative.

In over half of all cases, members of households claim that no other curative attempts preceded their first visit to the hospital and the medical practitioner, although clearly they often waited some time before the visit. The fact that sicknesses are often allowed to remain untreated for at least seven days is shown by the much higher attendance of people from outlying villages at the health center on the day of the weekly *shandy* (market). When we examined the history of individual cases, we came to the conclusion that mothers who were determined to get modern medical treatment for their children were assured of success in about one-third of all households. In another one-third they were not automatically assured of their husband's support but were likely to obtain the treatment if they could convince him. In the balance of households there were real traditional decision makers, and it was necessary to win the support, or await the decision, of someone who usually made health decisions (more commonly in the stem or joint families which form one-third of all households (see chap. 5). Power in these households was not the same in the area of health as in the case of economic decisions. With regard to treatment, the patriarch's wife more commonly made decisions than her husband, and there were sometimes even more knowledgeable and influential figures with regard to health, such as the patriarch's sister.

Traditional methods of cure are dominated by *yantras* worn around the neck and *mantras* (chanted prayers by priests or other wise men), and nearly half the community claim to employ one or the other or both (the anthropological approach suggests a much higher proportion). One-half as many claim to undertake visits to the temples to leave offerings (often rice, curds, coconut, betel nut, or flowers), pay for *pujas* (religious services), or make sacrifices of goats, chickens, or sheep. Often the visits occur after the illness if over, being the fulfillment of a vow made at the time. Sometimes rice, coconut, eggs, turmeric, or limes are not taken to the temple but sprinkled at the crossroads. Many households still obtain herbal medicines or more commonly make their own, but only a handful of families employ Ayurvedic medicines. Most Hindu families participate in some temple ceremonies during the year to protect their families and their villages from ill health. The temple of the village deity has a special significance here, although clearly not that of 60 years ago, when the goddess was seen as virtually the sole defender of the village from threatening disaster from all sides.[38]

Brown glass bangles play a major protective and curative role. (They are also important in temple ceremonies, especially those concerned with fertility, and are the symbol of currently married women.) They may be broken so that their ends can be heated in a flame to burn marks on the abdomen of a baby for protection against the evil eye and demons, or adults may have burn marks made on each side of the temple to cure persistent headaches (known as *sondu*). Sores which will not heal may first be cauterized; then a broken bangle is ground on

38. Whitehead, "Village Gods of India," 46.

the stone doorstep of the family house and the resultant glass powder is rubbed across the surface of the sore.

The great majority of households denied that there was any discrimination by generation or sex in feeding or in health treatment. One problem is that behavior which appears to the outsider to be discrimination is justified by household members as meeting specific needs or deserts. It was argued frequently that males needed extra food because they had to do harder work in the field. Similarly, certain foods, such as onions and spices, were omitted, on the grounds of danger, from females' diet during menstruation, pregnancy, or lactation.

Two-fifths of all households contained some pharmaceuticals which are frequently employed for home treatment. In two-thirds of cases there are only modern types, and in most of the rest of the households they are both modern and Ayurvedic products. The major source of Western pharmaceuticals was, until 1981, the dispensary attached to the health center. In that year a cloth merchant, reacting to what he described as a steeply increasing demand, converted his shop to one selling mostly modern pharmaceuticals, together with a few of the better-known Ayurvedic preparations, and brought in a trained pharmacist as dispenser. Almost half the pharmaceuticals examined in the households are described as being for headaches, and around one-quarter are for colds. Some households contain malarial suppressants, pain killers not meant primarily for headaches, and medicines for asthma and bronchitis. In order of frequency, the pharmaceuticals listed were a camphor preparation, Amrutanjan (sold as Vicks in the West and increasingly in India), Anacin, and Analgin.

Two constraints on the use of health centers were mentioned. One was the cost in money, and the other the cost in time. One of the reasons government health facilities have only limited time available for treatment is the proportion of time spent by some medical officers, and many of the multipurpose health workers, on family planning activities. A visit to an Ayurvedic doctor is usually cheaper, but Ayurvedic treatment can take months, with repeated visits; in the study area this involves a considerable journey. However, traditional healers are usually willing to have payment deferred, and they do not assume the formal attitude of modern practitioners which frightens the illiterate and poor.

Many of even the religious measures taken by Hindus have also been adopted by the Muslims in the society. Nevertheless, the evidence in the study area is that the use of modern medical facilities constitutes a considerably larger proportion of all health care among the Muslims than among the Hindus.

A Note on Death

The following statement, written a quarter of a century ago, is probably still reasonably accurate:

> Both Hindus and Muslims understand the physiological causes of death. It is generally attributed to natural causes, such as disease or old age, but in all cases where the circumstances or manner of death are unusual it is attributed to supernatural factors such as the wrath of gods and ancestor spirits, witchcraft and black magic.[39]

In the study area, the few Brahmins are the only ones who regularly cremate their dead. Among the rest of the population, in all but one village, burial is the common practice. However, where the circumstances of the death or the nature of the fatal disorder suggested possession or divine vengeance, the body is burned. It was suggested by some of the richer peasants that they would like to adopt the Brahmin cremation as a sign of their understanding of the best Hindu practices (i.e., Sanskritization) were it not for the identification of burning with the destruction of a body rendered impure or unnatural in some way. Deaths in childbirth are always the result of the presence of spirits, sometimes in the child, and the bodies of women who die in this way are always burned.

The easternmost village is one of a group of about seventy villages where many bodies are exposed on the rocks for birds to consume the flesh. This is strikingly similar to the practice of Parsees. However, such burial methods are apparently ancient in south India and are motivated by a philosophy of the continuing chain of life whereby flesh, rather than decaying, should help produce new flesh. In other areas, in nearby Andhra Pradesh for instance, the same philosophy leads to the bodies being placed in rivers so that the fish may be fed. This treatment of bodies in the study area village is a privilege and is reserved only for persons over 40 years of age, who have led a virtuous life and whose death was not of the type calling for cremation.

Of recent deaths, 8 percent have been cremated (half Brahmins and half because of the nature of the death), 8 percent have been exposed (all in the village employing exposure, making up half of the deaths there), and 84 percent have been buried.

Deaths caused real distress in about half of all cases. There was a great degree of acceptance in the other cases on the grounds that the deceased were either very old or very young, and hence death was not something unexpected.

39. S. C. Dube, *Indian Village* (London: Routledge and Kegan Paul, 1955), 124.

Of the recent deaths, three-quarters of those dying had been seen at some stage by a modern medical practitioner but in only one-third of cases were they patients at the time of death. The reason was that the family had decided to seek no more treatment. It is felt strongly that modern practitioners continue to treat and charge long after they are aware they can do nothing more, and, unlike traditional healers, they refuse to predict both the certainty of death and its timing.

A Perspective on Health Change

The persistent decline in mortality over the last 60 years is very far from being a simple case of a progressive increase in the supply of modern doctors and their medicines. The nearest example to that picture is the success of the great campaigns against epidemic disease. Yet there were problems about the acceptance of vaccination, and theological reasons why acceptance was easier at one time than another.

The progress of modern medicine is even more a question of demand rather than supply. For many diseases the growth of that demand has been made possible only by a reinterpretation of essentially religious concepts of illness and its cure.

The nature of Indian and Hindu society, with a greater degree of pluralism than probably any other society, has been a factor that has permitted much of the change. Yet what is happening is fundamentally a transition from one type of society to another, essentially to a Western type of society. Those who accept modern health services most readily are persons who believe that they have to a considerable extent joined this new and different society.

By far the most potent instrument of change is modern schooling. Mere attendance in institutions which pyramid as far as modern medical schools convince both the educated and their relatives that they have a commitment to a different kind of world, which includes modern medicine as an integral part. There are other conduits for contrasts with Western society or for heightening the belief in an identification with that society. Thirty years ago a practitioner in north India reported that modern medical services were accepted most readily by returnees to the village from the town or from army service.[40] This is true today in the study area if one adds to the army service work with the railways, the police, or a range of other government employment. Over fifty years ago, two missionary medical practitioners in rural north India found that the first villager who felt himself linked to

40. Carstairs, "Medicine and Faith," 133.

their type of cure was a Christian.[41] Undoubtedly, the high proportion of Christians in the society and the long contact with the West of the Malabar Coast do much to explain the marked degree of success of health services in Kerala.

The decline in mortality is, then, part of the political, social, and economic revolution of the last 40 years. At the official level, independent India has always identified with the new imported society and has given little more than lip service to the most fundamental of indigenous concepts of illness, its cause and cure. If mortality rates are to continue to decline in India, one of the central bastions of its religion and society will have to be successfully assaulted. The concept of pollution will have to be radically changed so that it approximates to circumstances where disease is most likely to be transmitted.[42] Indian society is so flexible that this may well be done without any real awareness of just how sacrilegious that transformation has been. Yet such a change is necessary because it is largely the present interpretation of pollution which makes India more polluted from a bacteriological point of view than most of Southeast and East Asia. Sales of soap are rising steeply, but the main reason is the replacement of the services of the *dhobi* (washerman) by the household washing of clothes. The practice of attaining high levels of "purity" by plastering floors, walls, and grain containers with mud enriched with cow dung has hardly begun to decline.

Changes in the family have already had profound health effects and these will probably accelerate. In a range of matters in the area of demographic decisions, the oldest generation has been slowly ceding power to their adult children, and health treatment and feeding practices are in this domain. At the same time, increased buying of food and an intensification of the concept of child dependency has meant that the weakest are less likely to succumb during periodic food crises. There is clearly also a move toward a child's mother being the main decision maker with regard to its safely and health, and this, too, will undoubtedly help to reduce infant and child mortality rates.

Declining mortality has been part of a profound social revolution, and even of a theological one in terms of moving ever more areas of behavior into the secular domain.[43] There are areas where major

41. W. and Charlotte Wiser, *Behind Mud Walls* (Berkeley: University of California Press, 1971), 3.

42. Cf. R. S. Khare, "Ritual Purity and Pollution in Relation to Domestic Sanitation," *The Eastern Anthropologist* 15, no. 2 (1962): 125–39, who points out that food is often abandoned if it is ritually polluted by a human hair or nail clipping falling into it but not if rat feces, which are not ritually impure, are found in it.

43. For a parallel process in England, see K. Thomas, *Religion and the Decline*

reductions in mortality can still be achieved relatively easily. Perhaps the most obvious is that related to antenatal and postnatal care and to infant malnutrition. Family size is beginning to decline, and there is clear evidence from the study area of lower child mortality levels in smaller families (see chap. 2). These arise not mainly from a greater concentration of parental attention originating merely in smaller numbers, but because the family planning program by its very nature has made a decisive attack on the nature of the traditional family, especially in the area of demographic decision making. It has also made both parents and the health service workers apprehensive about the possibility of deaths among the children of sterilized parents.

Modern medicine has also made slow but persistent gains when it has been able to demonstrate success. The fact that this has occurred more often in respect of adult disorders than the diarrheal or nutritional complaints of children has certainly played a role in confirming that the latter are more certainly the concern of the gods. This has been reinforced by the feeling that infants have only recently come from another world and accordingly still retain links which may draw them back again.

Our study of social attitudes to sickness and its care made two points clear. First, any new injection of modern medical technology or services will not have its full impact at once, but may take many years to achieve its full potential as the interpretation of sickness changes. This change is largely the product of a broad social transformation secularizing many aspects of social life and tending to remove medical explanations and cures from the area of theology. The latter process is probably accelerated by some of the successes of the new technology. Secondly, even if medical technology were to stagnate at its present level, mortality levels would almost certainly decline for many years to come.[44]

There is probably a limit to mortality decline unless nutritional levels can be raised. It may be possible to extend longevity to an expectation of life at birth of around 60 years, given sufficient social change, but doubts must remain about how much progress beyond this level can be achieved without very considerable rises in living standards, particularly in nutrition.

---

of Magic: Studies in Popular Beliefs in Sixteenth and Seventeenth Century England (London: Weidenfeld and Nicolson, 1971).

44. Ghana, over the last 20 years, probably provides an example of this. For evidence on the continuing decline in mortality, see S. K. Jain, "Mortality in Ghana: Evidence from the Cape Coast Project Data," *Population Studies* 36, no. 2 (1982): 271–89.

Chapter Seven

Educational Transition

Education is moving to center stage in both mortality and fertility transition theory. In a comprehensive examination of reported findings on the relation between fertility and education, Susan Cochrane concluded that although increasing educational levels may at first be associated with rising levels of fertility in a community, as the process continues fertility ultimately falls.[1] One of the authors has argued that historical data support the thesis that the onset of sustained fertility decline is associated with the attainment of mass education.[2] The authors have adduced evidence from rural south India that the cost of educating successive children over a short period of time is, in the presence of an active family planning program, the most significant element in controlling family size (see chaps. 2, 3, and 10). It is the purpose of this chapter to explore further, in the context of rural south India, both the reasons for growing school attendance and the related costs.

Education offers at best only a partial explanation of demographic transition. Education is clearly an "intermediate variable." A more satisfactory explanation can be provided only by taking a step backward, and explaining not only why nations provide schools but why parents, in circumstances where compulsory school attendance is not enforced, send more children to school and for longer periods. Our

---

1. Susan Hill Cochrane, *Fertility and Education: What Do We Really Know?* (Baltimore: The John Hopkins University Press, published for the World Bank, 1979).

2. John C. Caldwell, "Mass Education as a Determinant of the Timing of Fertility Decline," *Population and Development Review* 6, no. 2 (1980):225–55.

earlier research in rural south India produced a picture of change that embraces the provision of additional schools; the reduction of land size to the point where, in conjunction with declining mortality, there was an emerging surplus of child labor; and a move toward reducing risk from periodic famine by recourse to urban or other off-farm employment for some family members in circumstances where education was necessary for some types of employment and an asset for others. The circumstances in which families moved to give their children more education and the determinants of the duration of schooling have recently been a major focus of our research program.

There are fundamental questions to be answered, in spite of the fact that many educational and development theorists assume that education, as a good thing in itself, will tend to expand in the absence of extreme national and individual economic restraints. This assumption is presumably the reason for the extraordinarily limited treatment in the educational literature of the circumstances in which schooling spreads.

Yet this impression has not, in the past, been the one received by participant observers in Indian villages and elsewhere. Gerald Berreman wrote of rural north India in the late 1950s.

> School is thought of as a place for children with nothing better to do. In most families only children who are not needed elsewhere are allowed to go. Most families consider education for girls to be entirely useless and actually detrimental. . . . Often one or two boys of a large family are educated and others are not. The educated one is usually one who shows some liking or aptitude for school or, perhaps more often, who dislikes other work or is unable to perform it. . . . A small family, especially if it has much land, cannot afford to let boys go to school who might otherwise be helping to farm.[3]

M. N. Srinivas reported that the same sentiments were held by village leaders in south India. He recalled the attitude of a headman, a Vokkaliga, the dominant peasant caste in his area of research (and in ours, which is only a hundred miles distant):

> In the summer of 1952, a government bulldozer was busy levelling a knoll, five acres in extent, on the headman's estate—the flattening out of the knoll enabled it to become valuable rice-land. Electricity had come to the village, and powered two rice mills. The headman's enthusiasm for electric power and the bulldozer contrasted with his feeling that a new build-

---

3. Gerald D. Berreman, *Hindus of the Himalayas: Ethnography and Change*, 2d ed. (Berkeley: University of California Press, 1972), 331.

ing for a "complete" middle school was not important, to say the least. "A school will only teach the poor to be arrogant," he told me. Many other villagers, including the young men who were opposed to him, felt that he did not want a school because it would shut off the supply of cheap and obedient labour.[4]

Even in the city of Bhubaneshwar in Orissa during the late 1960s, Alan Sable found that laborers usually did not send their children to school, and that among the poor the dropout rate in the early years of schooling contrasted even more starkly with the pattern among the economically better-off than did the school entry rate.[5] Nevertheless, Srinivas's observations show that as early as 1952 there was also a demand for schooling, and education was seen as being antithetical to agricultural labor, at least in the latter's traditional form.

Such evidence is not confined to India. T. Marimuthu found that poor Indian families on Malaysian rubber estates derived little benefit from educating their children.[6] In Africa, Lwechungura Kamuzora has reported that schooling in Tanzania interferes with children's work, especially in the case of older children, and that it also raises their material demands upon their parents, and Enid Schildkrout found that when northern Nigerian girls attended school their mothers' and their families' productivity suffered.[7] There is a persistent idea that children may go to school without damaging family production if the children are very young or if the family is large. Haile Abeje reported of the poor in Dhaka city in Bangladesh that although there are monetary costs in sending children to school, attendance may be chosen if the school hours or the pattern of daily schoolgoing does not interfere with household production.[8] Judith Ennew found in Jamaica that domestic and agricultural work takes precedence and that children are withdrawn from school, partially, temporarily, or permanently, to

4. M. N. Srinivas, *The Remembered Village* (New Delhi: Oxford University Press, 1976), 63–64.

5. Alan Sable, *Education in Orissa* (New Delhi: S. Chand & Co. Ltd, 1977), 44.

6. T. Marimuthu, "Schooling as a Dead End: Education for the Poor Especially the Estate Children," in *Ethnicity, Class and Development* [Kauni Kelas Dan Pembangunan], ed. Husin Ali (Malaysia: Persatuan Sains Sosial, 1984), 265–73.

7. Because the mothers became more involved in child-minding when this task was no longer performed by older sisters. C. Lwechungura Kamuzora, "High Fertility and the Demand for Labour in Peasant Economies: The Case of Bukoba District, Tanzania," *Development and Change* 15, no. 1 (1984):112–14, 118; Enid Schildkrout, "Children's Work Reconsidered," *International Social Sciences Journal* 32, no. 3 (1980):487.

8. Haile Y. Abeje, "Innovative Approaches to Universal Schooling," *Development Digest* 21, no. 2 (1983):84–86.

meet these needs.[9] David Levine has shown that the British working classes reduced their opposition to compulsory education only when the industrial revolution reached a stage at which factory employment was replacing outwork production and children's labor was becoming redundant.[10]

Clearly, circumstances, and hence attitudes, may change or may differentially affect the society. As early as the 1950s, Aileen Ross reported that business and professional families in Bangalore city had high educational ambition for their sons: "A good deal of the anxiety for sons to do well is due to the belief that the son's success will reflect back on the family and eventually bring it a higher standard of living."[11] She believed that there was greater pressure for the education of sons in a society like India, where sons are obligated to provide support for parents in old age, and she noted greater skepticism about the need to educate daughters. Other contemporary developing societies report a growing demand for children's education—for example, in Thailand as a means of economic improvement for both children and parents, and in Fiji as a necessary preparation for migrating to work elsewhere.[12] In the densely settled core of eastern Nigeria, Stephen Ekpenyong reported that when land pressure made some children (or children for some of the time) surplus to family labor requirements, schooling was an obvious investment for rendering them a productive asset beyond the household economy.[13]

We find education in rural south India to be favored both as a route to a nonfarming job and as a means of securing literacy and enlightenment. The educated can cope with the modern world and its bureaucrats more easily. Dube's comment of 30 years ago is still relevant: "Education is now regarded as important because it provides the key to the understanding of the wide world and equips one better to

9. Judith Ennew, "Family Structure, Unemployment and Child Labour in Jamaica," *Development and Change* 4 (1982):559.

10. David Levine, *Unstable Population Theorizing* (in press).

11. Aileen D. Ross, "Education and Family Change," *Sociological Bulletin* 8, no. 2 (1959):41–42.

12. Chancha Suvannathat, "The Inculcation of Values in Thai Children," *International Social Sciences Journal* 31, no. 3 (1979):481; Muriel Brookfield, "Resource Use, Economy and Society: Island at the Cross-roads," *UNESCO/UNFPA Fiji Island Reports* 5 (1979):181–82; see also Isireli Lasaqa, *The Fijian People: Before and After Independence* (Canberra: Australian National University Press, 1984):81–82, 95–97.

13. Stephen Ekpenyong, "The Effect of Mining Activities in a Peasant Community: A Case Study," *Development and Change* 15, no. 2 (1984):255.

assert one's rights and claim one's due from officials and the cunning townspeople."[14]

The Situation in India and the Research Area

Education continues to spread in India, and given the present impossibility of enforcement of school attendance, this clearly reflects expanding demand. The available census statistics series for India are for literacy rather than schooling, but the relationship is close. Of the population over 10 years of age, 6 percent were literate in 1891, and only 9 percent 40 years later in 1931.[15] The proportion of the total population (i.e., of all ages) who were literate increased more rapidly after Independence in 1947, from 16 percent at the time of the 1951 census to 24 percent in 1961, 29 percent in 1971, and 36 percent in 1981.[16] In Karnataka, where the Compulsory Primary Education Act of 1961 makes it in theory mandatory for the authorities to provide elementary schools and for parents to send their children to them, the literacy level for these four census years was always somewhat higher: 19 percent in 1951, 25 percent in 1961, 32 percent in 1971, and 38 percent in 1981. By the last date, 31 percent of Karnataka's rural population were literate compared with 56 percent in urban areas. In rural areas 42 percent of males and 22 percent of females were literate.[17]

In our research area, educational levels were somewhat higher, with 46 percent literate in 1981. But this is explained by the fact that the site had been chosen to include one large village, with a population of 2,500 (61 percent literate), and eight smaller hamlets typical of India's rural population, with a combined population of 2,500 (29 percent literate). It might be noted that "large" villages are those most frequently studied by anthropologists in India.[18] Because of these con-

14. S. C. Dube, *Indian Village* (London: Routledge and Kegan Paul, 1955), 165.
15. Kingsley Davis, *The Population of India and Pakistan* (Princeton: Princeton University Press, 1951), 151.
16. Asok Mitra, *India's Population: Aspects of Quality and Control* (New Delhi: Abhinav Publications for the Family Planning Foundation, 1978), 404; Census of India 1981, *Series– 1, India Part 2, Special: Report and Tables Based on 5 Percent sample Data* (New Delhi: P. Padmanabha, Controller of Publications, 1984), 78.
17. Census of India 1981, *Series–9, Karnataka, Provisional Population Totals, Paper 2 of 1981* by B. K. Das (Bangalore: Government Press, n.d.), 73–74.
18. The large village may have been somewhat larger than the typical anthropologist's village; see Bernard S. Cohen, *India: The Social Anthropology of a Civilization* (Englewood Cliffs, N.J.: Prentice-Hall, 1971), 144: "The model of structure most

trasts we often report the two populations separately. Among those over 5 years of age, the proportions with some schooling were 54 percent for the whole population, 70 percent for the large village, and 34 percent for the smaller ones. There were major differences by age and sex, although the latter were diminishing: among males, the proportion of the whole population with schooling among those who were of elementary school age in the 1930s was 49 percent; in the 1940s, 52 percent; in the 1960s, 67 percent; and in the 1970s, 73 percent. Among females these proportions were 15 percent, 25 percent, 40 percent, and 54 percent (and, in the smaller villages alone, among females, 3 percent, 7 percent, 16 percent, and 37 percent). By 1981 close to three-quarters of all boys and three-fifths of all girls started school, even if, in many cases, attending only for a short time. The questions addressed in this chapter are, then, why did so many start and why did they leave again?

A simple answer to the first question would cite the availability of schools. The large village has had an elementary school, established by the government of the princely state of Mysore, for over fifty years; and not far from it a college, established by sympathizers with the Gandhian movement 30 years ago, provides secondary schooling. Since Independence more elementary schools have been established throughout the area, together with an intermediate school in the large village. By 1981 all but one of the hamlets had schools. In most, the language of instruction was Kannada (the Dravidian language of Karnataka), whereas in the large village and in one smaller village there were government Urdu schools (Urdu, the language spoken at home by Karnatakan Muslims, is an Indo-European language close to Hindi but with more Persian words and written in Arabic script), and the college taught some classes in English.

The establishment of schools over the last four decades owes much to the ideology of the independence movement, which assumed, as all government reports still do, that schooling, essentially according to the Western model, was the major road to modernization and rising

---

common in anthropological literature on village India is a village of 800 to 2,000 people." Analyzing studies of 13 villages in India, Frank Zimmerman showed that the populations ranged from 384 to 2,869 with an average population of 1,113 (personal communication); in contrast, our eight hamlets range in population from 77 to 587 (averaging 297), and even with the inclusion of the large village the average is only 569. At the 1971 census, around one-sixth of the rural population of both India and Karnataka lived in centers with fewer than 500 inhabitants, and two-thirds in centers with fewer than 2,000 (but smaller hamlets were often grouped to appear as a single larger village).

incomes. Most people with any education accept this view. However, the educational system has taken decades to set up and is still far from complete. Where it has been regarded as a vote-winner, as in Karnataka and much of the rest of south India, the spread of schooling has been fastest. Whether a school is placed in a specific village depends on the activity of the local politicians and leading citizens, and on pressures exerted upon them by *panchayat* councils, caste organizations (which, at the state level, are very concerned with the increased access to education of their own caste members), and other groups. Thus, the existence of schools cannot be regarded as a fixed element in the situation, as a given external to the attitudes and strategies that we are investigating.

Several features of the research area are touched on here as relevant to educational transition. It is a dry farming area with no riverine irrigation. There is limited rice cultivation below the earthen walls of tanks formed by damming small streams. The dominant crop is *ragi*, unaffected by the "green revolution"; and the size of the annual crop is dependent on the vagaries of the monsoon. The population is deeply conscious of the pattern of periodic drought-induced disaster, and an important security strategy has been to seek, for some of the family, local off-farm employment or full-time urban occupations (see chap. 9). The latter, particularly, has been facilitated by the increase in the local school facilities, and by the rapid growth of Bangalore, now the fifth largest city of India, about 80 miles away. Another strategy has been to marry daughters to men with such jobs, or with education promising access to urban employment, and this is rendered more likely if the daughters have received some schooling (see chap. 4). There is an awareness that land size has declined (land per capita was 2.5 times greater at the beginning of the present century) and that agricultural productivity is growing slowly and unevenly. Some increase in agricultural production has occurred as the result of the introduction of sugar cultivation and the extension of coconut groves, both involving considerable investment in power-driven water pumps. Tractors have not yet challenged ox plows, but motor transport, small rice mills, iron plowshares, and other such innovations have substituted capital for human labor. One result has been that employers of agricultural labor now hire adults for sustained periods of farm work rather than using the services of whole families with their mix of ages.[19] Except in

19. This change is reported in other developing countries as well. M. W. Tilakaratne, "Economic Change, Social Differentiation and Fertility," in *Population and Development: High and Low Fertility in Poorer Countries*, ed. Geoffrey Hawthorn (London: Frank Cass, 1978), 196.

periods of peak labor demand, children under age 12 now find it difficult to secure paid daily work (although some are bonded for more permanent work). Something similar has been happening on the family farm, influenced not only by changes in production techniques but also by fundamental shifts in the relations between the generations. Children's work is not disdained, but, compared with adult labor, its need is not felt quite so strongly and it is not taken so much for granted as it used to be.

A new concept of childhood is emerging that is partly related to the existence of schooling: the existence of schools and school children makes parents see their children more as immature dependents, while the fact that they see them this way is more likely to result in sending them to school. Fathers are less likely to make their adolescent sons work from dawn to nightfall, as both generations become aware of job opportunities in the towns, as bus transport becomes easier, and as social attitudes change (a result, we are constantly told, of the cinema). Although fewer than 10 percent of the adult male labor force of the smaller villages engage in work outside agriculture as their major employment, over 50 percent of those in the large village do so (as merchants, artisans, bureaucrats, road laborers, etc). These parents feel particularly strongly that their children's future, and indeed the whole family's future, depends on the children using education as a route to secure, reasonably well-paid employment.

The Investigation

In 1981–82 we undertook a survey of parents' attitudes toward education and of the educational strategies they followed with their children. The findings, supplemented by responses from less structured discussions with village residents, are detailed in the remainder of this chapter. For the survey, a 50 percent sample of households was drawn in each of the nine villages and questions were then put to intact couples with one or more living children (thus eliminating orphans, who almost certainly fared less well). The total population surveyed consisted of 364 couples with 1,294 surviving children. In addition, questions on the success of educational strategies were put to 197 couples where the husband was at least 60 years of age and one or more children had reached age 21.

Among all couples surveyed, the average age of husbands was 41.8 years and of wives 32.7 years, with an age gap between spouses of 9.1 years, the usual pattern in Karnataka (see chap. 4). The women averaged 4.7 births with 3.6 surviving children, a survival rate consistent with an expectation of life at birth of around 45 years. Among 49 percent of the couples reproduction had now ceased because one spouse—almost invariably the wife—had undergone sterilization; just over half of these operations had been carried out since the end of the Emergency in 1977, five-sixths of them soon after the birth of the youngest child.

Among respondents' children, 70 percent of the boys and 55 percent of the girls had experienced at least some schooling. Boys and girls had on average begun school at ages 6.0 and 6.1 years respectively and had left at 12.2 and 11.6 years—schooling durations of 6.2 and 5.5 years. Nevertheless, because of a system in which progression depends on reaching specified standards of achievement, the median grade reached by both sexes was only fourth standard. One-third dropped out by the time they were 9 years old.

Table 7.1 shows the erosion of age cohorts (actually the amalgamation of the experience of overlapping groups) as school proceeds. The erosion rate of girls is no greater than that of boys until after age 12 years. There remain major social differentials: although 62 percent of all children started school, only 44 percent of Harijans (untouchables) did so, even though most Harijans lived in the large village, and though they had access to special government funds to assist with tuition, books, clothing, and subsistence. Muslims have high rates of school attendance in the large village, where they are the merchant class, but comparatively low rates in the one hamlet where they are small farmers and agricultural laborers and may have been Harijans until two centuries ago during the rule of Mysore by Muslim sultans.

The age at starting school shows no great differential by parents' socioeconomic characteristics, varying only from around 5.2 years for the least educated (Harijans or agricultural laborers, depending on the measure) to 6.3 years for those with considerable education (the chil-

Table 7.1. Percentage of Children Starting and Continuing School among Those Aged 5 Years and Above: Surveyed Families in Nine Rural South Indian Villages, 1981–82

	Boys	Girls
Started school	70	55
Continuing school at age		
10 years	59	46
12 years	47	34
15 years	34	11

Note: Percentages in each cohort (total surviving children equals 634 boys and 660 girls).

dren of Brahmin and Jain parents or of the bureaucrats and land-lords—categories that greatly overlap). The poor are more inclined to use school as a child-minding service, often while both parents carry out agricultural labor, and as a source of children's food (various governmental and international programs provide a midday meal). They are also aware just how soon children may have to be withdrawn because of family labor needs. In contrast, the economically better-off are more concerned that their children should be sufficiently mature to perform well from the outset and thus impress teachers and ensure their continued upward progression (many receive paid coaching out-side school hours, usually from their teachers).

The major differentials are by educational duration and hence are reflected in the age of ceasing education. This ranges from 9.0 years for those children of agricultural laborers who go to school at all to 11.8 years for farmers, 12.4 years for merchants, 14.3 years for bureaucrats and professionals (mostly school teachers), and almost 16 years for the Jain and Brahmin landlords. This is in keeping with most reported findings for India[20] and is also in accord with historical information as to the early near-monopolization of educational opportunities by Karnataka's Brahmins.[21]

The Educated and the Uneducated

We learned early in the research program that education is far more than a tool for economic advancement. The latter may be the case in educationally more advanced societies where families make choices about the duration of education; it is not so where contrasts are being drawn across the gulf that separates the literate from the illiterate. It was not so in Ghana in the 1960s;[22] it was not so in nineteenth-century

20. For example, the findings of Richard Anker, "The Effect of Group Level Variables on Fertility in a Rural Indian Sample," *Journal of Development Studies* 14, no. 1 (1977):66; but our data differ from those of Ajit Dasgupta and Jandhyala Tilka in neighboring Andhra Pradesh (where the results may have been distorted by the use only of an income measure, which is difficult to secure accurately, and by the disregard of such social measures as education and caste, which may indeed be better measures of true income). See Ajit K. Dasgupta and Jandhyala B. G. Tilak, "Distribution of Education Among Income Groups: An Empirical Analysis," *Economic and Political Weekly* 17, no. 33 (August 13, 1983):1442–47.

21. Chitra Sivakumar, *Education, Social Inequality and Social Change in Karnataka* (Delhi: Hindustan Publishing Corporation, 1982), quoted in Krishna Kumar, "Education and Society in Karnataka" (review article), *Economic and Political Weekly* 17, no. 28 (July 9, 1983):1230–31.

22. J. C. Caldwell, *Population Growth and Family Change in Africa: The New Urban Elite in Ghana* (Canberra: Australian National University Press, 1968):104–10.

America, as the humor of Artemus Ward attests;[23] and it is not so in India today. The starting point for meaningful research is the investigation of this attitude.

There is great sensitivity to direct questions about literacy versus illiteracy, especially when talking about neighbors and, a fortiori, one's own children (although not when talking about other caste groups living elsewhere). Nevertheless, in long, rambling discussions the matter comes up repeatedly. In the survey only 54 percent of respondents agreed that there were differences in behavior between literate and illiterate children, but 84 percent discovered that they could spell out quite clearly very substantial differences. Similarly, 26 percent said the two types of children were not treated differently, but 65 percent described quite different work patterns during the childhoods of the two types.

Two points are of great significance. First, when talking about education and literacy and their effect on people, only 10 percent of all respondent comments were critical of the impact of schooling. Education is overwhelmingly seen as a good thing for the individual, the family, the community, and the country (although parents are often despondent or impassive over whether their children will be able to stay long enough in school or receive sufficiently good teaching to achieve their ambitions). Second, only 10 percent of comments referred to the economic value of education as a means to jobs and income (doubtless because the question referred to education's effect on people, but nevertheless this is evidence that most people are highly conscious of the noneconomic impact of education, while still being mainly motivated to send children to school because of the enhanced job prospects). Most attention was paid to changes in personality and behavior, and the illiterate were often likened to the beasts of the field in their ignorance and in where they were usually to be found. The educated were repeatedly said to be more gracious, to know how to behave, to know the correct way of doing things, to know how to plan, and to be able to decide their own destinies. Illiterates were characterized as rude, rough, unpolished, suited only to agriculture, unable to plan or save money, and given to drinking and gambling. They were regarded as immobile and as requiring help from others in any unfamiliar environment. They were felt to be clumsy, careless, and unsystematic.

Most parents were clearly proud of their schoolgoing children. Some dissidents, often illiterate themselves, regarded the educated as

---

23. Artemus Ward (Charles Farrer Browne), *Artemus Ward, His Book* (London: Hotten, 1865); idem, *Artemus Ward's Lecture* (London: Hotten, 1869).

arrogant. They could not be asked to do dirty but necessary tasks like cleaning out the cow shed. Another criticism was that educated sons were likely to listen to their wives rather than their parents and to seek an undue share of independence prematurely. Some argued that only the educated can really achieve happiness, and others quoted a Kannada proverb to the effect that while the illiterate possess, as man anciently did, two eyes, the literate have four. "An educated person can survive anywhere in this world." There was also an awareness not only of the greater economic potential of the educated, but of the fact that they were less likely to be cheated in commercial transactions, that they could handle bureaucrats and bureaucracy, and that they could send and receive communications without having to breach privacy by consulting outsiders.

The views of the community generally support Jack Goody's argument as to the fundamental difference that literacy makes to a society.[24] These views are probably felt more strongly in India than in many other parts of the Third World because of the hierarchical organization of society and because any movement toward behaving more like Brahmins (Sanskritization, in Srinivas's phrase)[25] is a movement toward purity, education, and gentility.

Srinivas's observation (noted above) of over a third of a century ago retains its point: the Vokkaligas, the largest peasant caste and a majority of the population in the smaller villages, were more likely than others to stress the negative side of education; those with only one or two sons were afraid that no one in the younger generation would wish to continue farming. In terms of occupation, the least convinced about schooling were the small farmers, not the agricultural laborers, although uneducated parents were always worried about the impact of education on parent-child relations. Nevertheless, even farming families often seek guidance with regard to family strategies from their most educated member.[26] Most parents believe that educated children behave differently, but only a minority said in answer to a survey question that they are treated differently (always with the important exception of the work they are asked to do). On the other hand, in ordinary conversation parents revealed more (and much more indeed

24. Jack Goody, ed., *Literacy in Traditional Societies* (Cambridge: Cambridge University Press, 1968; idem, *The Domestication of the Savage Mind* (Cambridge: Cambridge University Press, 1977).

25. M. N. Srinivas, *Social Change in Modern India* (Berkeley: University of California Press, 1966):6–45.

26. See Sarah Hobson, *Family Web: A Story of India* (London: John Murray, 1978).

about their neighbors). They said of others that once parents had educated their children they had to continue to treat them well so as to safeguard their investment and ensure that relationships remained good and that returns would come. They said that parents respected sons who earned money more than those who stayed to help on the farm. With regard to themselves, parents had a different form of affection for their uneducated farming or laboring sons who would always be with them. Nevertheless, the only hope for a different way of life was through their educated children. They often said that in their families and in the community, attention was turning toward children and their education. It would intensify over time, for in "educated families parents always pay more attention to their children than their children do to the parents."[27]

When parents with both educated and uneducated children were asked directly in a survey whether they pinned more hopes for the future on their educated children, over three-quarters said they did, whereas only one-twelfth denied doing so. The reasons given by the former were almost entirely in terms of town jobs, government employment, and guaranteed incomes. But was this economic motivation, in fact, the reason parents sent their children to school?

Why Families Sent Their Children to School

Among sampled families, 587 children had started school (irrespective of whether they were currently attending). The parents' primary stated reasons for sending children to school are listed in table 7.2; frequently, parents also supplied supplementary motives.

The most striking aspect of the response is that nearly all parents have clear views on why they send their children to school, and that the reasons do not vary greatly according to the size of the village or its level of economic development and social change. In no village is school attendance yet regarded as officially or socially mandatory, although the large village is further along that road. The dominant reason is economic, almost always spelled out as increasing the chance of gaining government, urban, or off-farm employment. The economic argument is often put in terms of helping the family, but additionally parents stress that educated children will not have to perform the drudgery that agriculture entails and endure the misery in its periodic crises.

27. Caldwell, "Mass Education"; this is consistent with the argument in J. C. Caldwell, *Theory of Fertility Decline* (London: Academic Press, 1982), where a reversal of wealth flows between parents and children is posited (152, 333).

Table 7.2. Primary Reason for Sending Children to School (Percentage distribution)

Reason	Sex of child			Size of village	
	All children	Sons	Daughters	Large village	8 smaller villages
To equip the child for a job	50	65	29	52	49
For the sake of knowledge; to achieve literacy	33	23	48	28	37
Now the usual pattern; a duty; need to do what others in a similar position do; the government expects it	6	6	6	9	4
To prepare for marriage or motherhood (daughters only)	4	—	9	6	2
Child bright and clearly suited to education; or weak and not suited to manual work	3	2	3	3	2
As a means of child-minding; or because food is provided	2	3	2	0	4
No response; "don't know"	2	1	3	2	2
Total percent	100	100	100	100	100
Total number	587	355	232	274	313

Most of the less frequently cited reasons are of supplementary importance. Indeed, the education of daughters so that they are more suited to better-educated, nonfarming husbands, or so that they are better equipped for rearing children, is an important theme in the society,[28] but many parents include such aims under the broader one of producing literate, more refined, and more capable daughters. In this respect, it is possible to regard the findings in the table as representing a modern adaptation to the traditional structure of the society: sons are being educated as breadwinners and daughters as suitable wives for this new type of breadwinner and as mothers for the next generation of such men and women. From this point of view, perhaps the most surprising finding is that over a quarter of daughters were

28. These issues are discussed in chaps. 4 and 6.

reportedly educated for better employment. There are very few paid positions, outside agricultural labor, for women in the villages. In large part, this desire to educate daughters reflects an awareness that young men destined for town jobs are increasingly likely to favor wives who are employable. Another reason given occasionally was that only education and subsequent access to town jobs would enable the children to break out of their position in the caste hierarchy. One would have anticipated that this would be a more frequent reaction, in light of how often the case for education in nineteenth-century England was given as overcoming the class system.[29]

An examination of reasons for sending children to school over the last 30 years reveals a remarkable stability. Among boys, the primacy of preparation for a job has slowly declined (although it is still the most important reason) as education has become more general and as the decision that one's children will remain illiterate has become more of a social anomaly. Among girls, the concept of schooling to prepare for a job is a feature solely of the last 15 years and, even among the younger cohorts, is not the major reason for education.

The clearest differentials in response are by socioeconomic class. The better-off and those higher in the caste hierarchy stress jobs less and the virtues of literacy more, particularly with regard to daughters (whose education they tend to favor more than do other members of the society). This is true of the Jains, Brahmins, and Lingayats, of landlords and large farmers, and also of the Muslim merchants. In contrast, most of the peasant castes, particularly the Vokkaligas, together with the Harijans, backward castes, and artisan castes, place more emphasis on securing employment. There is also a clear association with family size: the larger the family, measured either by surviving children or the number still living in the household, the greater is the emphasis on education for jobs.

In the survey we did not specifically ask why children were not sent to school, although we did so frequently in informal sessions. We were told that given the family's station in life, it was pointless and even harmful for children to go to school, or that it would make daughters unmarriageable. Often parents just said that school was not for people like them or that the teachers would not treat their children well. They said they needed their children's help, or could not afford school costs, or could not dress their children properly. They sometimes said it was obvious that a child would not do well at school.

Yet the anthropological approach revealed a more complex pic-

---

29. Caldwell, "Mass Education," 226.

ture than these responses, which blur decisions at various stages of a child's progress into a single decision. Parents today feel they no longer have much choice but to let a child start school: the community takes it for granted, as the child increasingly does. During the first years there is only limited parental ambition for the child and only a slowly growing feeling of a drain on the household's labor resources (although this can change dramatically if the household structure alters), but a greater, and increasing, awareness of the financial cost. By the end of elementary school, if the child (especially a son) is doing well, likes school, and perhaps is developing scholastic ambitions, then the family may think of preparing the child for nonagricultural employment, anticipating a substantial return on their investment. Relative to many other Third World countries, the rate of economic return to primary education in India is low and that to secondary education is high.[30]

The economic motivation—training the child for a job as a form of investment—is complex, and its articulation varies from family to family. Some parents emphasize immediate returns, but many more stress delayed returns and the provision of security. The form of security most often cited is that against periodic risk, but some parents emphasize ensuring greater support in their old age. There is also the type of risk avoidance provided by educating a girl so that she can be married to a man with a secure job; this ensures less that help can be received from her during an emergency than that she and her husband will not need help and so drain family resources.

From another perspective, in many ways the commitment to education, and the conditions under which children will be allowed to stay at school, are more clearly evidenced by the reasons given for withdrawing children from school.

Why Children were Removed from School

Of all children sent to school, 280 had left by the time of the survey. The stated reasons for this withdrawal are set out in table 7.3.

These bald categories cover a wider range of responses. Two-thirds of those needed for work were needed to work on the farm, as agricultural laborers or in the house; those destined for nonagricultural employment were kept at school as long as possible. Sometimes, especially in the case of girls, the next higher school is farther away and

30. Jonathan Kelley, "Social Mobility in India: A Cross-National Perspective" (Paper presented to the International Sociological Association, Social Stratification Research Group, Budapest, 1984).

Table 7.3. Primary Reason for Children Being Withdrawn from School (percentage distribution)

Reason	Sex of child			Size of center	
	All children	Sons	Daughters	Large village	8 smaller villages
Failed; not doing well; or incompatible with school	46	55	35	47	45
Needed for work	31	31	31	29	32
Cost prohibitive	13	13	13	11	15
Menarche	9	—	20	12	7
Education complete; or planned level reached	1	1	1	1	1
Total percent	100	100	100	100	100
Total number	280	150	130	138	142

there is apprehension about their walking there. The fundamental problem of interpretation is that the three major grouped categories are interrelated: the need for labor or the cost can often be ignored if the child is doing especially well and there are great hopes for his future.

Very few children are educated as far as would have been desired had there been no financial constraints or had the child proved capable of surmounting all educational hurdles. (Only 1 percent go on to university.) One-fifth of all females are still withdrawn from school at menarche (around half of those who are still at school at that age), usually to be married as soon as possible, either because menarche is taken as a sign that marriage should be arranged or because of the disgrace and danger of an unmarried pubescent girl being in public. A girl may even be withdrawn from school just before examinations that have been eagerly anticipated by parents, children, and teachers. She will also be withdrawn from field labor, even on the family farm. Menarche is still a major reason for the cessation of daughters' education among Muslims, peasant castes, and artisan castes. The exceptions are the educationally most advanced groups—Brahmins, Jains, and Lingayats—and the least advanced—the scheduled and backward castes, among whom the honor/shame aspect of premarital virginity has always been less stressed.

The majority of children are withdrawn for two interrelated reasons: because the cost, whether direct or in labor forgone, is felt to be prohibitive or because the investment in education is perceived to have failed. Clearly, as the chance of a child doing well at school fades,

there is rising bitterness about the labor forgone. Cost is more important in the case of daughters because the returns from education are
much less certain; among sons it is more common for the investment
to turn sour. There is another form of apprehension about a girl's
schooling. She must be married to a male with at least as much education. If parents become worried about their ability to arrange a match
for a schoolgirl, they may suddenly withdraw her from school so as not
to compound their problem.

Those who stress work needs are mostly the families who allowed
children to attend school because there was no great point in their not
doing so. Girls' work is now not greatly valued until they are around 8
years of age and boys until nearer 10 (unless there are animals to be
pastured or specific low-level tasks to perform, as in artisan families).
In this case school will do no harm, and further investment in it may
prove profitable. Nevertheless, this situation holds good only so long
as the family labor force is adequate and is balanced to sex. Even
young girls are frequently withdrawn from school because an elder
sister has married and left home or a mother or grandmother has
become disabled or the mother has become pregnant again, while a
young boy may end his school days as soon as his elder brother goes to
town to seek work. What is most striking to the outside observer is how
suddenly, when circumstances change, the family decides that the
child must be withdrawn from school and immediately acts on the
decision. The child is very rarely warned or consulted, and most families do not believe these decisions and actions are in any way the
child's business.

Where school performance was the deciding factor, the initiative
was that of the school in about one-third of cases, exercised through
failing the child or suggesting withdrawal. In the remaining two-thirds,
families decided that the child's level of achievement warranted no
further support. Some were fairly satisfied with what had already been
achieved; others, mostly with regard to daughters, felt that the next
higher school was too far away.

Cost and work needs were dominant among peasant, artisan,
backward, and scheduled castes, whereas school success was more
important among Brahmins, Jains, Lingayats, and the Muslim merchants. School success is also given greater importance among large
families because labor crises arise much less frequently (as Chayanov
observed)[31] and among the rich (as measured among farmers by the

31. A. V. Chayanov, "Peasant Farm Organization" (originally published in
Moscow, 1925), in *The Theory of Peasant Economy*, ed. Daniel Thorner, Basile
Kerblay, and R. E. F. Smith (Homewood, Ill.: Richard D. Irwin, 1966), 29–269.

possession of more than ten acres of land). The urgency artisans feel about educating children depends on the extent to which they feel their craft to be dying; in the research area this fear was strongest among the washermen, who felt that wider availability of soap, and declining fears of pollution, were encouraging more families to wash their own clothes.

There is surprisingly little variation in the reasons for leaving school by the age at which this occurs (that age itself being largely determined by socioeconomic class and caste), except among girls where the onset of puberty is involved. Otherwise, at every age a similar balance between work needs and failure obtains, perhaps because, although children's labor is more valuable at older ages, so is the significance of the educational investment made.

Over the last 30 years there has been a persistent decline, in the case of both boys and girls, in school withdrawal because of family labor needs and a rise in withdrawal because of the children's reaching their educational ceiling—a reflection of both the declining demand for child labor and the longer duration of schooling.

Are Educational Aims Achieved?

Given that only half of all children are sent to school to equip them for a job, and that many are sent only until their labor is needed, one might expect that parents' expectations were achieved in a large proportion of all cases. This is not so. The level of disappointment and frustration with the educational success of the children is high. There is disappointment both with levels of literacy and sophistication reached and with the grade achieved and hence employability, the greatest dissatisfaction being with the last of these.

Such disappointment cuts across socioeconomic class, with parents feeling that their educational aims were not achieved for 71 percent of children, and were only partly achieved for another 2 percent. There is a marked difference by sex, with parents regarding their educational aims as having been achieved for only 14 percent of sons who were sent to school but for 42 percent of daughters. The most interesting finding emerged when the analysis took both the educational aim and the sex of the child into account. When the chief reason for schooling was to prepare the child for employment, the sex of the child was unimportant, with only a 10 percent level of satisfaction for children of either sex; when literacy was the chief reason, satisfaction with sons' achievements was still little more than 10 percent, but daughters reached almost 60 percent. Clearly schooling still means something very different for boys than for girls. Nevertheless, satisfaction for both sexes was most closely associated with how long the child could be kept at school: where aims had been achieved, the students had usually attained some secondary education; where the aims had not been achieved, the children had usually left during primary school.

The situation of the oldest son and oldest daughter in a family is quite distinctive with regard to education: they are somewhat more likely to be sent to school, stay there longer on average, are more likely to be withdrawn because the family can no longer do without their labor, and are less likely to satisfy their parents' hopes in education.

The Cost of Schooling

As we have seen, two aspects of cost are central: the partial or complete withdrawal of labor during school, and the extra costs incurred by going to school. Table 7.4 shows parents' assessments of sources of costs of educating children among the two-thirds of parents who felt able to make such assessments.

Almost two-thirds of responding parents agreed that school children contributed less work to the household or farm and almost three-quarters that greater expenditure had to be made upon them. Our informal conversations convinced us that these views are almost universal; the resistance to registering agreement in the survey arises largely because the survey structure does not permit the respondent to argue that it should not be so and that such differentials in treatment are unfair.

School takes up time both during its formal hours and because children insist that they have a great deal of homework to do, a claim that uneducated parents find hard to assess. The changes wrought by school mainly fell into two groups. The first was a belief that school made children softer, weaker, or more genteel—another aspect of the civilizing force that we earlier noted was so often praised—and that they could not be expected to do hard or unpleasant work, or that they were simply incapable of it. Of equal importance was the charge (not always disapproved) that school taught children to play and that they resisted or skimped work in favor of recreation. The type of work performed also changes: school children work more in the house and spend more time running errands than working in the fields.

We have argued elsewhere that schooling broadens children's horizons and encourages them to demand general increases in their consumption expenditure and standards of living.[32] Our research in India

32. Caldwell, *Theory of Fertility Decline*, 60.

Table 7.4. Parents' Responses to Questions on the Labor Contribution of School Children and Costs of Educating Children (Percentage distribution)

Question/Response	%
Whether the children sent to school contributed as much work as those not sent[a]	
School children contributed just as much work	34
School children contributed less work	63
No children are made to work	2
Only the girls contributed as much work	1
Total percent	100
Total number	243
Why school children did not contribute as much work[b]	
Children are sent to school only when too young to work	15
School work and homework take up so much time	66
School changes children so that they cannot be made to do so much work	12
No response	7
Total percent	100
Total number	153
Whether more was spent on children sent to school[a]	
More was spent on those sent to school	72
No difference in expenditure	23
More was spent on those not sent to school[c]	5
Total percent	100
Total number	252
Why more was spent on school children[d]	
Fees, books, stationery, clothes	83
Fees, books, stationery, and clothes plus transport and/or accommodation	10
Clothes[e]	3
More expenditure in every way (including general expenditure)	2
Because the girls are being prepared for a better marriage	1
Because the children contribute no labor	1
Total percent	100
Total number	181

[a]Percentage distribution of those parents who felt able to make the comparison.
[b]Percentage distribution of those families stating school children did less work.
[c]E.g., parents tried to invest in a job or land for them, and in a few cases, higher dowry.
[d]Percentage distribution of those parents who stated more was spent on school children.
[e]For some Harijan parents, all other costs are covered by the government.

did not fully support this proposition except that it was taken for granted that school children must have better clothing, partly to keep up appearances and partly because either the school is likely to persuade a ragged child to leave or the child himself will become reluctant to go to school. Beyond this, all parents complain of the cost of books, stationery, and fees. Below senior secondary school no formal fees are charged, but a large proportion of the children receive some paid tutoring, usually by their own teachers outside school hours.

The differences in parents' response by sex of the child were not as great as might have been anticipated from studies elsewhere, and hence the table does not show a breakdown by sex. The type of work done by school children seemed to vary less for boys than for girls. Those who were most conscious of the withdrawal of labor were farmers and agricultural laborers, the farmers particularly stressing homework as taking children away from household tasks. There were no significant differentials by sex with regard to complaints about cost.

The Link with Family Planning

Since the end of the Emergency in 1977, 89 of the couples surveyed had been sterilized (women in all but one case, a decisive shift from the earlier pattern). This number was in keeping with the pattern in the whole community, where almost 50 percent of couples are covered by sterilization by the time the wife is 36 years old or has experienced five live births. This situation explains a fertility decline in the area over the previous 15 years of almost one-third and a birth rate just under 30 per thousand per year (see chap. 10). Of the sample couples who had undergone sterilization, 5 percent reported that they had responded to pressure from the family planning program or from relatives, 8 percent that they sought to protect the wife's health or to ensure that past difficulties with pregnancies or childbirth were not repeated, and 23 percent that they desired to cease having children. However, 63 percent gave as their reason the aim of raising (or maintaining) family living standards, usually with fairly strong reference to what could be done for their children. Over half said that economic problems associated with educating or training their children and setting them up in jobs had played a part in their decision for sterilization. The more educated the parents, the more likely it was for the need to educate children to have played a role in the decision. This motivation was also important among agricultural laborers, partly because pregnancy and caring for infants may reduce the wife's earning capacity.

When respondents were asked why sterilization should play a role in promoting education, the answers were clear: the number of children a family can afford to educate is restricted, particularly over a limited number of years. Many parents insisted they were able to keep the children in school only because of the mother's tubectomy. This was particularly the case among younger women sterilized since 1980.

Discussion

The situation in rural Karnataka is not as Linda Dove described it among the poor in Bangladesh, where schooling is regarded as irrelevant and costly, but more as she found the general position to be in developing countries, where schools are accepted when they fit in with the society and seem to offer a path to jobs.[33] The suspicion of education as eroding the culture, which Dove noted, is not found in the survey area, perhaps because of Karnataka's choice of Kannada-medium and Urdu-medium schools, the latter almost inevitably staffed by Muslims teaching Muslim children. Certainly the schools bring a modern, and even Western, message. But this is accepted by the government and most of the community as representing a desirable future. Indeed, 20 years ago the Indian Education Commission began its influential report by stating, "The destiny of India is now being shaped in her classrooms. This, we believe, is no mere rhetoric . . . it is education that determines the level of prosperity, welfare and security of the people.[34]

Education is certainly seen as a route to jobs, with some of the obsession and some of the disastrous rebuffs that Ronald Dore has described.[35] But this is not the whole story. The society has learned, in the words of John Oxenham describing the situation in Ghana, to "value the skills of literacy and numeracy, the access to a wider world of knowledge and experience and the socially disciplining effect of the school."[36] Indeed, as the proportion educated grows, and as the illit-

33. Linda A. Dove, "Educational Policy in Bangladesh 1978–81: Promise and Performance in Political Perspective," *Comparative Education* 19, no. 1 (1983):73–88; idem, "The Role of the Community School in Rural Transformation in Developing Countries," *Comparative Education* 16, no. 1 (1980):67–79.

34. Indian Education Commission, *Report*, quoted in Ronald Dore, *The Diploma Disease: Education, Qualification and Development* (London: George Allen and Unwin, 1976), 1.

35. Ronald Dore, "Deschool? Try Using Schools for Education First: The Educational Impasse in the Developing World," IDS Discussion Paper no. 6 (Brighton: University of Sussex, 1974); idem, *Diploma Disease*.

36. John Oxenham, "New Opportunities for Change in Primary Schooling?" *Comparative Education* 20, no. 2 (1984):212.

erate are contrasted ever more disparagingly with those who have been
to school, education tends to become a conventional necessity so that
parents will scrimp and save to educate their children even though no
certain gains are in sight and even though most parents are dis-
appointed by the returns from their educational investments. This
transformation has been clearly described in the northwest Kenya by
C. J. Martin, although in a more homogeneous society than in India,
where minimum consumption needs are often dictated by caste rather
than by the whole community.[37] Families, as well as governments and
labor economists, think of literacy and education as producing more
competent and efficient people, so Christopher Colclough may well be
right in finding positive returns from educational investment even in
rural areas.[38] Yet, unless the rural labor structure changes radically,
one might note the fear strongly expressed by many parents in Karnataka that schooling destroys the ability to be an agricultural laborer.

To the extent that the future differs from the past, however, this
fear may gradually be dispelled. One of the keys to the growing
demand for schooling is fundamental change in the rural economy. As
population has grown, average farm size has fallen to a point where
many farming families do not need the labor of young children. Young
children are also less likely to be employable as agricultural laborers,
partly because of changing rural technology, partly because of a breakdown in traditional patron-client relations in which the clients were
whole families, partly because both parents and employers tend more
to look upon the young as "children" (a change related to increased
schooling), and partly because older children themselves are increasingly able to resist endless work (the intergenerational social change
that determines the direction of the wealth flow). In our research area
an increasing number of children are allowed to go to school up to
around 10 years of age because they are no longer very useful at
younger ages, because it gets them out of the way, because their literacy will be an asset to them and their families as well as a good in itself,
and because they may do well enough to justify prolonged investment.
That they are allowed to attend school because they are not really
needed is demonstrated convincingly by the speed with which they are
often withdrawn once they appear to be more physically capable or

37. C. J. Martin, "Education and Consumption in Maragoli (Kenya): Households' Educational Strategies," *Comparative Education* 18, no. 2 (1982):139–55.
38. Christopher Colclough, "The Impact of Primary Schooling on Economic
Development: A Review of the Evidence," *World Development* 10, no. 3 (1982):167–
85.

when a genuine need suddenly arises. A similar phenomenon has been identified in Kenya by Martin.[39]

Nevertheless, a serious investment in education, especially for boys, is increasingly tempting. Sole reliance on agriculture has always haunted the rural population because of periodic drought-induced famine. The spread of schools, together with the growth of the urban job market, especially in Bangalore, and of off-farm employment as the economy develops, has made it possible to diversify income sources by having one or more sons work outside agriculture. Schooling makes migration easier and urban employment more likely. Education for girls also renders them more likely to marry men employed outside agriculture, an important point in south India where crisis assistance may well come from affines. Labor emigration, usually preceded by some schooling, has been sufficiently great in the last few years to offset natural increase and at least temporarily halt local population growth (see chap. 10).

In the thesis we originally put forward to account for a rise since 1978 in the demand for family planning, we posited a triangle: falling demand for family labor among both farmers and agricultural laborers because of declining farm size; increasing demand for education in a situation where schools were more available and a growing labor market offered the possibility of diversifying sources of income; and financial problems in keeping many children at school (see chap. 10). This research was aimed at testing two sides of the triangle: the reasons for growing school attendance and the related costs. Our findings appear to go far toward verifying this portion of the broader hypothesis.

Clearly, key elements in the fertility-education relationship vary among different communities in India and in the Third World more generally. In parts of north India, such as Bihar, there may be a smaller urban job market than is provided by rapidly expanding Bangalore. Caste conflict may undermine local unity in demands for schools; and certainly, in contrast to Karnataka, fewer small villages have schools. The desire to educate children in India may have a more immediate impact on the demand for fertility control than would be the case in sub-Saharan Africa, because the cost of education in India is largely borne by the household, whereas in Africa it can be spread among a wider circle of relatives (indeed, in Africa there may be little escape from such expenditures through restricting the number of one's children).[40]

39. Martin, "Education and Consumption."
40. Caldwell, *Theory of Fertility Decline*, 36, 41–43; J. C. Caldwell, "Extended

Yet there have clearly been changes in Karnataka society too. In our large village over half of all sons have received some schooling for half a century. Why, then, did fertility not fall sooner? Most of the population offer a simple answer: there was no way, the family planning program did not exist earlier. The real position is probably more complex. Until recently, only the economically well-off sent their sons to school, and society was differentiated more clearly between the haves and the have-nots. Nor did most attend school for as long as is now the case.

Finally, there is still, as in much of the rest of the Third World, tremendous capriciousness about educational chances. Our family histories reveal that children stayed at school or did not do so largely because a brother's leaving school or the hiring of a laborer or the division of the household and its property mean that there was or was not a demand at a given point for their work. The deeply rooted suspicion that much depends on whether the teacher likes a child probably has some substance and can play a critical role. One force remains constant: sons are likely to receive no less education (and usually more) than their fathers, while daughters are even more favorably placed compared with their mothers.

Family Obligations and Education: A Study of an Aspect of Demographic Transition Among Ghanaian University Students," *Population Studies* 19, no. 2 (1965):183–99. In Africa the fact that one has fewer children is often taken as evidence of greater ability to educate nephews and nieces.

Chapter Eight

The Support of the Aged

From the viewpoint of this chapter, the most important analysis previously reported in this book is that of family structure (see chap. 5). The central institution of the society is the stem family, which, if unbroken, consists of an older couple and one married son together with his wife and children. Nearly all young couples start their married lives in such families but may be displaced later as other sons marry. Joint-stem families are few and are usually a transitional form, having come into existence for the period between the marriage of a second son and the departure of one of the married sons with wife and children to form a separate nuclear family. If, during this transitional stage or in the case of the relatively few continuing joint-stem families, the older couple are broken up by death, a joint family may be formed. In a society which has until recently averaged three sons born and two surviving to their parents' old age, this precipitation of nuclear families by partition has meant that somewhat over half of all families are nuclear in residence, one-quarter are stem families, and the remainder are made up of a range of other forms. However, nuclear families are smaller in average size and only two-fifths of the population at any given time are found living in them. Very few persons have lived in no other form of family.

This system is very flexible. When fertility remained constant while mortality was slowly falling, the proportion of the population resident in nuclear families slowly rose. Now that fertility is falling, the proportion resident in stem families will again increase. The important point is that the stem family is the familial situation where all but about 5 percent of the population over 60 years of age is found. The older people are usually there not because they have joined a married child in old age but because they are continuing to live in the house where they have always lived and have with them the married son and family who found such co-residence either most congenial or more economically advantageous. In these larger family residences there may be emotional strains, most commonly between daughters-in-law and mothers-in-law, but there is little problem as yet of old-age care. The system still seems stable and we could find little evidence that it was beginning to erode. It has always been subject to some demographic threat, largely the failure to have sons or to raise them to adulthood, but one solution is to tempt a son-in-law with little or no land to bring the couple's daughter back to create a stem family consisting of the old couple and their married daughter together with her husband and children. One is told that young husbands do not like this and that such families are rare, but in fact around 5 percent of all stem families are of this type. The real threat to the system is posed by continuing declines in fertility, by a greater proportion of the younger generation migrating to the towns, and by rising levels of schooling inducing greater numbers of educated young wives to demand separate residence early in marriage.

The Situation of the Aged

In the study area, 6.0 percent of the population were over 60 years of age, 3.8 percent over 65, 2.1 percent over 70, and 0.6 percent over 80. These proportions match those that would be predicted by quasi-stable population theory[1] and our reconstruction of past demographic trends (see chap. 10). It is a surprising attestation of relatively good age statement even among the old, among whom only a minority of males and very few females have had any schooling. The age structure of the older population provides evidence that mortality rates have in general been higher among females than among males. Thus, 58 percent of the population over 60 years of age is male, a strikingly different situation from the position now found in Western countries. Even in rural India, however, female propensity for survival begins to predom-

---

1. Cf. United Nations, Department of Economic and Social Affairs, *Manual IV, Methods of Estimating Basic Demographic Measures from Incomplete Data*, ST/SOA/ Ser.A/42 (New York: United Nations, 1967); and A. J. Coale and P. Demeny, *Regional Model Life Tables and Stable Populations* (Princeton: Princeton University Press, 1966).

inate in extreme old age. Thus, the proportion of males falls to 54 percent among those over 65 years of age, and to 47 percent above 70 years. The proportion of the aged and their balance by sex differ little by caste or other socioeconomic characteristics.

Of the 304 persons over 60 years of age, only 20, or 6.6 percent, are living alone. Of these, 16 (four-fifths) are females. The lack of a residential spouse is explained in fifteen cases by widowhood, in four cases by desertion, and in one case by one woman who failed to marry. In addition, there are an equal number of persons living as ten old couples on their own because they had no children or all children have migrated. It should be emphasized that the majority of old intact couples and three or four of the individuals living alone are happy to be in this state because they are continuing to live in houses that they have known and have relatives residing close by. In fact, all the villages in this area are residentially segregated by caste (except in government quarters or *janata* housing projects). This means that most relatives live close by, even by village standards of distance, and solitary individuals or couples do have some caste group support. Nevertheless, nearly all the distressed aged, by both their own estimation and ours, belong to the small group who live on their own.

We selected a 30 percent sample of persons over 60 years of age so that we could examine their situation in depth. In this sample, 8 percent lived alone and 10 percent as couples. Those living with at least one son constituted 68 percent and those living with a daughter another 6 percent, while grandchildren gave support in 3 percent of cases. In some cases the old parents each lived with a different married son. In the stem families, most of the older males described themselves as the head of the household, whereas only half of widows did so, naming a son in the other cases.

The old are not without assets and indeed this is often the economic lever which explains their situation in life and even the continuation of the stem family. Although only 13 percent of those over 60 claimed to own any significant amount of money or gold, 70 percent of individuals or couples described themselves as owning the house in which they lived and 67 percent as owning some land. Almost half described themselves as having some source of income outside the family of residence: 16 percent got regular remittances from sons living elsewhere; 14 percent had nonagricultural sources, usually businesses which they ran or in which they had an investment; and 8 percent received government pensions. It might be noted that the landless were twice as likely to be destitute as even those with the smallest amount of land. Old persons often explained their ability to survive economically by what they grew on very small pieces of land as a supplement to some income from agricultural labor. The monthly government pensions were not large, being Rs 40 in half the cases and averaging somewhat more than twice this amount. The smaller pensions were for the needy and the choice was made by the Taluk Board, whereas the larger pensions were the result of past government employment. The government also gave loans for building on the *janata* housing estate, but this was available mostly to intact families.

The major component of support is demographic. The sample of persons over 60 years of age have averaged 3.1 male births and 3.0 female births, with an average completed family size of 6.1. Of the sons born, 75 percent were still alive, on an average of 2.3 per respondent. Again attesting to higher female mortality, only 65 percent of daughters were still alive, averaging 2.0 per respondent. Thus, for all children, there had been a 70 percent level of survival so that on average 6.1 births meant 4.3 children still alive.

These averages hide considerable differences in distribution. The real fear is that even six births will not result in a son surviving to old age either because of the capriciousness of the sex ratio at birth or a low level of child survival. Among all the old, 14 percent had no surviving sons. This reached 30 percent among Harijans because of higher levels of child mortality, 25 percent among Brahmins and Jains, because of lower fertility, but only 6 percent among Muslims who are characterized both by higher fertility and by a determination not to restrict family size as long as there are no sons.

Condition of Life and Destitution

The respondents were asked whether the standard of living that they had managed to maintain was largely a function of their children. Those who had no doubt that their condition of life stemmed directly from the help of their children (or, in some cases, grandchildren) amounted to 57 percent of the total, and a further 8 percent (bringing the total up to 65 percent) said that children played a significant supplementary role. The remaining 35 percent said children were not a crucial element, although the proportion declined with age. Half this group reported that they had no surviving children or sons, or that their children were no good or unsuccessful, or had gone to distant places. The other half said that they did not need help as they were still active and prosperous, although it might be noted that much depended on the perspective, because a disproportionate number of this group had sons working on their land or in their business. Those saying that children played either a central or a significant role in their economic well-being, although averaging 65 percent, reached 90 percent among Harijans, but fell to 60 percent among Vokkaligas who mostly owned land, and to 59 percent among Muslims who were mostly merchants still playing an active role in their businesses.

The position of those with land or businesses is of interest. Most are assisted by children who usually do much of the work. But the older people are well aware of their ability to employ others as labor, and even some widows do this on a significant scale. Not all the propertied group still own all their land, for most have long since agreed to partition land to married sons. But many have kept at least a share of land as a security (often worked by day laborers), for, as a Vokkaliga assured us, "without property, children do not look after their parents well." What is striking is to what advanced ages many agricultural laborers, women as well as men, continue to do at least some paid work. Most claim that this is not an act of desperation but their job, their way of life, and, indeed, their predestined role.

Education and migration for jobs to Bangalore and elsewhere have rendered the situation more complex. An increasing amount of money is remitted from these migrant children and this is one of the reasons for parents educating them. It also raises problems. Some of the old have joined their children in Bangalore, while others have refused to do so in spite of repeated requests. Some landowners and merchants have induced nephews and grandchildren to join them to replace their children's labor and have in effect adopted these other relatives.

We enquired of the old whether their condition was comfortable, less than comfortable but not destitute, or destitute, and assisted them to arrive at an assessment with which both we and they agreed. The final assessment was: comfortable—75 percent; less than comfortable but not destitute—8 percent; destitute—9 percent; no agreed assessment—8 percent.

The primary cause of destitution is quite clear. Of those with no living sons, 40 percent are destitute and a further 30 percent less than comfortable, whereas among those with any surviving sons these categories amount to only 4 and 6 percent respectively. In fact, those with no sons are half the destitute and half the group who are less than comfortable. In some cases daughters have a softening effect on the prevention of disaster, and some sons-in-law are helpful, but where there are no sons the existence of surviving daughters has not had as great an impact as we anticipated. Furthermore, the absence of surviving sons has an unequal impact, and it is far less disastrous on couples or widowers than on widows. Widows constitute 63 percent of the destitute and 80 percent of the combined group of the destitute and the less than comfortable. The fact of a woman having no surviving sons was largely a product of low fertility and a low masculinity ratio among her births; differentially high mortality to women giving birth to an average number of sons was of lesser significance. Thus, fore-warnings of disaster were present long before and were noted by all. The chances of disaster increased as the likelihood of widowhood did, and were greater among women with much older husbands. Desti-tution also depended on the caste group from which one came and on the resources that the whole group commanded and those likely to characterize individual members. Thus, although Harijans and Vok-kaligas formed only 39 percent of the population, they included 73 percent of the destitute old.

Lifelong Benefits from Children

Children, particularly sons, were so clearly of benefit to the old that we decided to survey all older people in the community to see if they believed that this characterized only their present situation or whether it had been true earlier as well. We interviewed couples or surviving partners where the husband was over 60 years of age (or would have been were he still alive) and who had at least one surviving child over 21 years of age, and obtained information from 438 couples or sur-viving partners.

Although the great majority felt that their present situation owed much or everything to the fact that they had raised children in ade-quate numbers and of sufficient masculinity, they were less convinced of their profitability over a lifetime. Certainly, we deliberately focused the questions on economic return and omitted social return and the extent to which children made viable living arrangements possible. This restricted focus almost certainly alienated a proportion of the respondents. Only 21 percent of the parents believed that their chil-dren had been clearly profitable, with returns outweighing costs. How-ever, 28 percent said that this had been the case with their sons, in contrast to only 5 percent reporting this of daughters. Furthermore, in spite of a strong, largely economically based, and growing determi-nation in the community to educate children, only one-third of the old parents reported that they had derived greater net gains from sons who went to school than from those who did not. The fraction reporting this for daughters was much lower still, but we did not ask about indirect gains through better marriages.

There were caste and related occupational differences. The Muslim merchants and the Jain and Brahmin landlords believed that there had been economic returns—possibly to the whole family—from the education of sons, but the Vokkaligas and Harijans, predominantly farmers and agricultural laborers respectively, were much more ambivalent. Most Harijans felt that economic loss followed the education of daughters, largely because either they would be more reluctant to spend all their time doing *coolie* labor or prospective parents-in-law would be deterred by the suspicion that this might be so.

Finally, we tested the firmness with which they held to this assessment of lifetime returns (inevitably mixed inextricably with the need for children toward the end of life). When asked what family size would have produced the maximum economic benefit for them compared with the one they actually raised, 11 percent said more children, 41 percent the same number, and 27 percent fewer, whereas 21 percent failed to reply directly but answered that now couples would receive greater economic benefits by having fewer children. Most of those who replied "more children" had experienced lower than average fertility, especially with regard to sons, through subfecundity, early widowhood, or imbalance of sex ratios in their births. It is clear that most feel that large families in the past, as evidenced in their own histories, were no economic disadvantage but that the prospects now facing young couples probably do discourage unrestricted fertility, at least on economic grounds. There were marked differences by caste and these were clearly occupationally based. Only 22 percent of Harijans and service castes believed that economic benefits would flow from smaller families either in the past or in the present, whereas the figure for the combined categories was 42 percent for Vokkaligas in contrast to 57 percent for Brahmins or Jains. Indeed, one-third of all Harijans believed that families would economically benefit from increasing their number of children.

Conclusion

India—at least, rural south India—has little in the way of a crisis arising from aging. The proportion of old people is still far lower than it is in countries where fertility is low or began to decline earlier. Indeed, the proportion over 65 years has probably not risen greatly in this century. The stem family system has proved remarkably capable of caring for the great majority of the old. Furthermore, given that it has traditionally existed by producing more nuclear families than stem families, it could remain viable as a method for housing the old for decades to come in spite of sustained fertility decline. The system would be jeopardized by out-migration only where it occurred on a massive scale. The real threat, although not much in evidence as yet in the study area, is not from demographic change but from social change. There is a fear felt by many mothers-in-law that rising levels of education among daughters-in-law may lead to such strains that there is a move toward separate residence for young couples from the time of marriage or shortly after.

There are some distressed old people, but their number is small. They are mostly women, nearly all widowed, and distinguished by having no surviving sons. Most had fewer sons than average because of subfecundity or early widowhood. The age gap between these women and their husbands was on average well above even the large gap (around ten years for this age group) usually found in Karnataka (see chap. 4). It was this age gap that made them more prone to widowhood. Men are rarely affected in this way because even widowers usually control more resources. More important, widows are discouraged from remarriage, whereas there is no discouragement for widowers and those who find themselves in economic or social difficulties are the most likely to seek remarriage.[2] Some communities are more supportive and less likely to produce destitute old women. This was true in the study area particularly of the Brahmins, Jains, and Muslim merchants in the largest villages. They were all relatively prosperous and characterized by marked group solidarity. The Brahmins were more inclined to live in large joint-stem families which could incorporate additional women and where there was often an assumption that female relatives had a right to a place. Among Harijans, one mitigating circumstance was the higher level of widow remarriage, but this option was most open to those widowed early in marriage.

Declining fertility certainly raises the possibility of more marriages without surviving sons and hence of possible destitution. There are two demographic factors working in the opposite direction which may do something to mitigate this effect. First, declining mortality—although only slowly declining at present—will do something to ensure that an increasing proportion of children survive until their

2. Widow remarriage appears to be on the increase and one-third of the widows in India may now remarry; cf. P. N. Mari Bhat and Ramesh Kanbargi, "A Preliminary Note on Levels, Trends and Differentials in Widow and Widower Remarriage in India in the Twentieth Century" (Bangalore: Population Research Centre, Institute for Social and Economic Change, 1981), mimeograph; the proportion is around 40 percent in the study area.

parents' old age. Second, there has been some narrowing of the age gap between spouses. This change, together with declining mortality and more social acceptance of widow remarriage, should significantly reduce the number of widows in the community.

Chapter Nine

Periodic High Risk as a Cause of Fertility Decline in a Changing Rural Environment: Survival Strategies in the 1980– 1983 South Indian Drought

In the attempt to explain persistent high fertility in much of the Third World, attention has been drawn both to current returns from child labor and to the mitigation or avoidance of future risks. The latter can be subdivided into meeting emergencies while the parental generation is still of working age and providing for old age or even safeguarding the transmission of family property on parental death. The problems of old age have recently received most attention and they may well be of paramount importance in many societies.[1]

Yet, in our research program in rural south India, the reasons given for demographic behavior have more frequently emphasized the

---

1. See Jeffrey B. Nugent, "The Old-Age Security Motive for Fertility," *Population and Development Review* 11, no. 1 (1985):75–97. On the transmission of property, see Mead Cain, "The Household Life Cycle and Economic Mobility in Rural Bangladesh," *Population and Development Review* 4, no. 3 (1978):421–38.

need to plan strategies to meet periodic crisis than to ensure old-age support (see chap. 2). Nevertheless, one should not underemphasize the latter merely because the problem is predictable and the solutions understood. In the study area, for the great majority of the aged, the support system still worked well (see chap. 8). In contrast, in our investigations of marriage, fertility control, and education, we repeatedly discovered that a fundamental consideration with regard to parental decisions in these areas was to strengthen the ability of the family to withstand periodic crises (see chaps. 3, 4. and 7). By far the most important type of crisis in this dry, drought-prone area was recurrent famines resulting from crop failure during one year or a succession of years with abnormally low rainfall.

There is no other way of studying the efficiency of such defenses except during drought-induced famine. Such a study has value not only for testing the success of the traditional strategies in mitigating disaster but in examining why new strategies—made possible by changing occupational and educational opportunities—were being increasingly employed. Indeed, we already had some evidence that these social and economic changes might completely reverse the strategies for obtaining the same end and that, far from reinforcing the supports for high fertility, they might undermine those supports.

The examination of defensive measures taken during drought provides not only the opportunity to test the soundness of demographic and other strategies adopted earlier but to identify the supplementary behavioral changes taking place in the course of the crises and the demographic sequelae of the measures employed.

Mead Cain compared risk and fertility in India and Bangladesh in a paper published in 1981.[2] The Indian data were from three villages in the Maharashtra-Andhra Pradesh border country, and attention was paid to retrospective information on the experience of the 1970–73 drought, especially during its climactic final year. Cain categorized the various possible sources of crisis support in the absence of institutional forms of insurance and well-functioning capital markets. He also raised the question of the impact of household composition, especially as determined by the life cycle. This question was first addressed by A. V. Chayanov in terms of the Russian peasantry and has since been investigated in the case of hunting and gathering and shifting cultivation societies by Marshall Sahlins.[3] Recently, Susan Green-

2. Mead Cain, "Risk and Insurance: Perspectives on Fertility and Agrarian Change in India and Bangladesh," *Population and Development Review* 7, no. 3 (1981):435–74.

3. A. V. Chayanov, "Peasant Farm Organization" (originally published in

halgh has analyzed the situation among families in a rapidly developing Asian economy, Taiwan, and has concluded that even there the life-cycle stage is an important determinant of relative economic well-being.[4]

Cain decided that risk insurance was more effective in rural India than in Bangladesh, as judged particularly by distress land sales, and also that the childless and those with only very young children did not suffer greater privations than others during the Indian drought. He concluded that high fertility was probably not the most rewarding strategy in the Indian situation because of the life-cycle pressure when most of the children were young and because the investment in future sons for the defense of the family property was not a critical consideration in the relatively secure conditions of the Indian countryside.

Jodha had argued in 1978 that periodic drought crises and the resulting sale of assets, especially farm animals, together with subsequent slow restocking rates, meant that agriculture in India is usually undercapitalized and that farmers are reluctant at all times to invest too much in their farms.[5]

There was, then, a need to explore the whole matter further during a crisis. Was Cain correct in identifying two aspects of the family, life-cycle problems and the declining need for physical protection, as sufficient discouragement to very high fertility? Was the only effect of increasing risk insurance a reduction in the optimum family size or did it play a more complex and dynamic role in promoting fertility reduction? Were the undercapitalized farms slowing down fertility decline since such decline was likely to be most rapid when economic development was fastest? How did their findings fit in with ours that one of the major concerns of the rural population was its deep suspicion of the periodic nature of rural incomes and that the commonest reaction was not to improve farming or storage so as to attempt to make returns

Moscow, 1925), in *The Theory of Peasant Economy*, ed. Daniel Thorner, Basile Kerblay, and R. E. F. Smith (Homewood, Ill.: Richard D. Irwin, 1966), 29–269; Marshall Sahlins, "The Intensity of Domestic Production in Primitive Societies: Social Inflections of the Chayanov Slope," in *Studies in Economic Anthropology*, ed. George Dalton (Washington, D.C.: American Anthropological Association, 1971), 30–51; Marshall Sahlins, *Stone Age Economics* (Chicago: Aldine Publishing Co., 1972).

4. Susan Greenhalgh, "Is Inequality Demographically Induced? The Family Cycle and the Distribution of Income in Taiwan, 1954–1978," Center for Policy Studies, Working Paper no. 103 (New York: Population Council, 1983).

5. N. S. Jodha, "Effectiveness of Farmers' Adjustments to Risk," *Economic and Political Weekly* 13, no. 25 (June 24, 1978):A-38–A-48; see also N. S. Jodha, "Famine and Famine Policies: Some Empirical Evidence," *Economic and Political Weekly* 10 (October 11, 1975):1609–23.

more constant but to invest effort and money in securing the best marriages for daughters, preferably into nonfarming families (see chap. 4)?

We found ourselves in a situation where we could test some of these conclusions and explore risk mitigation further in an Indian rural locality 400 miles to the south of the villages on which Cain reported. In our study area of nine villages in Karnataka, each monsoon was progressively poorer from 1980, culminating in an almost complete failure of the 1982 rains, which should have occurred in the second half of the year. As a result, most farmers harvested no crops at all at the end of 1982 or during most of 1983, and crisis conditions had been reached by mid-1983, when the special study reported here was undertaken. Adequate rains did come in late 1983 but did not affect the food supply before the November harvest of that year began.

Increasingly, farming households are seeking to insulate themselves from the seasonality of the agricultural cycle and its proneness to periodic disaster. Three-fifths of all families now have at least one member working outside the area. In fact, the effort to achieve this situation lies at the heart of the family educational and demographic strategies (see chap. 10).

The 1983 Drought Study

The 1983 study was carried out at the appropriate time to detect support mechanisms under maximum strain. After two dry years had reduced food stock and savings, if any, from crop sales and *coolie* employment,[6] the monsoonal rains, which should have begun in June 1982, had been an almost complete failure. The farmers continued to postpone the planting of the staple *ragi* crop, hoping until it was too late that adequate rains would begin, and ultimately very few planted at all. The state government ruled that the water level in the only big tank, which is near the largest village, was dangerously low, and accordingly the normal annual release of water in December to allow rice to be grown on the downstream irrigated land did not take place. Because this low-lying irrigable land retains some moisture from the previous year and receives some seepage through the tank wall, some of the landlords who own the area successfully planted a substitute *ragi* crop there. The whole district was seized by a crisis outlook, and the outsider was repeatedly assured that times had never been as bad.

The study was carried out in June and July 1983, while it was still

---

6. Laboring, usually agricultural labor (the term is used in south India to mean both the work and, more frequently, the wage earned for it).

too early to be certain that the rains would be adequate to end the drought and five months before any relief could be expected from the *ragi* harvest even if the rains were to continue. The work consisted of both a detailed survey and in-depth discussions with families previously well known from the continuing study. The survey aimed at sampling 50 percent of households in each village, but, because of dislocations and movements arising from the crises, as well as our focus on households that we had previously known and for which we had continuing information, full data are available and are reported here for only 45 percent of households or 387, of which 194 were in the large village and 193 in the eight smaller villages.[7]

During the six months preceding the survey, 21 percent of households had secured incomes solely from nonfarming activities (36 percent in the large village and 6 percent in the smaller villages), whereas 32 percent had no other source of income apart from their own land (17 percent in the large village and 48 percent in the smaller villages). These figures exclude loans and crisis help from relatives, which are examined below. The much greater resistance of this remote rural community to drought, as the old repeatedly told us, than had been the case 40 or 50 years ago, was based more than any other factor on this diversification of income. Such diversification is increasingly possible because of the growth of the economy and the accompanying development of a monetized exchange system, with subsistence production playing an ever smaller role. In rural India this process has been abetted by governments since Independence, progressively increasing the bureaucracy and services in rural areas. Thus, even during the downturn in the local economy during the crisis, one-fifth of families were employed outside agriculture, and a further 47 percent had some employment outside their own land—36 percent if *coolie* labor on others' land is excluded. If this nonfarming and nonagricultural *coolie* labor is analyzed, it is found that 44 percent is in commerce (both the tiny shops, which are appearing in the villages, and the trading of products from or to different places), 24 percent in jobs that require no education (road laboring, stone quarrying, *beedi* manufacture, traditional crafts), 18 percent in positions for which education is required (bank clerk, hospital orderly), and 14 percent in positions where employers would probably give preference to the educated (factory hands, where literacy is often an advantage). The farming population

7. The distribution of most characteristics varies very little from that of the total population. The distribution of caste by families (differing slightly from the individual data quoted earlier) was as follows: Muslims, 18 percent; Brahmins, 4 percent; Jains, 3 percent; Lingayats, 7 percent; Vokkaligas, 34 percent; Harijans, 10 percent; backward castes, 12 percent; service castes, 9 percent.

is extremely conscious of the need to secure this diversification, and it is the major reason for the increasing number of children being enrolled in school (see chaps. 7, 10).

In turn, the costs of keeping children at school explain the largest demand for family-planning services (see chaps. 2, 3). The need for this education does not emerge forcefully from the figures quoted above for off-farm employment for at least three reasons. First, some of the employment sought for the educated involves migration to Bangalore and elsewhere. Second, some of the parental ambition is sheer optimism that vastly exaggerates the chance of securing a government position. Third, when aiming at local employment, some parental decisions are shrewder than may appear from the gross figures above because many jobs are created and filled by older, powerful, illiterate persons, whereas the young are competing for only a fraction of the employment market where, in a greater proportion, education is an advantage in securing the position. What is clear is that the diminishing size of landholdings alone is no measure of increasing risk during famines; in fact, the old believe that in the past, moderately larger farms provided little extra security once all the crops failed.

To provide a baseline for the study of the impact of the drought, we assisted the householders to assess the predrought food situation: 72 percent obtained at least some of their food from land they owned or leased, and a further 9 percent were paid part of their *coolie* wages in food. Of those with land, one-quarter normally met all their needs for staple foods (grain, pulses, milk, and meat, if eaten) and one-half met two-thirds or more. In a normal June/July, half the farmers would have in store at least 600 kilograms (1,350 pounds) of grain and pulses (calculated on the basis of 60-kilogram bags). Of those farmers, who, at this time in a normal year, would still have food in store, nearly half had completely exhausted their stocks in 1983 and only one in 25 families had sufficient food stored to last at their usual level of consumption until the next harvest.

The Impact of the Drought on Life and Welfare

The single most important reason for investigating the impact of the drought and the mechanisms that reduced the risk to life was our knowledge that even disaster of this kind resulted in only some of the demographic reactions that had been the normal experience in the past. Mortality did not rise but remained at a level corresponding to an expectation of life at birth around 50 years and an infant mortality rate probably below 120 per thousand live births (see chap. 6). On the other hand, few marriages took place, and we anticipate that the 1984 birthrate will be considerably lower than the 32 per thousand recorded before the drought.

In spite of the absence of a Malthusian impact from the drought, every respondent agreed that it was a period of acute community crisis, although 7 percent of households, mostly salaried professionals and larger businessmen selling essential commodities or those with prices that rose during drought, reported that their way of life was little affected.

Among the farmers, almost three-quarters reported that they would harvest no crop at all, and not a single one claimed that there would not be a major decline in his production. One striking aspect of the drought was the visible change from largely robust cattle and other animals, at least by Indian standards, to much thinner beasts. Only 70 percent of those with land had any animals (although the remainder were mostly those with very small plots), and, of these, all reported problems: over one-third, mostly the richer farmers, were actually buying grass or other fodder, while nearly all reported great trouble in pasturing animals or finding grass to cut for their feed. Only 2 percent reported that animals had died and 1 percent that some were probably already beyond recovery, although a further 7 percent said that they had sold their stock to prevent this situation.

Nearly three-fifths of all farmers said that they were working less than usual, the remainder reporting that they were keeping to normal schedules either because of the search for animal fodder (although this was largely done by children, some of whom were working unprecedentedly long hours cutting and fetching grass from distant hills or bush country for cattle or even tree leaves for goats and sheep) or because of utilizing the period for additional manuring and field preparation beyond what was normally possible. The latter was partly an insurance that, if the rains were good, there would an above-average harvest to replenish food stocks. Among those families of Harijans, poorer Vokkaligas, and others accustomed to working only by selling their own labor, nearly all reported a substantial reduction in their total employment, whereas 12 percent reported no employment for family members and 8 percent that this would have been the situation but for government relief work.

There was a surprising acceptance of the inevitability of such bad times and less bitterness than might have been expected. Perhaps the major reason for this was the explanation for the cause of the crisis. Of all households, 14 percent explained the drought tautologically as the lack of rain (as people in any society might); 32 percent said that they did not know or that it was not proper for people like themselves to venture an opinion on such cosmic events; 43 percent were convinced that the gods were chastising the population,[8] 12 percent proffered a scientific or naturalistic explanation. The religious explanations rarely took the form of a lack of religious observations, but nearly all asserted that the gods disapproved of changes in behavior. Those changes cited were the move toward individualism, selfishness, corruption, and other aspects of the transition from an older form of communal life based on family authority, a firm social structure, and subsistence farming—in fact, the move toward a capitalistic society and market economy, which we suggest was the main reason that the impact of the drought was mitigated. A few attested that the offending behavior was family planning or sterilization.

The scientific explanation was dominated by the belief that persistent low rainfall was an outcome of the reduction in tree cover, an interpretation of a widely promulgated government informational program and a message taught in almost every school. It was frequently stressed that rain continued to fall on the *malnad* (the wet Western Ghats) because the tree cover remained there. The religious explanation was given by half of all illiterates, declining with increased schooling and reaching zero among those with tertiary education. Education dominated religious or caste determination; only one-eighth of Brahmins or Jains provided such answers, compared with nearly half of the Harijan or peasant castes. The religious response was higher than could have been predicted from educational levels only among the Muslims, who are tending more than Hindus to resist secularization, and the service or artisan castes, such as washermen, barbers, or blacksmiths, whose duties also embrace religious ritual roles as among the first two castes, or who need divine help in their activities as among the last. The provision of a religious explanation by a family did not mean a lack of effort to ensure a better support system in a future drought.

Although drought is identified with water shortage, this was true for most people in this drought only with regard to the irrigation of crops. In recent years, the Karnataka government has extended the provision of tube wells to most villages, and, even though some are usually in disrepair, these plus other wells and ponds meant that nine-tenths of all households experienced no greater difficulty than usual in securing sufficient supplies for domestic use. Where it had to be sought

8. See also John C. Caldwell, "The Sahelian Drought and Its Demographic Implications," Occasional Paper no. 8 (Washington, D.C.: Overseas Liaison Committee, December 1975).

from an unusually distant source, the burden fell mostly on women and girls: entirely on females in four-fifths of the households, on males in one-tenth, and with at least some male help in another tenth. However, clothes and house floors became dirtier in some villages.

The true measure of the drought was hunger. In 35 percent of households (as assessed by families and checked as far as possible by the study team), there was by mid-1983 real hunger and the proportion was rising. It was general knowledge that the worst affected were those who had no income outside farming, largely the landless agricultural laborers or the smaller farmers, especially those where no member worked in a nonagricultural job or no son was so employed elsewhere. Thus, the hungry constituted 30 percent of the population of the large village but 40 percent of those of the smaller hamlets almost entirely devoted to farming. Among the hungry there were no large landlords, only 20 percent of those engaged in commerce (even with miserably small stores), 40 percent of small farmers, 60 percent of agricultural laborers, and 44 percent of illiterates (compared with 33 percent who had been to primary school and 23 percent of those with secondary schooling). There were some thought-provoking findings in the demographic sphere. There was no trend in hunger by household size or by total number of children born or surviving. However, the proportion of hungry households did increase with the number of young children (under age 12) in the household at the time: from 31 percent with no children or where all were older, to 33 percent with one to three dependent children and 39 percent with four or more. These differences were not the product of different parental characteristics, there being little in the way of differentials in fertility or family-planning practice (see chap. 10). The Indian drought provides support for Chayanov's analysis of the impact of the life cycle; families tend to be economically relatively deprived when they have a disproportionate number of young children in the household, but to improve their position as the children grow older. However, there was no difference in the situation of families practicing family planning (sterilization in almost 90 percent of cases) and those not doing so—a situation pointed out by a significant number of those sterilized.

Only 8 percent of families believed that the hunger was the cause of serious illness in their households, and this is in keeping with the mortality evidence. Most of what was reported was consonant with famine symptoms although also found readily enough in normal times: stomach pains, diarrhea, fever, and some intensification of anemia in three-quarters of all cases. The balance largely consisted of pain and swelling in the joints, put down by most sufferers to eating coarser grains, usually sorghum. When inquiries were made from male household heads as to who bore the greatest brunt of the food shortage, 43 percent repeated that all shared equally in the cutbacks; 35 percent that adults had taken the greater part of the ordeal on themselves (although none said "men"); and 22 percent that it was mostly borne by women, children, and the old. The investigators reported that women appeared to suffer to a considerably greater extent than these reports suggested, partly because, as they ate last, no one actually knew what they ate. Many of them felt that the family fortunes during the crisis depended on the adult men retaining their strength (see chap. 6). A truer picture of the situation might be provided by a breakdown of those afflicted by sickness attributed to insufficient food: 60 percent of families reporting such illness listed only women, children, and the old; 23 percent only adults; and 17 percent a broad distribution by age and sex.

A special investigation was made of the 15 old people in the sample who were either living alone or as a couple. There were five couples and five single-person households, the latter being two males and three females. These three women were all widows, two of whom were Harijans. Except for the widows, these residential arrangements were largely with the agreement of those involved, and relatives living close by provided adequate support systems. Two of the five couples and the single male still owned land. Only the two Harijan widows reported being hungry (i.e., 20 percent of households or well below the community average), and neither of them associated this with any increase in ill health.

The Avoidance of Disaster

How, then was wholesale disaster averted in a largely dry-farming rural area experiencing a series of dry years culminating in the almost complete failure of the harvest? Why were the majority of families not even really hungry, and why was there no significant rise in mortality even among those who were? We explored the latter in depth with the 365 of the 387 households who were cooperative and who were prepared to be analytical. The major strategies (including multiple responses) are given in table 9.1. That table does not include a numerical response for eating less than usual because this was universal, dictated by both care and rising prices. Equally important, the majority of households usually get some money or other help from family members working elsewhere; most felt that this assistance increased during the drought, sometimes in response to frantic appeals for help, but few felt they could exactly distinguish the situation from other years and we were far from satisfied about the accuracy of attempts to do so.

Table 9.1. Chief Disaster-Avoidance Strategies in 1983 Drought (% of households)

General type	Specific action	All villages (N = 365)	Large village (N = 182)	Small villages (N = 183)
Reducing consumption	Eating less food: all levels	Nearly all	Nearly all	Nearly all
	Eating less food: to point of hunger	35	31	40
	Changing type of food eaten	9	5	13
	Spending less on festivals	18	18	18
	Spending less on clothing	15	11	18
	Postponing marriages	7	6	8
	Spending less on entertaining and visiting	3	3	3
	Removing children from school	1	0	2
Selling possessions	Animals	6	1	10
	Valuables	2	3	1
	Land	1	2	1
Employment	Changing rural employment	3	3	3
	Changing to nonrural employment	3	4	2
	Working on natural resources	1	1	0
	Some family members migrating	2	1	3
Exchange transactions	Securing loans	13	9	16
	Food from members of their community	1	2	0

206

The important point in interpreting the table is that these are the major strategies. This can be understood when it is realized that few households indeed made no change at all in the type of food that they were eating, but only 9 percent regarded this as making a major contribution to their survival. Similarly, over twice the proportion shown believed that they would have arranged at least one more marriage but for the drought, but half this number were not completely sure or regarded such delay as not being particularly serious. Half the families secured a loan of some type, but most families regarded such action as marginal compared with the belt-tightening that had to take place.

The important point is that most families still regard their ability to weather droughts as being based on savage cutbacks to their living standards, dominated by reducing food to the minimum. The rich families moved from three to two meals a day, and many ordinary families from two to one. The rich gave up most milk and ghee (clarified butter) and ate more *ragi* and less rice. The poor moved increasingly from *ragi* to *jowar* (normally animal food) and attributed a good deal of physical distress to this change. Most of the *jowar* being eaten was not the animal food but white *jowar*, which was being brought into the district for sale through the fair price stores run by the *panchayat* or local council. By mid-1983 almost half of all households were eating some *jowar*. The nonvegetarians no longer had meat once a week but once every several months (although Harijans may have underreported eating dead animals).

The next largest saving, which filled many with deep guilt, was that on festivals, clothing, and entertainment and visiting. These categories cannot really be separated because much entertaining and visiting parallels religious festivals, new clothes are bought if festivals are to be celebrated, and those in rags are reluctant to attend. Even the postponement of marriage is largely similar to the failure to observe religious festivals because this too was done so as to stint on entertainment and clothing.

The sale of valuables, mostly jewelry, or land is a desperate measure. Only 3 percent of landowning households sold any land at all, and the proportion was higher in the large village, where the blocks sold were not regarded as ancestral possessions. In no cases was the land sold to relatives because, although this was the preferred sale, relatives were usually of much the same socioeconomic status and in equal difficulties. Animals were another question, not because there was much less anguish with regard to their sale, but because the cost of fodder was beginning to prove prohibitive or because there was a fear that the animals would die. One-quarter of all families with animals sold at least some, and while land was sold almost without exception to fellow villagers, most animals sold went outside the village and even the district.

Employment changes were complex. Small farmers who rarely worked for anyone but themselves took on *coolie* labor when they could find it, usually with neighboring landlords but sometimes with government relief schemes. Sometimes they displaced agricultural laborers who sought nonagricultural employment, such as on road construction, in increasing numbers. Some farmers established small shops, and these grew in number throughout most of the drought period, although in the later stages their numbers began to fall as money available for purchases declined significantly. Heads of households, or adult sons, increasingly looked for employment outside the district.

Demographic and Social Aspects of the Drought

The drought did little to change trends in either mortality or acceptance of family planning, the first stable, and the latter gradually rising from the low point following the end of the 1975–77 Emergency (see chap. 3). Some of the rise in sterilizations after 1980 can be attributed to the greater importance of the monetary "incentives" in hard times. It did, however, have a dramatic impact on marriages, and this will doubtless be reflected in a more subdued fashion in the birthrate. Because many anticipated marriages fail to take place when expected even in normal times (see chap. 4), it is impossible to calculate what proportion of marriages were postponed during 1983. Of all households, 15.5 percent claimed to have put off a marriage, and a reasonable estimate for the whole area might be that the marriage level was around one-quarter of what might otherwise have occurred.

Marriage postponement was not directly associated with poverty or the extent of suffering from the drought and hence was not a method of risk aversion equally open to all. It was greatest among those sections of society that paid the highest dowries and spent most lavishly on weddings—the landlord and peasant classes—reaching 20 percent among the Vokkaligas who canceled nearly all marriages (see chap. 4). It was little more than half that level among the Harijans and backward castes, many of whom do not as yet pay any dowry, and among the Muslims. In normal times, lavish marriages are related to landownership, and, during the drought, deferment rose regularly with the extent of land owned from around 10 percent among landless agricultural laborers to 15 percent among those with less than 4 acres of land, and to 30 percent among those with over 10 acres (slightly exaggerated because of increasing household size with land, although that increase is not steep in this area (see chap. 5). Some of the lower castes hastened their daughters' marriages to get them off their hands. For every family that said that raising the dowry was the main problem, two said that they could not afford the cost of the wedding celebrations.

The drought had no significant effect on accelerating or retarding household division, although there was a temptation to claim division in order to become eligible for separate bank loans. Nor was school attendance much affected, at least in the aggregate: a few had to leave school to be placed in bonded employment to places like hotels (small businesses selling drinks of tea and coffee and sometimes food), but others stayed on because there was little demand for their labor.

The Economic Impact

The self-assessment of the impact of the drought on the family is necessarily affected by conventional living standards, but this has definite advantages when estimating felt needs, and the assessments seemed in most cases to be accurate. These assessments are presented in table 9.2.

Those families providing a range of self-assessments from "managing reasonably well" to "not greatly affected" numbered 42 percent of the total. The major determinant of this response is clearly not usual living standard but the extent to which livelihoods are nonagricultural in origin. Thus, the large village did much better than the small farming hamlets. The peasant castes, many of whom owned considerable areas of land, felt almost as distressed as the agricultural laborers, and far more so than Muslim merchants or the artisan and service castes with their little businesses increasingly concentrated in the large village. In fact, the size of the farm made little difference until very large areas were achieved. The critical difference is found between rural families, whether farmers or agricultural laborers, with incomes solely from rural activities and those who have managed to diversify by having one or more family members working full- or part-time outside agriculture. In good times, there may be a net flow of assistance from farms to family members in the towns, especially in the form of food from the family land on which all family members have a claim. By mid-1982 the flow was solely an urban-rural one. The boom-bust cycle is far more accentuated in farming than even in the nonagricultural occupations of little rural villages that would seem to be so dependent on agricultural prosperity. The relative well-being of nonagricultural

Table 9.2. Percentage of Families Assessing Their Conditions as Result of Drought as Fair or Better than Fair, Mid–1983

Characteristic	%
Residence:	
All villages	42
Large village	55
Small villages	21
Caste:	
Brahmins and Jains	65
Muslims	60
Artisans	53
Peasant castes	33
Backward castes	30
Harijans	30
Occupation:	
Professional and managerial	78
Landowner	71
Merchant	61
Nonagricultural laborer	43
Farmer	30
Agricultural laborer	11
Source of income:	
Nonagricultural	58
Mixed agricultural and nonagricultural	45
Agricultural	27
Land acreage (farmers):	
≥ 10 acres	50
4–9.9 acres	32
2–3.9 acres	36
< 2 acres	37
No. of children in household:	
< 4	43
4–5	42
≥ 6	35
Family planning (wife of reproductive age):	
Practicing	51
Not practicing	35

laborers arises from the fact that a considerable part of the funding for their work is governmental and does not originate in the district; some of it took the form of higher allocations because of the drought. The number of children in the household does not appear to have any considerable impact until they are quite numerous. On the other hand, family-planning practice appears to help, although the major mechanism appeared to be the greater amount of assistance that the sterilized received from other relatives than did the nonsterilized. The major explanation appears to be a greater apprehension of child illness or death, arising from an acute awareness that dead children can no longer be replaced. This anxiety leads to a greater persistence in pressing relatives for assistance.

The Support System

Nearly half of all families had taken loans during the drought, and most felt that they had been a considerable factor in maintaining minimum living conditions. There was a small number who reported that they would have been forced to postpone a marriage but for the loan. Many of the loans from banks or cooperatives were sought on grounds that differed from their intended use (e.g., agricultural improvements instead of dowry). Table 9.3 presents an analysis of those who obtained one or more loans during the drought.

The securing of loans in times of crisis is a mixed measure: partly of need and partly of the ability to find a lender. This is well displayed in the distribution by caste, where there is a very clear inverted U-shaped curve with the fewest loans being to the least needy, the Brahmin and Jain landlords and the Muslim merchants, and to the neediest, the Harijan agricultural laborers. This does not appear so clearly by occupation because the large Vokkaliga peasant caste includes agricultural laborers as well as considerable farmers, and the former find it easier to obtain loans from the latter, because of reasons of community solidarity, than do Harijan laborers. Those with large numbers of dependent children may also find that lenders are more skeptical of their ability to repay (this differential is not lessened by controlling for other family characteristics). Below the landlord class, the size of holding makes no significant difference, but being dependent on it alone renders the need for a loan much more urgent.

The sources of loans (see table 9.4) throw considerable light on the changes in rural society and its economy. The government share in lending is rising, and, as a proportion of money loaned rather than the number of transactions, is close to one-third. Much of the loans extended through the cooperatives is in the form of credit for the purchase of fertilizer or other agricultural needs, but even this can be readily converted into cash by resale. The proscribed professional moneylender still exists, but the group defined broadly (including some kindly and not very rapacious employers) constitutes 28 percent of all lenders and accounts for another one-third of money lent. Relatives, somewhat surprisingly, made up only one-fifth of lenders, but they, together with other members of the same caste community, are a majority of those giving loans although providing only one-third of the

Table 9.3. Families Securing Loans during Drought

Characteristic	%
Residence:	
All villages	46
Large village	39
Small villages	53
Caste:	
Brahmins and Jains	31
Muslims	34
Artisans	47
Peasant castes	55
Backward castes	45
Harijans	35
Occupation:	
Professional and managerial	34
Landowner	14
Merchant	33
Nonagricultural laborer	43
Farmer	52
Agricultural laborer	50
Source of income:	
Nonagricultural	32
Mixed agricultural and nonagricultural	48
Agricultural	54
Land acreage (farmers):	
> 10 acres	50
4–9.9 acres	51
2–3.9 acres	57
< 2 acres	52
No. of children in household:	
< 4	48
4–5	48
> 6	43
Family planning (wife of reproductive age):	
Practicing	45
Not practicing	44

funds. This tripartite division in funding between government, private money lending of a traditional type, and funding influenced by social bonds means a certain diversity in the support system. Even in a district in crisis, two-thirds of the funds are still locally generated, and the government does not play as significant a role as politicians often suggest. It may play an even less significant part in warding off real disaster, as those groups securing the higher proportion of loans through the bank and the cooperative were the Brahmins, Jains, and Muslims, at 25 percent of the loans they secured, compared with the

Table 9.4. Sources of Loans during Drought

Source of Loan	%
Governmental (through bank or agricultural cooperative)	18
Professional moneylender	9
Less professional moneylenders:	
Landlord, employer, business associate	13
Other well-off persons	6
Relatives	20
Persons usually from same "community":	
Friends	22
Neighbors	12
Total	100

Harijans at 15 percent. It was the Harijans who continued above all to be the forced clients of the traditional moneylender at 31 percent of all loans. The peasant castes received a disproportionate number of loans from relatives and other members of the same community at 61 percent of all loans. Thus, those with a great deal of land or considerable businesses in the larger village, near the banks and the cooperative, which are run by people like themselves and often of the same caste, employ government money. Some of them undoubtedly employ it in order to make loans at higher interest rates; thus government may finance traditional moneylending as well as competing with it. The peasant farmers of the smaller villages assist each other, and many have more money to do so now that cash cropping has increased and many households have nonagricultural sources of supplementary income. The Harijan and backward caste agricultural laborers are increasingly dependent on moneylenders because a growing proportion no longer have the traditional family links with a single landlord, which involved reciprocal obligations including loans when in need. The median loan was Rs 2,000 ($250), but the distribution of loans by size was not concentrated, for the poor received small loans and the rich larger ones: 20 percent of loans were for Rs 200 ($25) or less, whereas 40 percent were for Rs 2,000 ($250) or more. One family claimed to have received a loan from government money specifically allocated for drought relief (although 5 percent had at least one family member on relief work that would not have existed without such funding).

Table 9.5 analyzes the assistance given by relatives beyond the undivided family. Thus, it does not include unmarried children, even if adult and living in distant places, or married sons in cases where the property has not yet been formally divided (see chap. 5). Those

Table 9.5. Analysis of Assistance Sought and Received from Relatives in Drought

Characteristic	%
Families who sought and received help from relatives, by caste ($N = 378$):	
All families	18
Jains and Brahmins	15
Muslims	7
Peasant Castes	18
Artisans	17
Backward castes	13
Harijans	8
Families receiving help, by relationship to male household head ($N = 71$).[a]	
Siblings	13
Sons	6
Wife's relatives	43
Married daughter and her husband's relatives	13
More distant relatives of husband	25
Location of relatives providing help ($N = 71$):	
Same village	11
Other rural area	35
Bangalore	33
Other urban area	21
Occupation of relatives providing help ($N = 71$):	
Landlord or farmer	49
Agricultural laborer	1
Nonagricultural employment where education essential	21
Nonagricultural employment where education an advantage	22
Nonagricultural employment where education little or no advantage	7
Type of assistance received ($N = 69$):	
Loan of money	84
Food	12
General help (food, money, clothing, etc.)	4

[a]In the case of female-headed households, relationship to previous husband.

excluded in this way are part of the family, and, at least in theory, have no right to withhold assistance that is under the control of the family head as a single budget.

Once again, the curve by caste (and economic status) is an inverted U-shape, although relatives among landlord families do provide each other with loans, partly as a cheaper form of financing. The analysis clearly brings out the importance of marriage networks as a central mechanism in the insurance system against disaster. It helps to explain why the economic standing of a spouse's family is so important and why Indian families spend so much effort and money on a daughter's marriage (see chap. 4). In south India there is a very real obligation to help a married daughter if she and her family are in distress, and the analysis in the table shows that this occurs on a considerable scale. A high dowry can ensure that the daughter is economically well placed; a low one may mean continuing subsequent assistance. This situation has been confirmed in an area about 65 miles from our study district, as described by A. Shariff.[9] In terms of assistance from relations, India is not a lineage system but one where affinal networks play a key role.

In a district where 70 percent of adult males work in agriculture, only 46 percent of help comes from such families. Indeed, agricultural laborers can provide almost no help to each other in times of crisis and this is their plight. The nonagricultural help comes mostly from the larger urban areas, and Bangalore dominates the picture. Furthermore, those relatives in urban areas who do give support tend to be those in jobs requiring educational qualifications. There is support here for the growing belief that education provides a route to economic safety.

Finally, we returned to our detailed study of whether older persons living alone either singly or in couples were particularly badly hit by the drought. Only one of the five couples reported themselves as being in a fairly bad way. In fact, in all cases, for reasons specific to their families, they had somewhat accidentally found themselves living alone although not far from relatives, and there was little feeling of abandonment. The situation was different with those who lived alone; four out of five came from laboring families, and, although none feared starvation, all four were in a poor state. They blamed the drought for reducing the number of laboring jobs and so almost extinguishing the demand for older workers.

Discussion

The examination of the situation in the study district during severe drought is not an exotic or specialized concern. It is at the heart of rural demographic strategies and demographic transition. It was a crisis, above all, of peasant farmers and agricultural laborers—some of those in nonagricultural employment were almost as unconcerned as

9. Abusaleh Shariff, "The Beginning of Fertility Decline in South India: A Micro-Study of a Cluster of Four South Indian Villages" (Ph.D. thesis, Australian National University, Canberra, 1984).

the population of Bangalore, where the newspaper paid little attention
to the drought. One finding dominated our conclusions about these
rural Indian families, even in better times: their chief, all-pervasive
worry was the instability of rural incomes, both their seasonality and
their longer-term cycles from relative plenty to widespread scarcity.
They discussed desired marriages largely in these terms, much pre-
ferring daughters' husbands to have urban jobs with guaranteed continuing incomes than to be farmers of even substantial size. For the
same reasons, they preferred some of the family to work off the farm,
at least part-time, and felt safer if a son had a job in Bangalore,
especially a permanent position with the government or in a bank,
necessarily requiring education.

These emerging demographic strategies that underlie the gradual
fertility decline can only be partly understood by fair-weather research. Their basic sanity is revealed only by prolonged crisis. They are
"emerging" because they can only be undertaken on the present scale
as a mixed farming/nonagricultural economy develops. That mixed
economy works in two ways, in terms both of having some family
income originating in agriculture and some outside it, and of having
close contacts with individuals and families working outside agriculture. Some of the local nonagricultural work is in the off-farm local
economic sector; much is in distant urban areas.

When the agricultural sector was larger, and town communities
were more self-contained and took in fewer rural migrants, and when
the villages had scarcely any schools to assist the migrant to secure a
town job, rural security had to be achieved through unchecked fertility
and carefully arranged marriages, by farmers scrimping to acquire
more land and control over more labor, and by agricultural laborers
maintaining strong social links with patrons even if the latter were
often mean or overbearing.

This situation has changed because of the diversification of the
economy. It is now often safer to have fewer but educated children and
to marry them to urban or rural nonagricultural families. This strategy
is not equally open to all, for most Harijan families do not have the
kind of background that will allow a child to continue to do well at
school, and teachers and fellow students often discriminate against
them.

The conflict between schooling and family size is a temporary one
in the life cycle. Any resident of the study district would probably
benefit greatly by having three or four sons with university or other
tertiary qualifications and an equal number of daughters married to
such persons. This is possible for some of the larger landlords. How-

ever, most families testify that there is a real struggle, which may not be won, to keep all children at school in a large family (see chap. 7). The drought produced evidence of a Chayanov effect by demonstrating the likelihood of greater distress in families with young children. The effect is similar in normal times if the dependency status of children is prolonged by schooling.

Our picture of risk aversion during drought is close to that in the studies analyzed by Jodha.[10] Diets, change, festivals are forgone, clothes are worn until they become rags, marriages are postponed, animals are sold, and help is sought from where it can be obtained and often through channels established decades earlier.

The emphasis, however, is changing more rapidly in Karnataka than in some areas of India, particularly in an area such as the one studied, which is only a five-hour bus journey from Bangalore. Few families feel safe if all their income is derived from agriculture, and the securing of some of the family's income from other sources is increasingly regarded as a prudent and even necessary measure. The move out of sole reliance on farming has been necessitated by the reduction in farm size with population growth, which has not only made some family labor redundant on the smaller holdings but has replaced agricultural laborers with family members on the larger ones. Nevertheless, labor has moved out of farming not only because of the duress of population pressure but because diversification is safer. Thus, ratios of population to available land are inadequate measures of either distress or insecurity.

Such diversification is still far from being a complete insurance against drought distress. Loans were secured by half of all families in 1983. They were needed by more, for the most ironic finding from the study was the existence of an inverted U-shape curve, whereby fewer loans are secured both by those who need them least and by those in most need but who are bad risks and who have relatives economically like themselves, unable to provide assistance. In the area of financial assistance, government is not yet dominant. In terms of the volume of money lent, there is an almost equal three-way split: government through banks and cooperatives; traditional moneylenders, employers, businessmen, and large farmers; and relatives, neighbors, and caste group members. The patron-client relationship has largely broken down as lifelong family agricultural laborers have become more of an agricultural proletariat selling their labor to those willing to buy it. Nevertheless, laborers working frequently for the same farmer are

10. Jodha (see n. 5).

more likely to borrow from him than from others, whereas borrowing from businessmen is likely to be from those with whom one has regular contact in transactions or employment. In these cases, repayment may be made by the subtraction of a fraction of wages or commodity prices. Government relief work or food allocations were not a major feature of the 1983 drought, although purchases through ration shops were stated by many to be important to their budgets. Larger-scale governmental relief would probably have come in 1984 if the drought had persisted. The help received from relatives is changing quite dramatically. Major support in the drought came from urban-based relatives or those in nonagricultural employment.

Yet this is not a stable situation, and the pressures toward further change are intensifying. One reason is rising educational levels: between the 1971 and 1981 censuses, the proportion literate among all persons in India increased by one-quarter (one-third for females) and for those 5–9 years of age by one-third.[11] In the study area, the rate of educational growth had been even faster. There is an almost desperate realization that it takes more and more education for children to maintain a constant chance of securing a town job or a government position. There is also a vivid realization that an ever-growing proportion of grandchildren will not find employment in agriculture but will have to seek jobs in the nonagricultural sector.

The findings of the study broadly agree with the diagnoses of both Cain and Jodha. Nevertheless, a growing demand for fertility control was related not only to increasing security but to problems arising from promoting this improvement. So much of the improved security depended on family involvement through occupational shift and the building of marriage networks to nonagricultural incomes that the schooling of children was becoming an ever more central family concern, with substantial resultant economic problems during their dependent years arising from having too many children or having them too close together. There is little sign in the study area of any competition being offered to these risk-aversion strategies by a greater capitalization of farming, for the very reason that Jodha distinguished, a belief—almost certainly correct—that the higher the aim, the greater the fall.

No claim is put forward that this is a universal pattern for Third World fertility decline. There may be other parts of India, perhaps in

11. *Census of India 1981, Series 1, India Part 2, Special: Report and Tables Based on 5 Per Cent Sample Data* (New Delhi: P. Padmanabha, Controller of Publications, 1984), 78.

irrigated districts, where investment in farming improvement may stabilize incomes. It is likely, however, that most parts of the country are similar to Karnataka, in that land-reform provisions are sufficiently threatening to rule out substantial and continuing land purchases as a favored economic strategy. To take one example, this pattern is not applicable to sub-Saharan Africa for at least two reasons. First, the costs of schooling are frequently not borne by the parents alone and the costs of the younger generation are sufficiently diffused among relatives in the older generation to ensure that a life-cycle financial crunch usually does not occur. Second, support comes mostly from within the lineage rather than from marriage alliances and from decisions of old men whose power is increased by the prolificness of their descendants.[12] In rural south India, risk aversion is still a major determinant of individual and family behavior. Demographic behavior has changed only because there are new strategies for reducing risk that were not previously available. The major reason for this new availability is economic change, especially in the form of the growth of nonagricultural employment. The government has played a considerable role in reducing rural risk through extending credit facilities, creating work-for-food programs and assisting with food supplies during famine, and maintaining a very considerable measure of law and order through the bureaucracy and the police. Cain's contrasts with rural Bangladesh may all well be valid. Nevertheless, if we keep the focus only on India, the government's major contribution to the new risk-aversion strategies and the related decline in fertility has been the provision of rural schooling, and, at least in the short term, of the family-planning program. The motive force, which explains the effort put into risk aversion and the changes that follow from that effort, is the periodic occurrence of major rural disaster. In south India, this is usually drought-induced famine.

12. See John C. Caldwell and Pat Caldwell, "Cultural Forces Tending to Sustain High Fertility in Tropical Africa," Technical Note no. 85–16 (Washington, D.C.: World Bank, Population, Health and Nutrition Department, 1985).

Chapter Ten

The Causes of
Demographic Change

The Social and Demographic Conditions of Stable High Fertility

Our earliest fairly firm data, obtained by concentrating on the histories of the very old, are for the 1930s (315 people in the study area claim to have reached 20 years of age by the end of that decade). Even 50 years ago there was not complete demographic stability. By the mid-1930s the expectation of life at birth in the state of Mysore was probably already 30 years,[1] and the elderly claim that even in rural areas there was some awareness that life was a little less capricious (although ahead, in the later war years, lay upswings of smallpox, cholera, and bubonic plague, the last appearing for the final time in the study area in 1947–48). The birthrate may have dropped a few points, perhaps from the upper 40s,[2] but, if this were so, it was related neither to increases in the age of female marriage nor to greater marital fertility control but solely to an extension of the average length of the interval between births arising from declining infant and child mortality and hence to a reduction of the number of periods of breast-feeding cut short by the death of the child.

1. Based on child-survival estimated from the Mysore State volumes of the 1931 and 1941 censuses of India.
2. See Kingsley Davis, *The Population of India and Pakistan* (Princeton: Princeton University Press, 1951), 69.

Marital fertility was traditionally controlled almost entirely by two mechanisms, each employed solely to reduce mortality, very largely in the sense of maximizing the child's chance of survival, although now there is also reference to the mother's health.[3] The basic institution was postnatal sexual abstinence. Originally its duration appears to have been at least two years when the child survived, but by the 1930s the practice was already being modified. Indeed, among women who married in the 1940s, only 15 percent of those in the smaller villages and 5 percent in the large village abstained for two or more years, although most did so for more than one year. Among women who have married in the last 20 years, abstention for longer than 18 months has almost disappeared in the large village and is around 20 percent in the smaller villages.[4] Indians, like members of many other societies,[5] believed that semen poisoned the milk, but a unique aspect, allowing for change, was the Indian belief that the poisoning was greatest in the first months after birth, thereafter decreasing until the impact ultimately became negligible. The other mechanism was prolonged lactation, which in the study area was traditionally continued until three, five, or seven (auspicious odd numbers) months into the next pregnancy. Even in the 1940s, only women who had no milk or were very sick failed to breast-feed for two years, and many did so for three to five years. Thus lactation was normally longer than abstinence and not directly related to it, and only became important in terms of preventing conception by suppressing ovulation as abstinence shortened. The link between weaning and the subsequent pregnancy began to break in the large village in the 1950s and in the smaller villages in the 1960s. Nevertheless, the majority of women in the small villages still wean after 24 months, although the average duration of lactation in the large village has now been reduced to 18 months.[6]

A major thrust of the research has been the attempt to ascertain whether there were other mechanisms for controlling marital fertility,

3. See the parallel change reported in P. Caldwell and J. C. Caldwell, "The Function of Child-Spacing in Traditional Societies and the Direction of Change," in *Child-Spacing in Tropical Africa: Traditions and Change*, ed. Hilary J. Page and Ron Lesthaeghe (London: Academic Press, 1981), 82–83.

4. The average length of abstention in middle-class Bangalore is almost six months for the first birth and somewhat shorter for subsequent births.

5. On Africa, see Caldwell and Caldwell, "Function of Child-Spacing," 79; on Europe, see J. L. Flandrin, *Families in Former Times: Kinship, Household and Sexuality* (Cambridge: Cambridge University Press, 1979), 206.

6. This is similar to the duration recorded in a poor area of Bangalore.

partly in order to determine whether there was any desire to do so. The evidence suggests strongly that there was no significant practice of contraception or abortion as a form of family planning before the arrival of the government family planning program in the early 1960s. In perhaps one village in every half dozen, there was an old woman who had knowledge of herbal abortifacients, usually acquired from her mother, or a male herbalist who included such knowledge as one of his specialties. Such abortifacients were usually administered orally, and, within living memory, the demand was small. More important, there is consensus that such abortifacients were not used to limit family size. They were employed to hide the proof of sexual relations that should never have taken place: those before marriage, and, more frequently quoted by Hindus, those that would have resulted in a birth within 12 months of marriage, thus indicating that sexual relations had taken place during the first three months of married life and before the ceremony called *sobana*.[7] In the past 15 or 20 years there seems to have been a significant upswing in the demand for indigenous abortion arising largely from two causes: a demand for birth spacing that the sterilization program cannot meet, and a desire to remove evidence of extramarital sexual relations in the case of marriages that have reached the stage of little or no sexual activity.

In the past, the restraints on fertility have been this delay in consummation after marriage, long postnatal sexual abstinence, and —earlier of less significance for its impact on fertility—very long lactation, rapidly declining levels of sexual activity after the first ten years of marriage, and discouragement of widow remarriage. Every one of these restraints was intended to benefit the health of the individual or the society, and no one, in the past or present, has related them to the control of reproduction. Nearly everyone in this rural society still believes that after a man is about 35 years of age (when on average his wife will be 28 years) he can no longer easily stand the weakening effect of the loss of much semen, and male good health after this age is often ascribed to moderation or abstinence in sexual activities. Widow remarriage is discouraged partly because of the conflicting claims of children from two marriages but mostly because of a belief that the marriage may be sustained into the next cycle of life (because polygyny, although not common, is permissible, this possibil-

---

7. *Sobana* is the ceremony that allows *prastha* or the consummation of the marriage to take place. In the study area the majority of recent Hindu marriages have still not been consummated before *sobana*, only 25 percent of couples having sexual relations within the first month, compared with 95 percent of Muslims within the first 24 hours.

ity is not so prohibitive of male remarriage). Nevertheless, perhaps one-third of widows do remarry.[8]

The fundamental institution in achieving demographic stability—although this was not its primary purpose—was the family, its relationships, and its economy. The family was patriarchal, although an older man might hand over the economic management of the family to a son, usually the eldest. The patriarch's wife had very considerable powers of management within the woman's sphere, particularly over daughters-in-law. More important, the husband or wife—even the weak, who kept unswervingly to the traditional role—could resist or pressure others who wished to be at all deviant. Partly because land often remained undivided until the patriarch was quite old, and partly because of methods of payment in kind (the *jajmani* system for services, bonded labor, and the payment of agricultural laborers in grain and servants in keep and in access to some land), monetary transactions were few and economic transactions retained a large element of social relations.[9]

Nevertheless, the large, pyramidal, joint-stem family was not typical. Such families, together with joint and polygynous ones, now make up only 8 percent of all families, and the situation appears to have been similar for at least the last 50 years.[10] The old need a younger couple with them to assume the major burden of the harder physical work, and they also prefer to have some grandchildren in the house. Nevertheless, one married son, together with his wife and children, can satisfy this need. Most older couples feel that a more complex family imposes on them the unnecessary burden of numbers, especially as manifested in disputes between sons or daughters-in-law, and strains the physical capacity of the house in providing sufficient living space. Thus the older couple, or surviving member of a couple, typically lives in a stem family, while half the population lives, as has long been the case, in nuclear families. This is important in terms of decision-making. In the stem family there is agreement that nearly all decisions are in the hands of the older generation, provided that they

8. P. N. Mari Bhat and Ramesh Kanbargi, "A Preliminary Note on Levels, Trends and Differentials in Widow and Widower Remarriage in India in the Twentieth Century" (Bangalore: Population Research Centre, Institute for Social and Economic change, 1981), mimeograph, 29ff.

9. In the large village, *jajmani* relationships and the bonded labor of children have largely disappeared, and adult bonded labor no longer exists in any of the villages.

10. See chap. 4 for a discussion of how marriage change has affected family structure.

wish to exercise that right. Partition occurs when a family splits into one or more nuclear families; this is a formal occasion marking a division of land and some related property,[11] of budgets and cooking arrangements, and the abdication of some of the powers of the older generation. Such abdication is far from absolute because canons of morality remain and any person, especially a relative and more particularly a parent, may intrude where there is a possibility of indecent or immoral behavior.

We have placed much stress on securing testimony on the economic impact of children upon parents now and in the past. There is consensus that 50 or even 30 years ago, no one worried or complained about the economic implications of a large family. There is nearly as strong agreement that the large families prospered most. The most common description is of children working hard for long hours each day from a young age and offering little protest; their scant needs rarely involved cash expenditures. A major purpose of this chapter is to discover how this situation has changed.

The Nature of Change

The south Indian economy, even in remote rural areas, has been changing for centuries, and inevitably society has changed too. However, the belief in the study area is that change occurred somewhat faster with World War II and accelerated enormously with Independence in 1947 and the greater impact of government and politics that followed. Nevertheless, it is clear that at least three significant demographic changes were already under way in the 1930s.

First, mortality was falling, and the impact of the great epidemics was declining (there was yet to be a final upswing in 1943–47). Population was perceptibly growing, although the greatest pressure on land division did not occur for another quarter of a century.

Second, child marriage was disappearing. In the rural district in which our study was undertaken, the proportion of married females aged 10–14 years has been falling throughout this century, from 25 percent around 1901 to 20 percent in 1921, and to 5 percent in 1951. One reason is a waning of the belief that a transgression against divine law had been perpetrated if a daughter reached menarche unexpect-

---

11. Sometimes the land is in fact worked in common for a longer period, and tools may be shared longer still; nowadays, there is sometimes a pretense of partition to escape the implementation of the land-reform regulations.

edly and in an unmarried state.[12] Another was an awareness, at least by the influential leadership, of the 1929 Sarda Act, forbidding girls to marry before 14 years, and an increasing tendency to regard early marriage as contrary to the aims of the independence movement. Finally, and most influential, was a growing concept of childhood, dependency, and immaturity (discussed at greater length below).

Third, an increasing number of young couples were shortening the postnatal period of sexual abstinence, not because they either violated the instructions of the husband's parents or were instructed to do so, but because the older generation was beginning to abdicate their decision-making role in this area (also discussed below at greater length and more generally).

It seems clear that these changes, and the more massive ones to follow, were based jointly on economic changes, and on the existence of alternative models toward which to channel social change. It is significant that our respondents repeatedly refer to the impact of an external model, and they refer neither to modernization nor to Westernization but to "English ways." They employ the expression when pointing out the potential for social change found in the cinema, education, or urban society. They regard these three institutions, plus the impact of politics and politicians, as being the main instruments of social change, and the mechanism as being a molding of the younger generation so as to differ from its parents.

There is also an awareness that these social changes have rested to a large extent on economic and political transformations. Much emphasis is placed on the ability of the young, especially young men, either to obtain jobs outside the family or to appear as if they might do so. The lure of Bangalore is quoted, as is the growing labor market there during the first decade of Independence and since. Bangalore has continued to expand more rapidly in the 1970s than any other large city in the country. Less emphasis is given, probably because separation and exposure to city life are not involved, to the rapid expansion of off-farm employment opportunities in the district itself. A good deal of emphasis is also placed on the growing monetary economy, its

12. See Francis Hamilton Buchanan, *A Journey from Madras through the Countries of Mysore, Canara and Malabar Performed under the Order of the Most Noble the Marquis Wellesley Governor General of India for the Express Purpose of Investigating the State of Agriculture, Arts and Commerce: Religion, Manners and Customs; the History Natural and Civil and Antiquities in the Dominions of the Rajah of Mysore and the Countries Acquired by the Honorable East India Company* (London: T. Cadell and W. Davies, 1807), 1:52, 259–60; and chap. 4, this volume.

ability to suffer from inflation, and the impact of inflation on previously accepted economic and social relationships. It is widely appre-
ciated that political goals and ideologies lie behind many of the
changes of the last third of a century: the expansion of schooling, so
that all children in the study area have fairly ready access, and all but
the two smallest villages have primary schools; land reform, which has
had some success in Karnataka, and an even deeper impact in making
most larger landholders feel insecure; and the increase in modern medical facilities, so that by 1982 the study area had a small hospital, two
government doctors, and four multipurpose health workers (as well as
a private doctor and a pharmacy), plus other bureaucrats including
veterinarians, engineers, and police.

These are the basic forces and they impinged much more strongly
from about 1950. In order to explain how they affected demographic
behavior we consider five themes: secularization, dependency, the
changing relations between generation, the increasing cost of children,
and monetization.

Among religions, Hinduism is unique in the extent to which the
structure of society and human behavior are regarded as the manifestation of divine law. The little tradition, which has predominated in
the villages, assumes that every community or individual problem is a
sign of transgression against divine order or natural balance. For
decades, forces that might be described as blends of Westernization,
modernization, and the great religious tradition have been removing
areas of behavior into the secular zone, where human beings may
make choices in accord with their needs and the urgings of political
and bureaucratic programs. Demographically this is important because this secularization has been invading such areas as the cause and
cure of illness, the age of female marriage, widow remarriage, the
duration of postnatal sexual abstinence and lactation, and the accept-
ability of fertility control. The last is also now regarded as a secular
matter by some Muslims.

Concepts of childhood, dependency, and immaturity have gained
great importance within only a few decades. The existence of facilities
for mass schooling has played a role (even among families that do not
normally send their children to school), but the numbers in the schools
are also explained by the spread of these concepts. A generation ago
families tended to prefer very young daughters-in-law who were not
old enough to have become wilful. Now, many are apprehensive of
their sons marrying girls who have not attained menarche, or who
have only just done so, on the grounds that they are too immature to
fill adequately such roles as wife, mother, or even daughter-in-law.

Nearly every family testifies to significant changes in the relations between the generations both in the community as a whole and in their own family histories. Even the examples given above of charges of immaturity also evidence such changes, for once young brides were judged very largely as daughters-in-law rather than as wives, and children were reared more by their grandmothers than by their mothers (provided only that the grandmothers were still alive). There are considerable areas of demographic decision-making that many of the older generation are abdicating in favor of their sons and daughters-in-law; the duration of postnatal sexual abstinence and lactation, the employment of contraception or sterilization, and the treatment to be employed when the grandchildren are sick. Clearly, such abdication is related not only to changes in the power structure of the family but also to the transfer of types of behavior from areas where moral considerations are of the utmost importance to areas of greater moral ambivalence. It is also related to growing confusion about desirable goals in some of these areas (as described below). This abdication of powers is largely one between the married generations, and does not yet apply to the unmarried young, not even with regard to their own marriages, although by the time sons reach their mid-twenties some parents now concede a limited right of veto over proposed wives. Even among the married, very few of the younger couples would undergo sterilization without seeking permission from the husband's parents. However, they are increasingly likely to receive the answer that the decision must be their own (unless the older generation feels there are too few children or sons). There is not a complete parallel here with the abdication from decision making with regard to postnatal sexual abstinence, because family planning is an area with a competing new secular morality and there is pressure from both the state and the elites (discussed below) to reduce interference with a couple's acceptance of services. The successful application of such pressure, in that it supports both the young and the female, in its turn changes the family power structure further.

Most respondents explain the changing power structure in both general and specific terms. Generally, they say that the times are changing, that there are new models, and that patriarchs cannot remain austere, all-powerful, and fearsome while being deserted by their peers. Specifically, they argue that the old order rested on a nearly enclosed agrarian system with nearly all sons following their fathers' occupations. After Independence—the date overwhelmingly quoted —the growth of towns and nonagricultural employment meant that sons could more easily leave (or that their fathers believed that they could). Thus, over the years, fathers have insisted on ever less sustained work, and have conceded more rights of consumption as the family became slowly more egalitarian and as the purchase of goods in a more monetized economy became increasingly frequent. As is discussed below, changing ideas of dependency and of the nature of illness meant that children's food cost more in times of scarcity and their treatment more when they were ill. With almost three-quarters of boys and over half of girls now having some schooling, children are costing more because of labor withdrawn, because of the direct and indirect costs (such as better clothing) imposed by schooling, and because of the demands for additional expenditure that the educated, with wider horizons, impose. In another way, the younger generation has become less economically worthwhile: as the age at female marriage climbed, the female adolescents in the house changed from subservient, hard-working daughters-in-law to daughters who clearly expected more from family largesse and were more capable of resisting some of the work pressure. They may now also require expensive dowries.

At first we were surprised at the emphasis that most households placed on inflation in dissolving the old order, but it became increasingly apparent that they meant both monetization and inflation. It is only as commodities can be bought that the pressure of demands for expenditure by different members of the family builds up, and that a conflict is seen to develop between such demands and alternative expenditures or saving. Under the *jajmani* system, many services, such as haircuts or the washing of clothes, once cost no more for all members of a large than for a small family, whereas now the system has all but vanished in the largest village and has often been restructured according to household size in the smaller villages. Most respondents just do not believe that children could have been particularly costly when the main target of extra demand was restricted to the family store of *ragi*.

There is near consensus in the study area that large families were economically worthwhile to the older generation 30 or 40 years ago and that the position is now much more ambiguous. Much of that ambiguity is felt to arise from the extra expense originating in schooling. Villagers also argue that the schooling of children is becoming ever less an optional response for parents. It is a virtue and a duty when one's peers are ever more likely to send their children to school and to keep them there. It is strongly advisable to educate those sons who are to seek nonfarming jobs, and it is a necessity for daughters if they are to obtain the urban husbands with good jobs increasingly regarded by parents as their ideal picture of the desired son-in-law. With the growth in town jobs, and an increasing apprehension of further land division and of the more vigorous implementation of land-reform legislation, farmers are increasingly inclined to think of family strategies in terms of retaining the land as the core of the family economy but of moving all surplus family labor into nonagricultural employment, where any gains could be regarded as unqualified additions to the economic base. Similarly, if girls are married to a husband with a good and secure job, they are unlikely to again become charges on the family, as is the case even for married daughters facing poverty or destitution. The planning of family fortunes in this fashion is almost inevitable as long as parents retain control of their children's marriages, and hence their economic future, and as long as land and other possessions are regarded as patrimony. Nevertheless, strategies of this type necessitate schooling and inevitably lead in the Indian situation to choices between an unlimited number of children with a lower level of schooling and a limited number with a higher level.[13]

Demographic Transitions

Family Structure
We had anticipated that marked declines in mortality, greatly enhanced chances of migration for the young, and transition in the relations between generations would have led to major changes in family structure. All evidence is that this has not been the case, at least as far as household composition is concerned.

The reason is the great flexibility of a system in which the usual residence of older parents is in a stem family, while all the married sons of each older couple, except the one with whom they are living, reside in nuclear families. As mortality falls, the proportion of nuclear families may rise; as a result of fertility decline the proportion may eventually fall. The important point is that this system is still intact. Of all persons over 50 years of age, less than 4 percent (mostly widows) live on their own, and another 8 percent live as intact couples without other relatives. Not all are in distress, and some live near other relatives. Nearly all these cases are explained by either sterility or the

13. The situation is different in tropical Africa, where sibling chains of assistance can be established so that each child educated makes it more likely that the next will be educated. See J. C. Caldwell, *Theory of Fertility Decline* (London: Academic Press, 1982), 43.

death of all children,[14] and not by the breakup of stem or joint-stem families to leave the parents on their own.

Despite the fact that half the population lives in nuclear families, only one couple in 11 failed to begin marriage with the husband's parents, and only one in eight lived for less than the first five years with them. More important, two-thirds of all births and over half the sterilization decisions take place while the couple are still living with the husband's parents. In these circumstances, the significant family changes that bear on decision making are not those of family structure but of changing relations between the generations. We found, as has been reported elsewhere in Karnataka,[15] that such changes have been substantial. The younger couples do not seem to wrest decision-making powers from the old during overt conflict, but rather the old increasingly retire from various arenas of decision making. The most common explanation given in the study area is that old fathers grow increasingly apprehensive that their married sons will secure work elsewhere if they feel too dominated or if their wives convince them of such domination.

Five percent of families are joint-stem and 1 percent are joint. It would be easy to conclude that they are survivals from an older system. The evidence seems clear, however, that these are the necessary products of a stable stem/nuclear family system. The former are the products of the marriage of another son in what was previously a stem family, an occurrence often followed by a considerable period of joint residence before one of the younger generation couples moves out; and the latter result from the death of a parent in one of these usually transitional joint-stem families, leading to a period when married brothers live together while planning the partition of the property.

Too much stress should not be placed on the difference between stem and nuclear family residence. Even in the latter case parents usually live close by, often in the same partitioned residence where the partition may be solely the concept of separate management rather than a visible structure. In any case, partitioned land usually results in neighboring residence, and, among those without land, specific caste residential areas in even the largest village mean that relatives inevitably live within a hundred meters of each other.

14. Note that this does not specify only the death of all sons. Those widows facing destitution in this situation usually managed to get some assistance from surviving daughters and their husbands.

15. G. H. Conklin, "Emerging Conjugal Role Patterns in a Joint Family System: Correlates of Social Change in Dharwar, India," *Journal of Marriage and the Family* 35, no. 4 (1973):742–48.

Mortality

In the study area at the beginning of the 1980s, the expectation of life at birth was about 50 years and the infant mortality rate around 115 per thousand, levels indicating mortality somewhat above estimates for the whole of the state of Karnataka but probably not its rural areas. Thirty years earlier the expectation of life at birth was probably no more than two-thirds as great, while infant mortality was almost certainly more than double.

The answer to the question of what has caused this change is far more complex than we had originally anticipated. The explanation does not lie in the decline of epidemic disease, which had taken place earlier: the last death from bubonic plague in the area occurred in 1948, and all cholera and smallpox deaths since 1950 appear to total only a very small fraction of all deaths. Malaria was seemingly eradicated but is now common again, although apparently causing few deaths even indirectly. Nevertheless, even the decline in malarial mortality is only a small part of the explanation.

A significant part of the explanation appears to be the slow but steady penetration of modern (allopathic) medicine. However, the constraints on this penetration seem to lie far more on the demand than on the supply side. The largest village has had a health unit with a doctor for half a century, although it became a hospital with both a male and a female doctor only in 1982. Patients from the smaller villages tend to save up their complaints and to seek medical service on the day of the weekly market in the large village.

Nevertheless, the total attendance at the unit is low compared with what one might anticipate from patient rates in Western countries, and was lower still in the past. Even when patients attend, they have often tried several preferred methods of treatment first, although this has become less common in recent decades. When given courses of treatment, many patients do not persist with the full treatment. The reason is neither competition with allopathic private practitioners, for there is only one with few patients, nor adherence to Ayurvedic treatment (traditional medicine drawing on the explanations and treatments given in sacred writings), for there is no Ayurvedic doctor within 30 kilometers, as probably has always been the case. Certainly, some—but not a major—part of the explanation is that medical treatment costs people, who have little to spare, both time and money, the latter in transport and accommodation costs as well as for medicines and sometimes payments to the doctor.

The major explanation is not one of overcoming fatalism or aversion to the unfamiliar. It is, in fact, a question of conflict between philosophies or theologies about the nature of well-being and the meaning of illness. Traditionally, illnesses have been classified according to cause, with cause dictating treatment. Some disorders, such as accidents, are just ill luck or caused by the stars. Fevers, colds, and influenza are instances of the disorders of imbalance, caused by taking too much hot food with insufficient cold food,[16] or by excessive sexual indulgence or other immoderate behavior. The cures are clearly a more balanced life, and modern doctors are often regarded as isolated from their own culture for not realizing that this is the case. Infectious diseases arise from the displeasure of the village goddess or regional disease goddesses (such as Marayama, the bringer of smallpox and chickenpox, who, like other deities, causes the damage by her physical presence in the village or inside the persons), cures being achieved by appeasing their wrath or leading them out and away by a range of stratagems. Skin diseases, which are common, are specifically the domain of the snake god. Leprosy, skin cancer, and tetanus are divine curses for breaking religious laws, such as transgressions against the rule of incest or caste commensality (or eating together) in this life or the last. There are also problems of demons, ghosts, and the evil eye.

The important point is that these are not peripheral beliefs but the age-old, central religious tradition of the village, somewhat reinterpreted over the centuries to cast them within the framework of the great traditions of Hinduism and Islam.[17] These beliefs are still held to a greater or lesser extent by most villagers, although not as exclusively as half a century ago. Therefore, the most common first steps against a wide range of disorders are the chanting of religious verses or *mantras* by priests or other practitioners, and the making of *yantras* (which can be used for prevention as well as cure), which have verses or the numbers of verses written on them, and the name of the person blown onto them, before being affixed around the neck. Priests can be visited in the appropriate temple, or sacrifices (of goats, chickens, or sheep) can be promised at the appropriate temple if the complaint is cured. Demons or the evil eye can be warded off by subterfuges such as placing a black spot on a child's forehead, and goddesses can be discouraged from entering houses by appropriate messages on the doors.

16. Examples of cold foods in the study area are milk, curds, and most greens, while meat, chilies, and spices are hot. The concept of hot and cold foods is found throughout India, but there are some differences in the foods that fall into each category.

17. That is, the religious beliefs set out in the major religious works and approximating more closely the beliefs held by the more educated and urban residents.

In this situation, it might seem surprising that allopathic medicine has made much headway. However, India is a plural society with regard to health, as in many other ways. No one is quite sure of the nature, and hence of the cause and cure, of any disorder, and so, in some kind of hierarchical order (depending on background, social position, and education), a series of treatments will be attempted. Over the last 40 years an ever larger proportion of the populace has included allopathic medicine in that sequence, and a growing number place it fairly high in the order of alternatives. The likelihood of doing so is greater among those with more schooling, those who have been employed by the government, those who have lived in towns, and among younger parents. The acceptance of Western medicine is very much an acceptance of a wider, even a global, society. In terms of securing quick, allopathic treatment, the direction of changes in family decision making is important, because our investigation of the first identification of illness among children showed that mothers were convinced that something was wrong much more often than their parents-in-law or husbands.

The penetration of modern medicine is, then, as much a matter of social change as of technology and delivery system. Unless the society is torn apart, it will take time for mortality to decline in response to the greater availability of health services; conversely, even when that availability ceases to expand, death rates may well continue to fall for many years.[18] Nevertheless, the acceptance of the new system is uneven. Families are often surprisingly lax about seeking treatment for their older members, partly because of a feeling that they are already leaving this life for the next and that any action might be an interference with the divine plan. However, the greatest cause of excess mortality is a similar reluctance to bring young children to the health service. When sickness occurs, a boy or girl under ten years of age is much less likely to appear for treatment than is a person in the prime of adulthood. The reason is a belief that young children have only just emerged from the world of spirits and demons and are still much more likely to be attacked by evil forces. This belief has two effects. First, in order to protect infants from the evil eye and other manifestations of jealousy, there is a deliberate appearance of casualness about antenatal care, the conditions of child birth, and subsequent child care. The problem is that appearance inevitably has a considerable impact on reality. Second, a considerable fraction of children are said to suffer from *balagraha* (Kannada for "a divine visitation upon a child"). This

18. A possible example is Ghana. See S. K. Jain, "Mortality in Ghana: Evidence from the Cape Coast Data," *Population Studies* 36, no. 2 (1982):271–89.

covers a range of nutritional and alimentary disorders: dehydration from prolonged diarrhea, kwashiorkor, and marasmus, and the extremely common liver complaints that are so widespread that the hard abdomen caused by cirrhosis[19] is frequently taken to be a universal symptom of this complex of childhood disease. Because *balagraha* is regarded as being so clearly outside man's province, only a fraction of all cases are brought for allopathic treatment, while *mantras* and *yantras* are employed more widely than for any other single complaint. It might be noted that snake bite, because of the reptile's association with both Siva and Vishnu, is never subject to purely human antidotes and no case has ever been brought to the health center.

Nonmedical forces have certainly also been involved in the reduction of mortality. For a very long time, much of the population has not been particularly well nourished. Nevertheless, the main impact of food shortages was felt either in the annual lean period before the *ragi* harvest or more severely during years of drought and famine, and deaths from starvation or, more commonly, other complaints abetted by malnutrition, arose during those periods or in their aftermath. Such times have in the not too distant past been regarded as inevitable (and also a divine punishment necessitating religious ceremonies by the whole community at the temple of the village goddess), and one suffered them just as one ate better at other times. The suffering was usually greatest among those whose needs were thought to be least or who were not so necessary to the survival of the family: women, children, and sometimes the old. This situation has been improved by increased government help during famines and by better communications and a greater commercial availability of food. Yet it is clear from the interviews that there have been important complementary changes in family attitudes toward the purchase and distribution of food. Among farming families and others paid in grain, there is still a reluctance among the very old to purchase grain during periods of shortage rather than to try to battle through, but the younger men have adjusted more to an increasingly monetized economy. Because of that adjustment and also because of growing concepts both of child dependency and of the younger women being wives as well as daughters-in-law, there is a growing concept of minimum food needs during periods of crisis even if the household finances are severely strained by food purchases. In fact, there is some apprehension now of sending a child to school if he is too obviously malnourished. In other ways the con-

19. Amarjit Singh, S. S. Jolly, and Leela Kumar, "Indian Childhood Cirrhosis," *Lancet* 1 (1961):587–91.

cept of childhood is also having an impact. The testimony from the study area consistently argues that young children no longer work as long hours as they once did, and, more important, that they are much less likely to be forced to continue to work if they appear sick or exhausted. Women who have been to school are also more likely to insist on a more equal distribution of food within the family.

Another important, if slow, change is in the concept of pollution from one that is largely ritual to one that more closely approximates the conditions most favorable to the transmission of disease. The situation in which rats' feces in flour gave rise to less alarm than a human hair or fingernail clipping[20] is passing. Nevertheless, the cleansing effect of washing with any type of water is hardly questioned, and freshly peeled vegetables or fruit and clean, dry dishes or cups are usually doused in water that is frequently far from clean. Facilities for defecation are often so poor simply because these are not matters for consideration and discussion.

Even in south India there are still differentials by sex, age, and marital status in treatment and feeding. Boys are twice as likely as girls to be taken to the health center. However, more women than men attend, the whole surplus being explained by anemia, perhaps partly an indication of differential feeding, but doubtless also related to menstruation and childbirth. Women eat last in most households, so that men do not know whether they are stinted for food or not, and the young wife serves her mother-in-law, almost inevitably being forced to graciously give her the larger share.

The medical struggle, therefore, is with the basic spiritual concepts of the society. It tends to be resolved less by a decline in religion than by the secularizing of certain areas of behavior, in that the feeling grows that these are matters where man is effective and of little interest to nonhuman forces. There is no significant spiritual battle between officially recognized Ayurvedic medicine and allopathic medicine. The former has changed quite rapidly in this century, partly because of support by the independence movement and the growth of state-financed institutional training. Its practitioners deal in physical treatments and medicaments, differing only in type from allopathic approaches, and very likely providing intermediate experiences that lead people to allopathic medicine. The two government doctors most extensively investigated had both Ayurvedic and allopathic training, with more of the former; but, partly because they felt themselves to be

20. R. S. Khare, "Ritual Purity and Pollution in Relation to Domestic Sanitation," *Eastern Anthropologist* 15, no. 2 (1962):125–39.

part of an official system with worldwide links, they practiced almost exclusively the latter while praising the cultural benefits of the former. The demand for modern medicines, which tend to be respected more than modern doctors (who are often regarded as little more than retailers of these important substances), has become so great in the study area that in 1981 a cloth merchant in the large village converted his shop into a medical store and imported a qualified pharmacist to dispense medicines.

Infant and child mortality differentials in the study area by caste were unexpectedly small, largely because the scheduled castes were found mostly in the large village adjacent to the health center. The largest differentials in infant mortality were by mother's education, with a level of 130 per thousand where the mother had not been to school, 80 where she had only primary schooling, and 70 where she had some secondary schooling. Infant mortality levels by the occupation of the household head were 75 for merchants, 130 for farmers, and 165 for home duties (widows bringing up their children).

Marriage

Of major interest to the people of the study area are the very great changes that have been transforming marriage over the last third of a century. Those cited are a movement from a shortage of potential brides to one of potential bridegrooms, a transition from bridewealth (*tera*) to dowry, a diminution of the proportion of marriages between relatives, and a rise in the age of female marriage. These changes are believed to be interrelated to a considerable extent. There is no claim of any decline in the significance of arranged marriage.

Nearly every family believes that most of these phenomena spring from an unexpected changeover from a surplus of males to one of females. Certainly, the fundamental mechanism of the marriage squeeze, declining mortality and a resulting broadening of the base of the age pyramid in a situation where there is a considerable age gap between spouses has been operating.[21] Nevertheless, Indian sex ratios are high, being 105 males per 100 females in the study area in 1981, compared with 104 in Karnataka and 107 in India as a whole.[22] The

21. See J. C. Caldwell, "Fertility Decline and Female Chances of Marriage in Malaya," *Population Studies* 17, no. 1 (1963):20–32.

22. Census of India 1981, *Series 9, Karnataka, Paper 2 of 1981, Provisional Population Totals* (Bangalore, 1981); Census of India 1981, *Series 1, India, Paper 1 of 1981, Provisional Population Totals* (New Delhi, 1981).

explanation is relatively high female mortality, probably arising from sex differentials in nutrition and other treatment.[23]

Despite high sex ratios, however, there does appear to be a squeeze. The age gap between spouses declined in the first seven decades of the present century, but in 1971 was still five years in the whole country and seven years in Karnataka and in the study area. In the study area, the number of never-married females over 15 exhibited in 1981 a surplus over never-married males over 22 years (employing the minimum age at which any significant number of marriages now occur and the average age gap between spouses at first marriage) of 29 percent. The proportion is reduced, but not eliminated, by taking into account the much higher numbers of emigrant single males than emigrant single females, all available for marriages arranged by their parents. The key to the whole problem is the much greater number of women than men who are widowed (because husbands are considerably older than wives), the substantially younger average age at widowhood among females than among males, and the stronger pressures against the remarriage of widows than of widowers. (One study of the whole country showed that in spite of widows tending to be much younger than widowers, only one-third of the former remarried compared with two-thirds of the latter).[24] For the whole country (ignoring changing borders) in 1931 and 1971 respectively, comparisons of all females, regardless of marital status, over 10 years of age with all males over 15 years (India has a smaller age gap than Karnataka) reveal a female surplus of 12 million at the earlier date and 20 million at the later date. But, if we then subtract the surplus of widows not remarried over widowers not remarried (16 million at both dates, a tribute to declining mortality), we observe a transition from a deficit of 4 million women in 1931 to a surplus of 4 million in 1971.

This may not fully explain why the old attest that it was once easy to marry off daughters, whereas now it is increasingly difficult. The change in the nature of the marriage market toward a dowry system, while probably being at least partly caused by the squeeze, is also likely to increase the feeling of parents that it is difficult to find suitable husbands for their daughters. We were told repeatedly that boys' parents used always to make the first suggestion about a possible mar-

23. Asok Mitra, *India's Population: Aspects of Quality and Control* (New Delhi: Abhinav Publications for the Family Planning Foundation), 1978; Barbara D. Miller, *The Endangered Sex: Neglect of Female Children in Rural North India* (Ithaca: Cornell University Press, 1981).

24. Bhat and Kanbargi, "Widow and Widower Remarriage."

riage, whereas now girls' parents often do so. In fact, in recent marriages the first suggestion seems to have come from the bridegroom's side in about half of all cases, compared with around two-thirds a generation ago.

The only marriage payment in the past in the study area was a payment from the bridegroom's side to the bride's side, the *tera*. Thus it was a type of bridewealth, and, although in this century it has been a fixed and low amount, there is evidence that in earlier times it could be a deterrent to marriage.[25] Nevertheless, in one sense the *tera* system had the characteristics of a full bridewealth system. Only a generation ago, the expensive wedding celebrations were held at the house of the bridegroom's parents, and the latter met most expenses and were much more apprehensive about whether they could face the cost of another marriage at any given time than were the bride's parents. It was the bridegroom's parents who sought loans to meet their expenses and who might sell some land. Some possessions, gold or jewelry, the *stridhana* (female wealth), have always been passed from female to female, but this produced no strains at the time of marriage, for the existence and size of such family possessions were predetermined.

The major change was the coming of dowry. In the early 1950s the first dowries in Bangalore were paid by some Brahmin families.[26] Not until the beginning of the 1960s did the first Brahmin landlord family in the study area provide a dowry, and not until 1965 was this done by the first Vokkaliga family. It is still not paid by Harijans, although in the largest village they ceased paying the *tera* five years ago, and the payment is still small among some of the backward castes. Nevertheless, they all anticipate its arrival. In all castes, the bride's family now bears the major portion of the wedding costs, and it is they who seek loans and sell land.

Throughout the society this change is ascribed to two causes: the growing shortage of potential husbands; and the coming into existence of a class of more desirable husbands, characterized by education and usually by urban employment. Clearly, though the fact is little stressed, a key factor is also preexisting models in north India and in ancient writings. Once the sacrifice is made, individual families like it to be known that they paid a huge dowry (the highest total costs of dowry and wedding expenses in the study area approach Rs 100,000),[27] but nearly everyone regards the coming of the system and the subsequent

25. Buchanan, *A Journey from Madras*.

26. Dowries were apparently paid by some Brahmin families in Madras City as early as the mid-1930s.

27. Approximately $11,500 at the time of the research.

inflation of dowries as invidious, and no one believes that their caste has risen in the hierarchy of religious merit and respectability as a result—that is, the cause of change was not Sanskritization.[28]

In a society in which families do not make their greatest sacrifices in other matters for their young women, the determination to obtain, if possible, educated, nonfarming sons-in-law is not easily explained either by the researcher or by those involved. The latter argue that they wish their daughters to have a different life from their mothers, released from the drudgery of agricultural labor and the miseries of the annual cycle of sufficiency and want, with the possibility of famine years looming in the background. They deny that they gain anything personally, although it might be noted that educated sons-in-law can be influential or can give needed advice, and one's daughter is less likely to return home seeking the support to which she is entitled in times of need if her husband has a steady income. Some parents do admit to having received help from daughters in time of need.

Among south Indian Hindus, the preferred marriage for a man has been to his sister's daughter, but a shortage of suitable brides has probably always meant that cross-cousin marriages were the most common, in contrast to parallel-cousin marriages among Muslims. In the study area, 30 percent of all marriages have been between persons closely enough related to specify the exact relationship (one-third among Hindus and one-quarter among Muslims), half between first cousins, but only one in sixteen between uncle and niece. However, only 20 percent of recent marriages have been between relatives, fairly clear evidence that the widespread testimony of a decline in such marriages is correct. There seem to be four reasons. The first is the same reason as explains rising village exogamy and the expanding geographical borders of *jatis* (endogamous, areally defined subsections of caste that determine commensality and other social activities) if they are determined by intermarriageability, namely, that in a society increasingly heterogeneous in terms of education and occupation, parents have to look further afield for suitable marriage partners for their children. The second is the temptation of the parents of sons to seek the large dowries available in marriages between nonrelatives, in contrast to the small or negligible ones permitted within the family. Often opposed are the feelings of the girl's mother, who may place strong pressure on her brother to provide his son or himself for the marriage,

28. This explanation is given for the region in T. Scarlett Epstein, *Economic Development and Social Change in South India* (Manchester: Manchester University Press, 1973):194–200.

partly to reduce the expense but partly so that she will reforge a link with her family or household of origin. The third is a relatively recent belief that the children of relatives may be sickly, or even that such marriages may be sinful. Such ideas are clearly an import, from north India or the West, or more likely with ingredients from both. The fourth reason is that with the passing of child marriage, there may be some effective opposition to marriage between relatives from one or other of the proposed spouses.

Between the first quarter of the century and 1971, the mean age of female marriage in India climbed from 13 to 17 years and in Karnataka from 15 to 18 years (while that of males rose from 20 to 22 years and from 24.3 to 24.8 years respectively, possibly with some decline in Karnataka after 1961).[29] In the study area the modal age of female marriage by 1979–82 was 20 years. When analyzing the change in female marriage, it is necessary to distinguish two separate aspects: the disappearance of child or premenarchic marriage and the increasing gap between menarche and marriage.

The necessity for treating child marriage separately is not merely that it has no fertility implications but that, according to local testimony, it has no sexual implications, consummation being delayed until the *sobana* ceremony (which then allows *prastha* or consummation) some months after menarche (although the struggle in the last century to raise the minimum legal age of female consent leads one to wonder whether this were always so). At one time there were religious sanctions against marrying a girl too late, and, among some castes, disgrace befell the family, and the girl became unmarriageable, if she unexpectedly and precociously attained menarche while still single.[30] The situation has now been reversed, and most families would feel some guilt at marrying a daughter before menarche, largely because of the strengthening of the concepts of childhood and immaturity. Nevertheless, with few exceptions, schoolgirls are withdrawn from education at menarche, and all unmarried girls are withdrawn from the fields. Most families still feel an unease at having a single, menstruating female under their roof, and the search for a husband begins, the dowry payable mounting as time passes, clearly showing a concept akin to that of damaged goods. When mortality was higher, parents felt a responsibility for arranging all of their children's marriages early so that death would not catch them with some children still unmarried, but this pressure has lessened. In Karnataka, the proportion of 10–14-

29. Mitra, "India's Population: Aspects," 300ff.
30. Buchanan, *A Journey from Madras* 1:52, 259–60.

year-old females married was 25 percent in 1901, 20 percent in 1921, but only 5 percent by 1951. In our study area, it had declined to 1 percent in 1981.

Except for a handful of more educated families, members of the bureaucracy, or large landowners, parents of daughters go through at least some motions of searching for suitable sons-in-law once a girl attains puberty. But, in practice, the median age at female marriage is already around five years beyond menarche. This delay needs explanation, and, to obtain it, we examined the history of all women under 30 years of age. It should be emphasized at the outset, because of its significance for economic-demographic theory, that not a single person in a community of 5,000 people suggested, even as a supplementary consideration, that any marriage had ever been delayed so as to contain subsequent family size. On the contrary, it was widely averred that one advantage of postponing marriage for two or three years after menarche was that the bride would be physically more mature, that both she and her child would be more likely to survive childbirth, and that her subsequent fecundity would not be impaired by the damage done by bearing a child when too immature. The reasons given for the delay in marriage fell into two groups: the condition of the marriage market and changing concepts of maturity.

Most of the parents of daughters have experienced a series of troubles in arranging a marriage: difficulties in finding a potential husband of whom they approved, and whose parents approved of their daughter; disagreement about the size of the dowry; and problems with raising the money needed for both dowry and wedding. In ninetenths of all marriage delays, the primary emphasis is placed on these mechanical troubles arising from large dowries and the shortage of males. Nevertheless, it is clear that these negotiations are occurring in a society that is less apprehensive than it once was about later female marriage. The groom's parents are now worried about bringing into the household a girl who cannot play a full domestic role and who is not sufficiently mature to raise their grandchildren (an interesting change, for the mother-in-law would once have thought of herself as raising the grandchildren), while their son is increasingly likely to be concerned about having an immature wife (a sign of the strengthening of the spousal bond). The bride's own parents are more likely than before to regard their daughter at menarche as still largely a child, and to be less frantic than they once might have been about marriage delays. This is especially the case if she has been to school, for there is a widespread belief that the longer a girl has been to school, the later she should marry. This does tend to occur, and most of the delay is not mechanical in the sense of her not being able to marry while at school. Nevertheless, no one with whom we have discussed the matter has ever been able to explain exactly why schooling should be equated with later marriage, except that sometimes suitable husbands also marry later. But clearly they also seem to feel that the girls have become enrolled in a nontraditional society in which marriage occurs later. (They probably see it not in terms of this single theme but as a complex characterized also by earlier weaning, treatment of children's sicknesses at the health center, and, increasingly, by a greater tendency to restrict family size.)

There are very strong beliefs about the age at which a man should marry: in a survey 80 percent of all respondents, including the young men themselves, said 25 years, and most bridegrooms are in fact close to that age. Again and again we were told that younger men would not be physically mature enough to withstand their wives' sexual demands or to meet them without affecting their health. If a rural man goes much beyond that age without marrying (in contrast to males who are finishing higher degrees or training courses or securing advancement in urban employment), he is increasingly likely to be regarded as not having fully reached a man's estate and perhaps as being physically or emotionally defective. Both in Karnataka as a whole and in the study area there appears to have been a small decline in the average male age at marriage. This is mostly explained by local people in terms of increasing sexuality caused by exposure to cinema and the restless desire of some young men to marry, but an examination of the circumstances of each marriage suggests that a more important reason may well be the offer of a tempting dowry somewhat earlier than the time at which the young man's parents would have made their first move.

There is, then, a continuing significant increase in the average age of female marriage. In the study area it seems to have persisted and perhaps even accelerated during the 1970s, and this may be found to be true more widely when the 1981 census data on marital status by age become available. This increase has both demographic and social roots, but the relaxation of the demographic pressures may well reveal that older age at marriage has become culturally acceptable. The relaxation of the demographic pressure may arise from a narrowing age gap between spouses (declining fertility affecting the age structure in the age range where first marriages mostly occur), a reduction in the proportion of widows remarrying, or an increase in polygyny. The first two are likely to occur. If there really is a ceiling on male age at marriage, and the evidence suggests that there is, then the increasing age at female marriage (with marriages perhaps being brought about by ever higher dowries) will inevitably reduce the gap. Given that fertility decline appears to have begun in the early to mid-1960s, and to have steepened in the late 1970s, changing age structure may reduce the pressure on the marriage market slightly from about the present time and markedly by the end of the century. The latter two possibilities (i.e., an increase in polygyny or a decline in widow remarriage) appear improbable because the long-term trends appear to have been in the opposite direction. It seems doubtful whether changes will occur rapidly enough to allow the marriage of all the 3 percent of women aged 25–29 and the 30 percent of those aged 20–24 still single, and the society may have to accommodate itself to older unmarried women. Nor are dowries likely to decline in value until the grip of the marriage squeeze loosens, perhaps only in the last years of this century. A different problem arises from the narrowing age gap between spouses. The single main purpose of the undivided family has been over the last two decades to serve as an engine for generating enough wealth to marry off all the daughters before sons married and began to talk of partition. This was easy only when the girls married much earlier than the boys.

Fertility Decline

Both retrospective data and births recorded during the period of the research, 1979–82, suggest a birthrate in the study area no higher than 30 per thousand and possibly as low as 28 per thousand. Both the retrospective information and the age structure indicate a birthrate 20 years earlier in the range of 40–45 per thousand, probably nearer the higher end. Thus, fertility may well have fallen by as much as one-third over two decades, with the steepest decline being concentrated in the last ten years.

The mechanism whereby this has been achieved is clearer than the reason. Among married couples with the wife under 50 years of age, one-third were employing some method of family planning. Among this group, the method in use was sterilization in 86 percent of cases (female, 70 percent; male, 15 percent; both wife and husband, 1 percent),[31] the *nirodh* or condom in 6 percent, the IUD in 5 percent (with another 2 percent recent past users), and rhythm in 1 percent. One-quarter of all couples are now sterilized by the time the wife is 26 years old, and half by the time she is 36 years. In terms of parity, 36 percent of couples with three live births have been sterilized, and the proportion reaches nearly 50 percent with five births. Computer simulation

31. Emergency cases.

suggests that the incidence of birth control by age, parity, and date of commencement is compatible with the recorded birthrate of 30 per thousand, when combined with the proportions currently married and living together, the reported average duration of postnatal amenorrhea and sexual abstinence, and plausible estimates of fecundity and sexual activity by age.

No women in the study area has ever used oral contraceptives, and they have apparently never been available through the government program in the area. The use of IUDs and condoms is entirely concentrated in the large village, while in the smaller villages fertility control and sterilization are believed to be synonymous. The use of the IUD, fitted at the health center, is largely confined to the wives of salaried government employees, the doctor, the engineer, the veterinary surgeon, school teachers and policemen, and to their associates, educated large landowners and bank officials. These people all know one another, regard themselves as the village establishment, influence *panchayat* decisions, view themselves as somewhat responsible for the health service and the family planning program, and know what services are available. They are also usually apprehensive about the effect of sterilization, but they do not say so to the rest of the population. The use of condoms is very largely concentrated among the Muslim merchants, who are apprehensive of official pressure if they have too many children, but who fear sterilization and usually believe it to be against their religion. They obtain condoms through the market when making business trips to the towns.

An understanding of the fertility transition necessitates an understanding of the sterilization program, for most members of the community are offered nothing else. There has always been a degree of moral pressure, as is inevitable with a system of targets. The moral pressure is broader than the relationship between the health worker and the client. The rural elites, always a little apprehensive of the growth of the large poor section of society, have been convinced of the need for fertility control both because it is government policy and because of the worldwide debate on the population explosion. The need for fertility control is often expressed by officials and village leaders in public places and on public occasions, while opposition or doubts are voiced only privately. Indeed, a majority of the elite believe that the expression of opposed views should be prevented on public occasions. In the past all government employees had a duty to support the family planning program publicly, and, although the present position is a little obscure, nearly all assume this still to be the case. When the multipurpose health worker (previously the auxiliary nurse mid-

wife) or the female health visitor, a woman of above-average education and with an official position, suggests the operation for the first
time to a young woman with two or three children, there is little overt
pressure on her or her family, but rejecting such advice (which is
sometimes supported by the doctor as well) perhaps 20 or 30 times
over a two-year period is much more difficult. This is particularly so in
the Hindu society with its concepts of elite leadership and of religious
virtue arising from proper social behavior. This moral pressure partly
explains the rapidity with which sterilization decisions are often
made,[32] and also a degree of withdrawal by the older generation from
responsibility for the decision, which is facilitated by the long-term
process of ceding of power from the older to the younger generation
but which exceeds what one might anticipate. Indeed, in one-third of
cases the husband and his parents insist that the ultimate decision
must be made by the wife, a situation quite different from that found
with regard to other important decisions, and, admittedly, nearly
always confined to the matter of her own sterilization.

Decisions are usually made in accordance with what is deemed to
offer the least potential danger to the family, a wife arguing against her
husband's being vasectomized on the grounds that the household
could not survive his death or incapacitation or that his job requires
wading in deep water or riding a bicycle, activities held to be dangerous or impossible after a vasectomy. The family planning program,
aware of the potential impact of publicized disasters, often refuses
sterilization on the grounds of illness or weakness, most frequently
because of tuberculosis, anemia, or asthma. For the same reasons the
health service ensures quick treatment for the young children of sterilized couples. Wives do not have tubectomies without consulting
others, but about one-tenth of vasectomies were decided on quickly by
the man alone, often, but not always, because of the incentive offered.
Among Hindus there is no longer any discussion of the morality of the
operation, only of the balance of disadvantages in having it now or
later, and of having it done to the wife or husband. There is usually not
an absolute decision against sterilization but often an argument that
this is not the right time in terms of family composition or fortunes, or
sometimes the wife's age.

The assessment of the forces involved in fertility decision-making
is rendered even more difficult by the existence of the Emergency from
the end of June 1975 until the elections of March 1977. Although the

32. P. H. Reddy and K. N. M. Raju, "Psycho-social Impact of Sterilization on
Rural Acceptors," *Bangalore Population Centre Newsletter* 5, no. 1 (1979):1–14.

first sterilizations in the study area date back to 1962, half of all those carried out in the 18-year period from then until the beginning of 1980 were performed during the Emergency. Most of these decisions were made under substantial duress, and force was employed quite widely. Several points might be made. There was bitterness at the time and since, but no real resistance, perhaps because of a concentration on female sterilization. These actions did not destroy the family planning program, because the dramatic drop in sterilizations in the balance of 1977 and 1978 did not fall below the upward trend line established before the Emergency. By 1981 demand was rising quite steeply (sterilizations amounting to twice the 1976 level) and probably more spontaneously than at any previous time. The reason was probably largely continued social and economic change, but there is some evidence that the Emergency sterilizations had made the population more familiar both with sterilized women and with terminated childbearing. Certainly, the more spontaneous demand of the 1980s was entirely for female sterilization.[33] In spite of the fact that the family planning program had operated in the area for 13 years prior to the Emergency, a considerable number of families claim not to have heard of the program or what it was offering until the mass program of 1976–77.

The dominance of sterilization as a family planning method did not indicate that it was considered entirely satisfactory. Rather, the elite and health personnel were convinced that the masses could cope with nothing else and evinced little enthusiasm for offering them a choice. Nearly everyone believes that both male and female sterilizing operations may lead to permanent weakness. Even the health personnel accept the community wisdom on this point in their private capacity (it is the main reason the elite use the IUD), even though they do not say so in the public capacity nor state the community view in their reports. Half of both sterilized men and sterilized women believe that they never regained their full strength after the operation; just over half the males and almost half the females believe their sexual enjoyment was impaired, and hardly any reported improvement. Indeed, when the daughter-in-law of the household has agreed to sterilization, there is often the suggestion that she is making a sacrifice, although, in the Hindu tradition, it is frequently seen as virtuous or ennobling and as having been done for the family.

Perhaps because of greater pressure on the poor, especially during the Emergency, there are no significant differentials in fertility or

33. The demand was partly raised by a greater use of laparoscopy, which in 1981–82 was increasingly believed to have fewer after-effects than tubectomies.

family planning practice by socioeconomic status, caste grouping, or education. There is only one important differential, and that is by religion. Muslims are only half as likely to practice family planning as Hindus, and, except at younger ages, exhibit significantly higher fertility (which is completely explained by the lower levels of fertility control). They regard the family planning program as a creation of the Hindu State and, frequently asserting that sterilization is opposed to Koranic law, they say that they adhere to the morality of the Book rather than to changing social and political morality. They feel themselves to be an embattled minority, even more with regard to sterilization than on most other issues, to an extent that even research on the matter is very difficult. The pressures within the Muslim population against sterilization are often coercive. They range from refusal to eat with the sterilized, to accept food from them (there are clearly undertones of a Hindu type here) to have them as servants, or to allow them to be buried in the Muslim burial ground. The majority of Muslims stated the case against sterilization in terms of religious morality, either that it is forbidden or that Allah has committed himself to provide for children sent to this earth, whereas contemporary Hindu explanations are completely secular. It might be noted that there is a fertility differential between Muslims and Hindus in the study area, as has been widely reported in Inda,[34] but it can be largely explained by the differential in sterilization acceptance (hence it is greatest for fertility rates among women over 30 years of age) and totally explained by the addition of a differential in the period of postnatal sexual abstinence.[35]

Forces of Change

Although the existence of the family planning program and its considerable efficiency has been a major force in accelerating the fertility decline, there is little doubt in the community that there have also

34. K. Balasubramaniam, "Differential Fertility in India: Evidence from a Survey in Karnataka State" (Ph.D. thesis, Australian National University, Canberra, 1981); India, Office of the Registrar General, *Infant and Child Mortality Survey, 1979: A Preliminary Report* (New Delhi: Ministry of Home Affairs, 1980); M. A. El-Badry, "A Study of Differential Fertility in Bombay," *Demography* 4, no. 2 (1967):626–40; J. R. Rele, "Fertility Differentials in India: Evidence from a Rural Background," *Milbank Memorial Fund Quarterly* 41, no. 2 (1963):183–99; L. Visaria, "Religious Differentials in Fertility," in *Population in India's Development 1947–2000*, ed. A. Bose et al. (Delhi: Vikas, 1974), 361–74.

35. Muslims are enjoined to abstain for 40 days. In the villages many abstain for longer periods, often quoting the advice of Hindu neighbors on the ills that might follow short periods of abstinence.

been underlying forces reducing the value of unrestricted fertility. This has probably been true for decades, but the current upswing in the demand for sterilization is evidence of intensifying change.

People are aware of declining mortality, and point to it as one of the reasons for not feeling so strongly about the early marriage of children. They probably take it into account when deciding on sterilization, but they very rarely quote it as one of their considerations when making that decision.

The testimony of older persons in the study area is that the value of children ceased rising linearly with their numbers for three reasons: the value of their work declined, the cost of keeping them rose, and the maximum return from a child necessitated more investment in each than most parents could afford for a large number of children.

Children still work hard on farms and in businesses, and they appear to do what they are told without protest. Nevertheless, there is close agreement by the elderly that in their childhood and youth they rose earlier, worked longer hours, and were more severely punished if they faltered. There are various reasons why this system has eroded. Among younger children, the hours taken up by schooling and homework are obviously important, given that three-quarters of the children in the large village and half in the smaller villages now have some schooling. School starts late (10:30 A.M.), allowing farm work in the morning, but children are less likely to be worked excessively if they are to attend school subsequently. However, adolescents and young adults, especially males, are no longer compelled to work quite as long or as intensively as was once the case. Part of the reason is that because of the growth of the concept of dependency, they were not brought up from infancy to expect uncomplaining toil. There is substantial evidence that sick or exhausted children are not as likely to be made to continue working as was the case a generation or two ago. Nevertheless, the critical age range for work inputs is adolescence and young adulthood. Here, it is claimed, fathers are not as tyrannical as they once were, largely because they know that their sons are less dependent on the fathers' land or trade for employment, for both fathers and sons are always conscious of the urban and other nonfarm labor markets that have developed in the last few decades.[36] Fathers fear their unmarried sons wanting to migrate (especially an only son or one of the only one or two left in the village) or their married sons urging an earlier partition. There is actually very little evidence that

36. Between the 1951 and 1971 censuses the population of Karnataka increased by 51 percent, but male employment in the modern nonfarming sector (manu-

partitioning is occurring earlier, but many would argue that it is the changing nature of the patriarchy that has allowed this stability. Certainly, more general social change has also affected relations between the generations: it is frequently observed that patriarchs are now subject to greater strains, because, whereas approaches to them were once largely made through their wives or eldest sons, almost all members of the family now feel the right of direct approach. Finally, as the female age at marriage climbs, the adolescent girls, and even young women, in the house are more likely to be daughters than daughters-in-law, with all that this implies for the diminishing margin for work over keep.

However, those discussing the changing value of children more often place even more emphasis on the increasing cost of children than on declining labor or other economic returns. The discussions center on money and on inflation, and their kernel is the impact of monetization on the cost of children. The picture painted of conditions half a century ago is of family food stores, mostly grain and secured from the family's own farm or from daily or periodical payment for labor or services, from which children were fed. Their other costs were few: most clothes were hand-downs, although clearly purchases were sometimes necessary; and children's illnesses were usually classified as belonging to categories in which human action was of little avail. Monetization, together with changing concepts of care, means that most families tend over time to spend somewhat more on children's food, especially in times of adversity, and somewhat more on medical and other health treatment. However, it is the advent of schooling and the increasing proportion of children attending school that have accelerated these changes. There are minimum standards of dress and of feeding and health demanded of school children; there are pressures from teachers, peer group pressure on the children, and parental decisions that their sons and daughters should not appear noticeably worse off than other school children. Furthermore, school children make demands of their own, partly because the school has introduced them to a wider world. By 1982 a tent cinema had been set up near the large village, and school children were more likely than their illiterate fellows to plead for permission and for money to go and were more

---

facturing, construction, transport, and trade and commerce) rose by 243 percent or 2,263,496 new positions for males, and by 206 percent or 2,357,641 new positions (India Census, 1975) if we take the somewhat more suspect figures for both sexes. The examination of changes in the occupational proportions in the total work force is less revealing because of changes in the enumeration of agricultural employment.

likely to attend. It is not merely that money identifies more areas for expenditure on children, but that it does the same for adults. Questions of choice and potential conflict become ever more obvious, and the cost of children begins to be a subject of some concern.

It is probably the expansion of schooling that has brought all these changes into focus. Schooling has been available in the large village for over half a century, but the provision of schools for the smaller villages is only just being completed. Parents send their children to school for both social and economic reasons, and local leaders, encouraged by national attitudes, urge parents to do so. The family property or business is regarded as the patrimony by farmers, merchants, and those providing services (87 percent of all families, although some have only small holdings,[37] and many provide labor to others at certain times within the year). Anything earned over and above the patrimony is considered a kind of profit or windfall gain. The increase in urban jobs and in local off-farm employment[38] has meant that there is a potential for extra earning capacity. Farmers prefer one or more of their sons to hold such jobs both because of the surplus earnings and because some income or help may thus be guaranteed at times of crop failure. Many sons who have lived and worked in Bangalore for years still belong to families in the study area who have partitioned neither the land nor the house. Such members often provide some general assistance to the family, usually help in crises, and almost always contribute to costs associated with marriage, death, and various festivals. Of course, education is necessary for many such jobs and helps in securing others. This is the single most important reason for sending sons to school and for keeping those who do well in the educational system.

The move in this direction has been catalyzed not only by the establishment of schools but also by the reduction in the size of the average holding (at least halved in the last 50 years). The reduction in average farm size is basically a product of population growth and of division by inheritance. However, land reform, which has been more successful in both the study area[39] and Karnataka as a whole than in

37. Almost one-quarter of all holdings are one acre (.405 hectare) or less in size and almost half two acres or less.

38. Almost one-third of adult males work for at least some of their time outside agriculture, in the bureaucracy, as merchants or craftsmen, in the rice or sugar mills, or as drivers or road laborers.

39. The families in the study area who owned wetland have retained most of it through household partitioning and other devices. Most of the redistributed land has been dry and has gone to tenants rather than to the landless. Some land is now uncultivated because of fear of losing it if leased out.

most of India, has made even the larger farmers apprehensive about placing too much emphasis on their farms as the basis for the family's future fortunes. The largest farmers and landowners, who tend, especially in the case of the wetland near the large village and its tank, to be Brahmins and Jains, have long admired secular (as well as religious) education and have led the way in the education of sons. In these wet lands, where new varieties of rice are grown with increasing inputs of fertilizer, productivity has risen greatly over recent years; but in the dry lands, which make-up most of the study area, productivity gains in the growth of *ragi* and *jowar* (sorghum) have been small. Even if productivity gains had balanced land fragmentation, farmers would have needed fewer sons because of the greater efficiency involved in working more intensively in a smaller area and because of limited advances in technology.[40] In any case, more sons are now surviving to adulthood.[41] It would be wrong to think of farmers considering off-farm employment for one or more sons as resorting to a desperate remedy for worsening conditions. On the contrary, most regard the important change as an increase in the availability of off-farm employment with its opportunity to release the family from total reliance on the land and its vicious cycles of disaster. They emphasize that the growth of urban employment, together with the local availability of schooling, would have meant rural-urban migration even without land subdivision, although they admit that some way would have had to be found for working all the land.

The level of female education has also been rising rapidly. In the large village the sex ratio of those under 20 years of age with some schooling is now only 111 males per 100 females (in contrast to 184 per 100 in the smaller villages, where nevertheless the chance of a girl going to school has increased twelvefold over the last 20 years compared with only a doubling for boys). The reasons given by parents for educating their daughters are dominated by the assertion that educated men demand educated wives, and hence that there is no other way of securing a satisfactory son-in-law. Supplementary reasons are that educated women look after their children better, especially their health, and make better wives. Some people even say that if their sons have a right to education, so should their daughters.

40. For example, greater use of electric pumps for raising water, small mills for grinding grain, and metal ploughs. In addition, more tube wells and expanded bus service have reduced carrying and carting.
41. Males now reaching adulthood represent the cohort characterized by the lowest mortality before fertility began to decline.

The increase in nonagricultural employment and the provision of schooling have created a situation in which there are real choices to be made. No one doubts that there is economic strain imposed on a family by keeping their children at school, and that the strain becomes greater if the child's scholastic success is sufficient to warrant continuing education. However, the majority of respondents believe that there is still little economic handicap in raising children who do not go to school, who dress in the tattered way that illiterate children usually do, and who work from an early age. We repeatedly asked whether the solution was to send some children to school but not others, but were consistently told that families just cannot do this, although if a child performs badly at school, he or she can be withdrawn while siblings continue.[42] Thus, if a family opts for educating its children, there may well be economic problems if their numbers are too great. The potential for investing in rural-urban migration can mean expenditure in ways other than schooling. Once a child is educated, there is often a need for bribes or more legitimate expenditure in securing a town job. Even when the child is not educated, there can be expenditure—for instance, investing in a motorized tricycle that can be used to carry paying passengers in Bangalore.

Investment in children, however, is not the only reason for couples to eventually accept sterilization. There are problems peculiar to women. With higher parity and age, women complain increasingly about the problems of continued pregnancies, breast-feeding, and caring for young children. A significant number of women, largely from poorer families, also wish to cease childbearing because they either have to shoulder an unusual amount of family responsibility or fear having to do so because their husbands are unreliable providers, being given to drink, being regarded by employers as lazy or incapable, or tending to disappear to other women or distant places. These problems are accentuated by the fact that most women in the study area do fieldwork, many to earn money that is sorely needed by the family. They do not always decide that the solution is sterilization, because many anticipate even greater physical problems from the operation than from continued childbearing. There is little status conferred in the area for having a large family, and, after three or four children,

42. Nevertheless, among farming families there is a significantly lower chance of both the first son and the first daughter going to school or staying there for long than is the case for their younger siblings. This is so because of the urgent need for the eldest son to help his father on the farm and for the eldest daughter to release her mother from child care, usually for fieldwork.

women frequently begin wondering whether it is time to stop. There is no doubt that they do so more readily now, in part because the question is often raised in the first place by the multipurpose health worker. The intrusion of the state in this matter, and the fact that the female health workers talk mostly to married women of reproductive age, suggest that birth control is primarily a female matter. The state does a good deal to counterbalance, both in the case of birth control and in the treatment of sick children, the influence of males and the elderly. Not only is it becoming more common for the elderly to say that the final decision on sterilization is that of the young, but for the younger husband to say it is the decision of his wife.[43]

Partly because it is anticipated that sterilization may well have major and lasting physical effects, both the husband and the mother-in-law prefer the wife to make the final decision to undergo tubectomy, emphasizing that the operation is desirable but that the decision must be hers (thus giving the impression in surveys that wives are autonomous decision-makers with regard to sterilization). Women do increasingly choose sterilization for themselves, partly influenced by doctors who are much more confident of their ability to undertake female sterilizing operations than they were 20 years ago, but largely because of their fear that their husbands might die as a result of being vasectomized, an occurrence that usually leads through property partition to a dissolution of the family in its existing form and consequently often a disastrous change in the women's situations.

One would not anticipate economic and other problems impinging equally on all members of the society. Yet, within Hindu society, there are no significant differentials in birth control by occupation, education, or caste. One reason is that there has been greater pressure by the family planning program, especially during the Emergency, on the weaker groups, and they have had less will to resist. But this is not

43. Because of the maintenance of late weaning and the persistence of a considerable period of postnatal abstinence, the major demand for fertility control in both rural areas and urban slums is still for terminal methods. This is in striking contrast to the situation among the middle class of Bangalore city, where shorter periods of abstinence and a quite dramatic decline in the duration of breast-feeding (averaging around six months when the mother works and nearer twelve when she does not) present young married couples with the possibility of the second child coming close behind the first, followed perhaps quickly by the third. Here there is an almost frantic demand for means to achieve birth spacing. There is a rising demand for the condom, but a weaker reliance on the pill than might be anticipated (because of a widespread distrust originating among doctors). Various versions of the safe period are in common use, the abortion rate is rising, and there is a low incidence of experimentation with withdrawal.

the only reason. Because the Harijans have been agricultural laborers for the Brahmin landlords, most live in the large village (70 percent, compared with 23 percent of Vokkaligas), where there are more educational facilities and more social and political pressures for children to attend school. Furthermore, the landless—Harijans, other backward castes, and service castes—see possibilities of economic advancement through the education of their children, in contrast to the Vokkaligas, who feel more ambivalent because they fear that all sons will seek to leave the land and the stem family.[44] Thus, the proportion of children 6–14 years of age with some schooling is 72 percent for the service castes, 60 percent for both backward castes and Vokkaligas, and 56 percent for Harijans (compared with 100 and 95 percent among Brahmins and Jains respectively). However, the Harijans are largely concerned with the economic success of a son. Therefore, the sex ratio of their children at school is 189 males per 100 females, compared with 157 among the backward castes, 151 among Vokkaligas, and 120 among the service castes. One reason is that the main marriage qualification among the Harijan women is an ability to undertake a great deal of agricultural labor, and educated girls are suspect in this regard.

Among Hindus, the case for and against sterilization is now argued entirely in secular terms, concerning contending fears. There may no longer be a case for a large family, but there are strongly held beliefs about the minimum number of children. Clearly, there must be a son, and most would say two sons, frequently quoting a proverb relating a couple's need for two sons to the head's need for two eyes (the most colloquial form literally saying, "One eye is not an eye, and one son is not a son"). There are also very strong feelings that there must be a daughter (and a granddaughter), noting the role that she must play in many religious festivals, which, in rural south India, center more often than not on the temples of the local female divinities.

Many sterilizing operations would not have taken place but for the incentive payments (now Rs 125 or $15), even though many of the sterilized persons claim that much of the money was later spent on medical treatment or was needed to compensate for time missed from work. The incentives seem to have been particularly important prior to 1975 and may, together with the doctors' increasing confidence in their ability to perform tubectomies, explain the earlier predominance

44. Most parents live with only one married son in a stem family, and, if the son wishes to migrate, join the household of another married son.

of vasectomies in India and the frequency with which men decided on this operation at short notice without consulting any relatives.

A Final Note

Rural India often appears timeless. Yet there has been much social, economic, and demographic change, especially during the last third of a century. The demographic change has taken many forms: declining mortality, rising age at female marriage, reductions in fertility in recent years, and the shortening of the periods of postnatal female sexual abstinence and lactation. There has also been some demographic stability: in residential structure, which belies some of the changing relations within the households, and in male age at marriage.

It would be tempting to explain these changes as a demographic sequence whereby one demographic change compelled another. It is probably true that declining mortality has to a considerable extent allowed fertility decline and to a lesser extent the rise in the age at female marriage, but in neither case has it been the cause. The truth seems to be that a range of demographic changes occurred at much the same time neither because of close interrelation nor because of coincidence, but because they are all products of massive social and economic changes during the last half-century.

These changes have been neither wholly economic nor wholly social. Major roles have been played by the growth of nonagricultural employment, especially in the towns, and by the substitution of monetary or commercial relations for other forms of exchange and the expansion of exchange at the expense of home production and consumption. Institutional change has also played an important part: the provision of schools, the establishment of a denser network of health centers and doctors, and the attempt to implement land reform. Clearly the main vehicle here has been political decisions based on political ideologies and enthusiasms. Yet there has also been a model of social behavior and relationships at hand toward which the society might move spontaneously or have been directed by its leadership, for there is little difference between the two. The study area population has little doubt what that model is. They refer to it sometimes as urban society and at other times as English ways, the former more often when referring to what is learned at the cinema and the latter in the schools. They know that many aspects of these changes are favored by government, both in its political and bureaucratic form. They know, too, that there are implications of fundamental change in the relations between the generations and the sexes. What is now becoming apparent is that those changes in family relationships have profound demographic implications.

Some attention was given earlier to changes in family decision-making. This should not be exaggerated. The rural family, and indeed many urban families, are usually still patriarchal and often tyrannical. The young do not easily put their views to the old, nor wives to husbands, and decisions made by those with power are accepted. Furthermore, power, when possessed as by the ownership of property or the right to decide upon marriage or to set the size of the dowry, is exercised. Yet decisions, perhaps demographic decisions in particular, are frequently no longer made at the apex of the family power pyramid.

The reason for this abdication of power is not all altruism; it is frequently confusion and doubt. The control over the period of post-natal sexual abstinence was stable only as long as the very long periods were believed to be dictated by a theologically based morality. This was probably first undermined less by Westernization than by another product of modernization and urbanization: the challenge, channeled through the educated and the towns, of the great religious tradition to the little tradition of the villages, for the former was less concerned with such aspects of family behavior as duration of abstinence or lactation. Certainly, an increasing likelihood that the son would grumble about prolonged sexual frustration was the product of other forces, but the success of these complaints lay in a certain understanding by the patriarch that made him withdraw from the situation rather than give his wife the necessary backing to control the behavior and morality of the daughter-in-law. The hesitation of the older couple frequently also arose from an increasing fear that interference would be grounds for partition, a greater fear as off-farm employment increased. The reduction in the period of breast-feeding owed something to the fact that the period of sexual abstinence had declined, potentially lengthening the period of ambivalence when it was felt that there was a danger of damaging the milk. There was probably also a declining belief in the value of very late weaning, especially in households that were more willing to provide food for the young, even in times of shortage. Somewhat earlier weaning was progressively regarded as being better for the child, and also as freeing the mother for fieldwork.

The treatment of sickness is a more complex matter still. It is related not only to changing family relations, but also to the rise of education and the penetration of the area by government health services. At present, daughters-in-law are three times as likely to be educated as their mothers-in-law, and in the previous generation the ratio was nine times. There is a widespread belief that educated parents can look after their children better than the uneducated. Furthermore, even when members of the older generation are ambivalent about the value of modern medicine and are unwilling to make a decision to send their grandchildren to the government doctor, they are often relieved that their children are willing to make this decision.

The decision about sterilization is the most complex of all. We have stressed that there are often economic gains to be made by educating the youngest generation, but no one is quite certain of these gains, especially in the case of each individual. Perhaps the stress placed by the family planning workers on the probability of such gains convinces some people. Most of the community is in some doubt, and the elderly more so than younger members. The elderly are often inclined to believe that younger married couples are in closer contact with the new world and are more likely to make the right decision. Nevertheless, two other factors play a role. The first is some apprehension of the bureaucracy and the elite, for the family planning workers first approach the younger couple and convince them of the necessity of a positive decision. The second is an awareness that "the operation" is a major step, with the possibility of considerable physical consequences, and hence there is a growing belief that the person directly affected should make the final decision.

Many families have major and continuing arguments about sterilization although the dispute is more likely to be about whether sufficient children or sons have been born than about the morality of the operation. The state has made the latter decision, at least for most of the Hindu population. Resistance to ever having the operation is still strong, but it is based not on morality but on fear of its aftermath and doubt about the reality of economic or social gains. Only very rarely does a younger couple decide on sterilization without consulting the husband's parents, and almost equally rarely do they go ahead against overt opposition. Nevertheless, it is increasingly common for the older couple to answer that the decision must be made by the young. In a significant number of cases, however, the first suggestion of sterilization has come from one of the older couple.

The argument here that the intergenerational abdication of decision-making power is occurring faster in the demographic area than more generally is not a denial of the other broader, but slower changes. Young wives are increasingly seen as having a close relationship with their husbands and not only being daughters-in-law. The study area abounds with tales of husbands who took their wives' side against their parents. Education, later female marriage, and the beginnings of a sexual revolution, fanned by contacts with the towns and the cinema, have seen to that. These changes almost certainly will sustain declines in child mortality and probably in fertility. The later age at female marriage is almost certainly socially self-sustaining and is unlikely to reverse as the marriage squeeze weakens.

Finally, are the people in the study area correct in their economic-demographic conclusions? Has the wealth flow[45] really reversed? Why has it done so at such a low level of per capita income? Or, has it failed to do so, and is the fertility decline largely a product of the family planning program?

Perhaps the only conclusion that either the local people or the researcher can reach is that the marginal value of each extra child is impossible to determine. Some agreement exists that there is no economic point in indefinitely adding to family, and that there are women's reasons as well as reasons connected with a distaste for indefinitely fragmenting the patrimony that argue against it. Accurate research into the economics of the family is very difficult, partly because the respondents give answers that are neither wholly accurate nor wholly truthful about their economic prospects and hopes. Clearly one should take into account the concept of the family land and houses being patrimony, and earning above this as being in the nature of sheer profit. Clearly, too, one should distinguish between the periods before and after partition. Even before the partition, migrant children living in the town have their own budget as well as the responsibility to help their families of origin from their earnings. Help from sons does not cease even with partition, especially in crises or for dowry expenses for their sisters or for funerals and festivals. There are advantages even in a good marriage for a daughter. She will be less likely to return to the family in times of scarcity or of desertion, and she may be able to give some help to her parents in times of disaster or old age. Educated sons or sons-in-law can give advice or exert influence, while rich ones can provide loans. The family network is important even after partition, even if the Indian patriarch does not have a lifetime call on the resources of his sons, as is the case in some other high-fertility societies.[46] Nevertheless, it is clear that assistance in crisis is regarded as far more important than assistance in normal times. Even the investment in schooling is not a simple matter, because, as farms become smaller in size, the withdrawal of a child's labor is not as serious as it once was.

In this situation of uncertainty, the certainty of the family plan-

45. Caldwell, *Theory of Fertility Decline.*
46. As in tropical Africa; see Caldwell, *Theory of Fertility Decline.*

from limiting family size probably does contribute some influence, despite a good deal of skepticism. Equally, their view that the curtailing of indefinite reproduction is a social virtue and of value to the country appears to carry some weight, at least in the Hindu community. The people of the study area have not the slightest doubt that given these conditions of uncertainty about the impact of high fertility, the existence of the family planning program, with its ability to deliver sterilizing operations, has reduced fertility much faster than would otherwise have been the case. No one believes that in its absence there would have been an equivalent upswing, at least in the short run, in the spontaneous use of withdrawal and local abortion, together with the supply by the market of large quantities of condoms and pills.

In one sense, the area has, at least for the present, reached a kind of demographic equilibrium, in that its population size has not grown over the last few years, with net emigration equaling natural increase. It is possible that the end of land division has also been reached, for although land will continue to be divided in theory, migrants will tend to let their brothers back on the farm manage their share or will allow them to buy it. The movement toward smaller farms with a greater proportion of the family working off the farm has promoted both education and family planning while probably limiting changes in agricultural technology.

Appendix

Index

Appendix

Preliminary Note

We reproduce here the first part of a previously unpublished manuscript, "The Micro Approach in Demographic Investigation: Toward a Methodology." It was written at an early stage of our research and summarized the feelings that led to our beginning the work. We believe that its publication here is justified on three grounds.

First, it does make some points that need making and that may continue to be largely ignored.

Second, it puts into perspective the situation we faced when we first went into the field and experimented with different methodologies. Some of our attempts at innovational approaches clearly flow straight out of the deficiencies we have identified here.

Third, and more important, the manuscript is a significant social science document, not in terms of its content, but because of the reactions it caused. Our manuscript does say that there are problems inherent in the survey approach itself, but clearly maintains that the survey is an indispensable instrument that needs supplementation by other approaches. What it most firmly argues is that many surveys are carried out at a level of social science expertise far below that which is justifiable, partly because surveys do lend themselves very easily to a lowering of standards. We expected most people working with surveys to agree with this and to urge raising standards. After all, most of our criticisms were of faults identified by the authors of standard textbooks on surveys written 40 or 50 years ago. We expected much greater agreement with the proposition that the principal investigators in survey research should saturate themselves with knowledge of the specific society and the problems to be investigated before any move toward constructing a questionnaire is made. We expected much more support for the argument that the best interpretations are derived from work where those investigators have played a primary role at every stage. Instead, our work has always provoked extraordinarily defensive and even emotional reactions. We have been told repeatedly that it is unqualifiedly antisurveys, and, when we have suggested publication, we have been asked whether it were not possible to write something more constructive. It is true that in this Appendix we leave ourselves particularly exposed in that we reproduce only the critical parts of that manuscript, because the "constructive" parts, on our "positive" methodology, are all where they belong, namely, in the first chapter of this book.

The Need for a Micro Approach in Demographic Investigation

In no area of inquiry can research methodology be properly discussed except in terms of the fundamental goals of the inquiry. We assume here that demographers are basically concerned with the nature of the demographic change, and that they want to know why change occurred, the conditions in which new demographic trends might originate, and likely future trends. Accordingly, we further assume that they look for patterns and correlations in their data, not as ends in themselves, but as clues to underlying explanations.

The contemporary study of population is producing a great mass of patterns, some approximating reality and others the products of deficient methodologies. The challenge lies in how to jump even from the reliable material to an understanding of cause and sequence. We argue here that this cannot be done except with a historical perspective and a method for generating and testing hypotheses about change closely related to the particular society being examined and having a high probability of approximating the truth.

The discussion of experiences with satisfactory and unsatisfactory methodology must, to a large extent, be personal. The main experience employed here is work in south India from 1979, but much was also learned from earlier studies in West Africa[1] and Australia.[2] Experience has also been gained in Latin America.[3]

Limitations of the Survey

It would be more satisfying to begin at once with a discussion of the possible advances that can be made by employing a quasi-anthropological or micro approach to demographic investigation. However, the survey so dominates

1. Undertaken at the University of Ghana, 1962–64; University of Ife, 1969; University of Ibadan (Changing African Family Project), 1973, with Population Council funding; and the University of Ibadan (Nigerian Family Study), 1974–75, with funding from the Australian National University.

2. Department of Demography, Australian National University. Described in John C. Caldwell et al., *Towards an Understanding of Contemporary Demographic Change*, Monograph no. 4 (Australian Family Formation Project, Department of Demography, Australian National University, Canberra, 1976).

3. Particularly in Mexico in 1981 with a team from the Colegio de Mexico headed by Susana Lerner. All Latin American work has been funded by the Ford Foundation.

the present approach to demographic research that any deviation from it or supplementary research must be justified by arguing that the survey is inadequate.

The survey has one enormous strength. It can cover huge areas and tens of thousands of people (representing millions if the sampling is adequate). This yields the satisfaction that one is delineating a general phenomenon and not something that is unique or aberrant and confined to a single locality. It can produce patterns and correlations, which, even at the worst, suggest where relationships might be sought. Yet the patterns of value, in the sense that they represent something real and not misleading, are probably largely confined to unambiguous data which are quantifiable by nature and where reported behavior is not subject to different interpretations in different cultures.

What will remain from the era of comparable Third World demographic surveys (i.e., the KAP surveys—surveys of fertility and of the knowledge of, attitude toward, and practice of family planning—of the 1960s and the World Fertility Survey of the 1970s) is likely to be the outlines they have provided at the time of the survey of fertility and mortality levels, of the mechanical way these were produced by such intermediate variables as periods within marriage, postnatal amenorrhea and its quantitative relationship to breast-feeding, and postnatal sexual abstinence; and also of the use of contraception and of such characteristics as age, years of education, and occupation. It is unlikely that the knowledge or attitude data—even the ideal family size information—will stand up to rigorous examination in each individual society, precisely because it will be shown that there was a blurring of concepts or that the assumptions built into the questions were inappropriate at that time for many members of the society. Even if progress is made with the conversion of retrospective data into time series, it is unlikely that the necessary linking of two or more time series will prove to be satisfactory.

In many of the societies studied, much of the data will ultimately be shown to have been astonishingly inaccurate. Yet, this is not a particularly worrying problem. We will have an approximate idea of their magnitude usable for many purposes and when ordered (for instance, by size of residential center or education or parents) the rank order is likely to be correct. The real problem is that although such findings are an essential first step in seeking explanations, they do not get us very far (but they may stop us from starting off in the wrong direction).

For example, explanations of declining fertility in terms of later age of female marriage or rising fertility in terms of earlier weaning do not really get us any closer to understanding why society is beginning to change and what were the earlier movements that began a chain of cause and effect. Indeed, they may mislead persons not steeped in the knowledge of a particular society who may assume that females are postponing marriage in order to reduce the ultimate size of their families, although, curiously, such persons are less likely to conclude that early weaning is an attempt to raise fertility levels. Similarly, when we found an inverse association between the duration of parental schooling and infant and child mortality,[4] we concluded that the point was reasonably well established, even while suspecting that education was frequently overstated and mortality understated. It was, however, nonsurvey experience of the impact of education on families, and the results of a very small survey on the mechanics of health care,[5] that prevented us from placing too much explanatory emphasis on parents directly utilizing what the schools had taught them about health and child care.

Some of the failings of surveys are inherent in the approach and others arise because of forces which make most surveys very much less accurate than they might be. Much of the failure of surveys is linked with what makes them appear to be the most advanced weapon in the social science armory. An appearance of great efficiency is provided by their size, their organizational flow charts, the division of labor between persons with different skills, the extent to which they have adapted to the computer age, their suspicion of crude data from the field, apparent improvement of those data by "cleaning" techniques, and, above all, the magnitude of the operation with everyone involved working to their limit to meet deadlines. Such activity makes the participants proud to be part of an operation that has real standards and requires levels of professional skills that few can attain. It has all the excitement of a team effort by peers with unusual abilities. Yet, it is precisely this high level of professionalization that obscures just how little all this has to do with understanding societies and the reasons for social change and makes its practitioners so strongly defensive when doubts are expressed.

One of the curious effects of survey work, by people steeped in its practice, is just how seductive it can be. While experimenting with the micro approach in south India, for example, we are tempted quite regularly to confirm patterns we have begun to hypothesize by conducting a relatively small and highly focused survey. Before it gets under way, we intend to leave it largely to others and to continue with semistructured interviews and almost unstructured home visits. Usually, however, we are eventually caught up with the excitement and precision of the survey, and, for a period, cancel all other work (where standards are less obvious) in order to meet criteria of survey excellence. Most researchers feel guilty if they spend their day in a single household while a survey is in progress with all its logistic and other organizational problems. It is easy to understand why some researchers can spend a lifetime

4. J. C. Caldwell, "Education as a Factor in Mortality Decline: An Explanation of Nigerian Data," *Population Studies* 33, no. 3 (1979):395–413; J. C. Caldwell and Peter McDonald, "Influence of Maternal Education on Infant Mortality: Levels and Causes," in *International Population Conference Manila 1981, Solicited Papers*, International Union for the Scientific Study of Population, vol. 2 (Liège: IUSSP, 1981), 79–96.

5. I. O. Orubuloye and J. C. Caldwell, "The Impact of Public Health Services on Mortality: A Study of Mortality Differentials in a Rural Area of Nigeria," *Population Studies* 29, no. 2 (1975):259–72.

doing this work and feel that they have made a major contribution to social science.

These observations were necessary to bring us to some understanding of the basic weakness of most surveys, for it is a very strange phenomenon indeed. That weakness is their distancing effect from the very phenomena they are investigating. It is as if viruses or molecules were large enough to be examined without optical aids, but biologists and chemists still preferred to use the electron microscope because of the detachment it gave. Many demographers are distressed by the possibility of working for long periods in Third World rural or urban slum societies. If they do so, they wish to be managing teams of interviewers rather than spending most of every day talking with local people and behaving as closely as possible as they do. Others are disturbed, especially when in the field, by continuing to read anthropological and other social science material on the area, and turn to detective stories or science fiction in order to provide the necessary air of unreality and a kind of external link. Still others never go to the field at all but obtain chunks of partly processed data about people with behavioral patterns unknown and unimaginable to them and then proceed to produce social hypotheses from their analyses—hypotheses and sometimes analyses which are clearly at odds with what transpires daily in the society said to be under study. There is a ladder of command which means that an intimate experience with the study society is obtained only by the humblest employees and often not conveyed correctly to the "researchers." Those controlling the 1963 census of Nigeria believed the upward-flowing reports of the successful use of historical calendars for determining age; we discovered, almost by accident, by dint of reemploying the enumerators to observe them in the household situation, that the calendars could not be used in repeated interviews, and, far more often than not, had not been used.[6] The completion of questionnaires can be arranged, especially in literate societies, so that there are not even humble employees who are aware of what is happening.[7]

The very sampling which ensures the unique quality of the survey, its representativeness over a large population, also makes it impossible to study a single person or household in context. The survey usually chooses one type of person (or sometimes two; for instance, a wife and husband), commonly, in demographic inquiries, currently married women under 50 years of age. This restricts the study to the examination of households containing such persons (not a major restriction in this case, but in some surveys the households are clearly atypical of the whole community), and, more seriously, can mean that some or all of the information on the household and its relationships is obtained from a single type of person. Our evidence indicates that this situation results in a major distortion in information about fertility-control deci-

6. J. C. Caldwell and A. A. Igun, "An Experiment with Census-Type Age Enumeration in Nigeria," *Population Studies* 25, no. 2 (1971):287–302.

7. Shulamit Reinharz, "The Ritual of Survey Empiricism," in *On Becoming a Social Scientist* (San Francisco: Jossey-Bass, 1979), 50–125.

sion making. Even more seriously, except again as seen through a single pair of eyes, households cannot be related to their neighbours, or families to kin—the relationships which are central to the study of society. In societies based on tight social networks, the survey helps to create an apparently atomized society.

This artificial creation of a new society, different from reality, is furthered by many of the questions. Respondents, who are both wives and daughters-in-law, may be asked questions about contraceptive decision making and the timing of their marriages, even though they had little control over the former and none over the latter. The questions themselves are often artificial, largely irrelevant to the society, and, when they provide for a forced choice or a "yes-no" dichotomy, may well generate much of the spread of answers that later prove to be statistically significant (discussed at greater length below). Social researchers are never so embarrassed as when they agree to answer a colleague's questionnaire on working conditions, their research, or their reactions to a professional conference, and find that few of the questions have boxes that really represent their exact answers. In the Third World field situation these problems are compounded in two other ways. First, survey questions are quick in two senses. There is some pressure (arising from a limited budget and a large sample) to keep up pace when applying the questionnaire, and the questions are rarely embedded in the mass of closely related queries which would be the case in a long and detailed discussion. Second, there are language problems which are as much a matter of concept and vocabulary as of true translations. In our research area, surveys seem to get a wider distribution of responses than anthropological interviews, and the reason is almost certainly a lack of full comprehension of the questions by many of the respondents, some of whom become embarrassed or apprehensive, or just lazy and resigned, and blurt out almost any answer. The nonresponse or refusal, which is a feature of many surveys, is unknown in longer conversations.

Perhaps the most fundamental problem, and one which has been given far too little attention, is the generation of hypotheses or assumptions upon which survey questions are based. Questionnaire construction, even in the largest and most reputable of surveys, is rarely based on the concept of constructing questions which will rigorously test hypotheses put forward as a result of prior research on the culture. Questions are suggested by committees or are taken wholesale from earlier questionnaires used in other parts of the world. They are chosen because they have "worked" before or because there is a certain rigor in the order of questions and in their internal wording which is logically exact and which appeals to those persons with a penchant for flow charts and statistical analysis. It matters little that the exact word which provides this fine definition may not be translatable or may be rendered only in the form of a word or phrase not fully comprehensible to many interviewees.[8] Questions

8. On problems of language see J. C. Caldwell, *The Study of Fertility and Fertility Change in Tropical Africa*, Occasional Paper no. 7 (London: World Fertility Survey, 1974), 16–19.

tend to be favored when they yield clearly quantifiable answers, suited to coding and computers, and this undoubtedly tends toward the overemphasis of some aspects of behavior relative to others (for instance, how many more children one wants—a foolish question in many societies—rather than the much more meaningful degree of reluctance felt by all involved for there to be yet another birth and the extent of conflict over the matter). A most unfortunate tendency in the preparation of surveys or the framing of Ph.D. dissertations is to write down scores or hundreds of "hypotheses" mostly in terms of permutations and combinations, using the volume and coverage of all the suggestions to justify the lack of knowledge possessed of the society and implying that investigations of all these hypotheses will eventually sort out the plausible from the ridiculous. This approach merely dilutes efforts and lowers standards.

Survey analysis is dominated by the search for statistically significant correlations, which is a dangerous mire for more reasons than the few noted here. One is that it is very easy to be distracted from the socially most significant point. For instance, in our research area, we have confirmed (see chap. 2) what has been widely noted in India: that 68 percent of the landless or near-landless (those possessing less than one acre) live in nuclear families, compared with 54 percent of those with land—a fact that is statistically highly significant and shows what has been said again and again, namely, that those with resources need to be able to keep a large family together to exploit those assets. But why is it apparently never asked in the literature on India why 32 percent of the landless continue to live in joint families or why 46 percent of those with land are found in nuclear families? Another problem is that the greater comprehension of the more education (or richer or urbanized or those in nonagricultural occupations) or their different way of defining the intent of the question will frequently produce statistically significant differences in response by education, even for situations where the reality is much the same for all educational divisions. This is one reason why fertility attitudes show so much better correlations with education than fertility behavior does. Finally, there is a random chance element, especially when a computer is scanning hundreds of cross-tabulations, asterisking those which are significant at the 95 percent level.

Most surveys fall far short of what perfection could be even in terms of the macro approach. Funds are usually insufficient, and those providing them often want answers quickly and within a relatively confined focus. Pretests and pilots usually do not mean detailed micro-level research to identify the matters of most significance, but seeing whether questions "work" at all.

However, the strangest survey phenomena are those concerned with analysis and interpretation. The analyses rarely explain the hypotheses or reasoning upon which the questions—as well as the decision to include some questions and exclude others—are based. Of perhaps more importance is the fact that the best analyses are clearly based partly on information and concepts which do not flow from the survey tabulations. Indeed, the statistical data are often employed selectively to illustrate what the researchers already feel to be the truth. Edmund Leach, when criticizing the Ceylon University Socioeconomic Survey of Pata Dumbara in the mid-1950s,[9] wrote: "I believe that Drs. Sarkar and Tambiah have really arrived at their conclusions by intuitive methods, and that it is only because they are both by instinct first class anthropologists that their conclusions are fundamentally correct. The numerical apparatus in which these conclusions are embedded seems to me to be very largely a complicated piece of self-deception."[10] He might have added that they knew their own society from childhood and had incidentally learned more during the survey fieldwork.

A fundamental problem, then, of the apparently scientific survey is the generation of the hypotheses upon which their questions, and, less obviously, their analyses, are based. We have argued here that there are hidden hypotheses (sometimes, when questions are borrowed, some generations of surveys back) but that they are often formed in an astonishingly primitive way. A micro approach can develop such hypotheses, both as a major contribution to survey research and as a method of investigation in its own right. We do not, however, suggest that this input into survey research will prove sufficient to allow surveys to proceed as they often have in the past. If they seek causal explanations they must have an associated micro component, and, if they aim at the best standards of survey research, they will require preceding micro research to render them culturally specific and to make their questions appropriate and adequate. Nor do we suggest that one-time surveys will ever be able to handle change over time easily. With regard to fundamental changes in society, such as the onset of fertility decline, their role may be to test implications suggested by the micro approach (see chap. 2). The survey, transient as it is, can never become sufficiently familiar with any society to ferret out much that is relevant. Indeed, one anthropologist has defended the micro approach over many years against single anthropological visits lasting as long as a year: "Among Kapauka Papuans, for example, practice of black magic, knowledge of witches, one's personal savings and profits, and political plans and aspirations are not discussed. Among the Tirolean peasants personal income, savings, smuggling to Italy, and political intrigues are kept secret. . . . People are willing to surrender this information only to good friends. To make such friends in a short period is hardly possible."[11]

9. N. K. Sarkar and S. J. Tambiah, *The Disintegrating Village* (Colombo: University of Ceylon, 1957).

10. E. R. Leach, "An Anthropologist's Reflections on a Social Survey," in *Anthropologists in the Field*, ed. D. G. Jongmans and P. C. W. Gutkind (Assen, The Netherlands: van Gorcum, 1967), 76 (first published in *The Ceylon Journal of Historical and Social Studies* 1, no. 1 [1958]:10).

11. Leopold Pospisil, "The Tirolean Peasants of Obernberg: A Study in Long-Term Research" in *Long-Term Field Research in Social Anthropology*, ed. George M. Foster, Thayer Scudder, Elizabeth Colson, and Robert V. Kemper (New York: Academic Press, 1979), 129.

Toward a Micro-Macro Mix

In a demographic investigation there can hardly be a micro approach on its own, as this account of preliminary censuses and accompanying small focused surveys indicates, and there should not be a macro approach unsupported by detailed local knowledge. Perhaps the most disturbing experience in the social sciences is to meet a research team who have a large survey which they "have just got out of the field" and who have not the slightest idea of the direction in which their findings will lead because this will be revealed in the computer printouts. This means that no adjustments or changes were possible during the field work. In fact, they can be made only to the next large survey, if there is one. Another alarming experience is to find social scientists attempting to infer simple, easily ascertainable facts about societies from large data sets as if they were radio astronomers analyzing electromagnetic waves.[12] Seminars among demographers and quantitative sociologists often develop an almost surrealistic atmosphere as participants examine cross-tabulations and venture guesses about what the societies concerned must be like.

Where there must be a micro approach is in the period before a large survey, with the possible exception of the case where the survey is a repeat in the same area and culture of an earlier one which was accompanied by anthropological work. This is, of course, just a restatement of classical survey methodology—familiarize yourself with the group to be surveyed before designing the research instruments. However, in the last two decades this tradition has been largely abandoned, particularly in the case of large-scale, international, comparative surveys—in the case of the World Fertility Survey by dint of reducing social and economic data to a minimum. The near-elimination of preliminary work has resulted from an attempt by both funding organizations and investigators to save time and money in the one area that did not appear to be indispensable. This was, of course, more appearance than reality, and the surveys that abandoned such work will have produced findings that are almost certainly incomplete and hence are likely to be forgotten.

Most surveys would benefit enormously, and become much more scientific, if preceded by a substantial period of micro work undertaken by the principal investigators and not contracted out. Surveys suffer from inadequate questions, and questions embodying fallacious assumptions, but they are much more impaired by questions not asked and not even suspected as being necessary. Some early KAP surveys in Africa did not ask about postnatal sexual abstinence even in societies where abstinence probably accounted for 95 percent of all fertility control. This preliminary period should be devoted to thorough reading about the society and a great number of semistructured, long, probing interviews with a wide range of people.

There is also a good case for encouraging a tradition of village demo-

12. See J. C. Caldwell, "Review of *Population and Economic Change in Developing Countries*, edited by Richard A. Easterlin," *Journal of Political Economy* 89, no. 4 (1981):830–34.

graphic studies (or studies of component populations of urban areas), even if other people translate this work into larger-scale patterns or attempt to employ the larger framework to test hypotheses thrown up.

Nevertheless, there remains a need for devising a research strategy that achieves a mix of methods in the course of the main investigation. There seem to be two possibilities.

The first is employ micro methods to investigate a subsample of the original sample. This would be adequate both for testing the adequacy of the survey questions and for amplifying the information gained on the subject being investigated. It would also allow all persons in the household to be studied. But it would not get around two rather serious problems. One is that the households would still remain out of social context: there would still be insufficient knowledge of the neighbors and the community. The other is the high probability that the survey sample universe would not be all households but those characterized by containing persons with certain characteristics.

The second method is to design the survey sample so that the first stage selects whole villages or urban districts. Some of these can then be chosen—presumably by sampling—for micro studies. This might well prove to be the most satisfactory approach.

Whichever approach is used, micro work of this kind will be very similar to village studies. Such activities may, in fact, start much earlier than the macro study and serve as the preliminary work for it. Nevertheless, micro studies, when serving as one component of a micro-macro mix, have an additional function. That is to test each question in the survey and to estimate the extent to which adequate responses are being obtained. This will lead either to the changing of questions or to their full illustration from the micro studies in the reporting; it is probably unwise to aim at correction factors.

However, such a mix is not merely a way of securing adequate micro support to ensure ultimately that a better survey is undertaken. To a considerable extent, the purpose of the survey will change. Its additional new function will be to devise questions aimed at confirming or disproving hypotheses thrown up either by the preliminary micro research, or, more likely, by earlier village studies.

Discussion

One of the strongest cases for micro work is not merely that it can help produce an adequate and largely correct picture instead of a thin, partial, and often erroneous one, but that it can draw attention to important areas that otherwise might not have been investigated at all. Here again, it is easier to provide examples from one's own experience. In work prior to that in India (i.e., by the Caldwells), it was only participant observation within Ghanaian urban middle-class households of the early 1960s, while investigating fertility control at a time of rapid educational change, that focused our attention on the fact that educated children and other persons were being treated very differently from those who had not been to school[13]—an observation that has had some impact on everything we have subsequently done. It was participation in the fieldwork of the 1962 Conjugal Biographies study in Ghana[14] that taught us not only about the role of postnatal sexual abstinence but that we should have learned more about it earlier from a more thorough reading of the anthropological literature or by following up conversational leads with our colleagues. In India, the three of us were indebted to the micro approach for having our attention drawn to the role of monetization and inflation in changing the value of children, to internal changes in the family that did not result in measurable transformations in family structure, and to the concept of many illnesses being caused by sin and punishment as being an important component in explaining ambivalence toward modern medical services (see chaps. 2, 5, and 6).

Finally, the discussion of the micro-macro mix may have given the impression that survey work was the only way, or the major way, of testing hypotheses produced from investigations of an anthropological type. This is not the case. As our work on the origins of fertility decline in India progresses, we anticipate being able to confirm—or further explore—the hypothesized impact of monetization, the growth of the wage market, and land division from official records. The impact of the family planning program and changing decision making within the family may require a micro-macro mix, whereas changes in the balance of family labor will need a new micro study. The discussion may also have given the impression that the micro approach's purpose was solely to generate hypotheses. On the contrary, we regard the masses of testimony obtained as evidence in their own right (as individual observations are in anthropology, history, geography, and even biology and astronomy), and contest any assertion that the only demographic data must be that yielded from formalized questions stretched across the grid of a sampling framework and restricted further to include only those which can satisfactorily survive coding.

Perhaps a note should be appended on the problem repeatedly suggested in India of finding people to do this kind of work. It is true that demographic programs are mostly staffed by people with statistical backgrounds. Our experience has tended to show that it is easier to recruit persons with social science backgrounds and interest them in demographic problems that it is to convert statisticians into anthropologists. We have also been told repeatedly that it will prove impossible to recruit investigators, especially females, with the proper qualifications who will work alone in villages for a year or more. This has not proved to be the case in Karnataka in work undertaken by the Bangalore Population Centre.

13. J. C. Caldwell, *Population Growth and Family Change in Africa: The New Urban Elite in Ghana* (Canberra: Australian National University Press, 1968).

14. J. C. Caldwell, *A Study of Contemporary Ghana*, vol. 2, *Some Aspects of Social Structure* (London: George Allen and Unwin, 1967); Pat Caldwell, "Notes on Abstinence Fieldwork," mimeograph (Department of Demography, Australian National University, Canberra, 1976).

Index